Reprints of Economic Classics

NEW YORK IN THE CONFEDERATION

NEW YORK

IN THE

CONFEDERATION

AN ECONOMIC STUDY

BY

THOMAS C. COCHRAN

[1932]

AUGUSTUS M. KELLEY • PUBLISHERS
CLIFTON 1972

First Edition 1932

(*Philadelphia* : University of Pennsylvania Press, 1932)

Reprinted 1972 by

AUGUSTUS M. KELLEY PUBLISHERS

Reprints of Economic Classics

Clifton New Jersey 07012

Library of Congress Cataloging in Publication Data

Cochran, Thomas Childs, 1902–
   New York in the Confederation.

   (Reprints of economic classics)
   Originally presented as the author's thesis,
University of Pennsylvania, 1930.
   Bibliography: p.
   1. New York (State)—Politics and government—
Revolution. 2. New York (State)—Economic conditions.
3. United States—History—Revolution—Finance,
commerce, confiscations, etc. 4. United States
Continental Congress. 5. United States—Politics and
government—1783-1789. I. Title.
F123.C66 1972   974.7'03   72-77054

ISBN 0-678-00911-2

PRINTED IN THE UNITED STATES OF AMERICA
by SENTRY PRESS, NEW YORK, N. Y. 10013

NEW YORK
IN THE CONFEDERATION

AN ECONOMIC STUDY

———

A THESIS

IN HISTORY

PRESENTED TO THE FACULTY OF THE GRADUATE SCHOOL OF THE
UNIVERSITY OF PENNSYLVANIA IN PARTIAL FULFILLMENT
OF THE REQUIREMENTS FOR THE DEGREE
OF DOCTOR OF PHILOSOPHY

THOMAS C. COCHRAN

———

PHILADELPHIA
1932

To

MY FRIEND AND TEACHER

ST. GEORGE L. SIOUSSAT

PREFACE

AS a result of the work of several distinguished historians it has become generally recognized that the American Revolution was not only a Continental movement, but also thirteen separate State revolutions. It has now become the task of historical scholarship to analyze each of these separate revolutions from the standpoint of their effect on the revolutionary movement as a whole. Such studies as have already been made of these State backgrounds have altered some of our most firmly held conceptions of the history of the period, and those being made at the present time will undoubtedly continue to do so. This volume deals with the economic history of the revolutionary movement in New York as it affected relations with the central Congress and the other States. In other words, it is an attempt to coördinate the economic history of internal affairs in the State with the course of national ꞌvents.

New York was the most vulnerable link in the long chain of colonies that stretched along the Atlantic seaboard. The richest portion of it was indefensible in the face of a naval attack, and its inland regions were open by several routes to easy invasion from Canada. Had Great Britain possessed all of New York she could have prevented the co-operation of New England with the remaining colonies, and doubtless broken down the whole machinery of resistance. Therefore New York became the principal battle field of the war, and the one area that was continually occupied by large British armies. There was also a strong Loyalist faction, a separatist movement in the eastern counties, and three actively hostile Indian tribes within the State. Because of these conditions New York during the war affords an excellent opportunity for analyzing the revolutionary movement in its most complex form.

PREFACE

In the period after the war also the State was deeply involved in the major issues of the day. In the adjustment of western land claims, the questions of trade relations, and the struggle to add to the powers of the Continental Congress the attitude of New York was vitally important. The economic conflict between the mercantile and agrarian classes and the reaction of this on the Continental Congress should be emphasized as the clue to most of the political problems of the period. Unquestionably, the defeat of the impost by the New York Legislature in 1786 was a chief factor in bringing to a climax the movement for a new constitution.

I wish to express my sincere appreciation for the aid and advice given to me by Dean H. V. Ames, Professor W. E. Lingelbach, Professor R. F. Nichols and Professor St. G. L. Sioussat of the University of Pennsylvania, and by Dean M. S. Brown and Professor John Musser of New York University in the preparation of this study.

THOMAS C. COCHRAN

New York City, 1932

CONTENTS

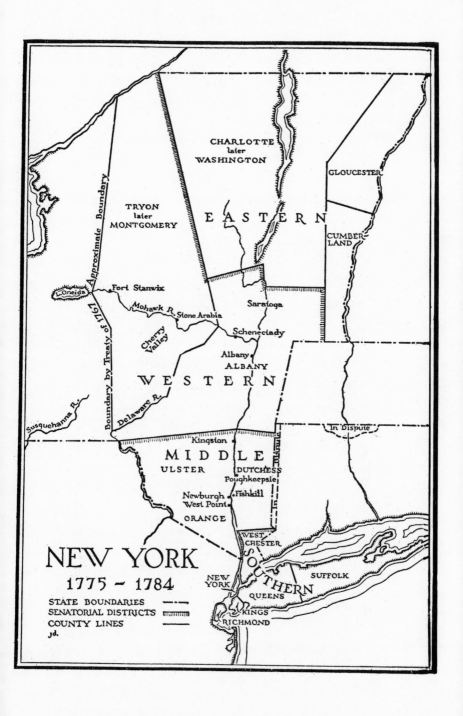

CHARLOTTE
later
WASHINGTON

GLOUCESTER

TRYON
later
MONTGOMERY

E A S T E R N

CUMBER-
LAND

L. Oneida

Fort Stanwix

Mohawk R. Stone Arabia

Saratoga

Cherry
Valley

Schenectady

Albany
ALBANY

W E S T E R N

Susquehanna R.

Delaware R.

In Dispute

Kingston

M I D D L E

ULSTER

DUTCHESS
Poughkeepsie

Newburgh
West Point

Fishkill

ORANGE

WEST
CHESTER

NEW YORK
1775 ~ 1784

S O U T H E R N

NEW
YORK

SUFFOLK

STATE BOUNDARIES
SENATORIAL DISTRICTS
COUNTY LINES

QUEENS

jd.

KINGS

RICHMOND

Approximate Boundary

Boundary by Treaty of 1767

CHAPTER I

INTRODUCTION[1]

GEOGRAPHY OF THE STATE IN 1775

AS a basis for understanding the economic relations of New York State during the Revolutionary period we must make a survey of its geography and area of settlement. The valley of the Hudson River, and its principal branch the Mohawk, which empties into it from the west at Albany, comprised the most fertile area of the old colony and naturally formed the nucleus of settlement. The county of Tryon, large in area but small in population, marked the westernmost limits of the Revolutionary State, extending from the Canadian border to the headwaters of the Delaware, and eastward to within twenty-five miles of Albany. Beyond the headwaters of the Mohawk at Lake Oneida stretched the lands of the Six Nations, embracing all the western part of the present State. Despite its small population the upper Mohawk Valley was already an important farming area.

The territory on both sides of Lake George and Lake Champlain was included in Charlotte County, practically uninhabited north of Lake George, much of it permanently uninhabitable because of the Adirondack Mountains. The eastern part of this area was eventually to be lost to Vermont. Still further east, lying along the western bank of the Connecticut River, were the long thin counties of Gloucester and Cumberland which were also to form a part of this new State.

The heart of New York during the Revolution was Albany County, which extended in irregular shape from the southern tip of Lake George to just above Kingston on the Hudson, and from the head waters of the Delaware to the Massachusetts

[1] Most of the material in this chapter is merely a combination of the information contained in the writings of: A. C. Flick, Carl Becker, Allan Nevins, W. C. Abbott, and others.

boundary. This county had a larger population than any other except New York. It was here that the Livingstons, Van Rensselaers, and Schuylers lived. Below Albany County lay Dutchess on the east bank of the river and Ulster on the west, Dutchess being the more thickly populated. Orange County was a wedge-shaped area extending from around West Point south to the New Jersey line along the Hudson, and west to the Delaware. South of Dutchess lay the comparatively small but wealthy county of Westchester extending from Tarrytown to the Harlem River.

The five southern counties—New York, Kings, Queens, Suffolk, and Richmond—were so continuously under the control of the British that we may disregard them during the Revolution despite the fact that they embraced about three-fifths of the total wealth of the State. Suffolk County included all of Long Island east of Huntington, and Queens all the western part to the present-day limits of Brooklyn, which occupies all of Kings. Richmond County was, and still is, Staten Island; quite prosperous and very Dutch in those days.

New York presented a greater mixture of agrarian and mercantile interests than any of the other colonies. At least four distinct classes of people could be distinguished in the provincial social body: first, the large landowners, limited in number but great in influence; second, the wealthy lawyers and merchants, mainly in New York City;[2] third, the small shopkeepers and laborers in New York and Albany; and fourth, the small farmers and tenants who made up the bulk of the up-state population.

Agrarian discontent in New York was not primarily regional as in the case of most of the other colonies. There was in general no great frontier antagonism toward the provincial legislature. The frontier counties were fairly repre-

[2]It appears probable that most of the New York merchants were independent operators, rather than factors for British concerns. A. M. Schlesinger, *The Colonial Merchants*, pp. 25-35.

sented, and in the case of the Pontiac Conspiracy, at least, had received reasonably prompt and effective protection from the provincial government. It must also be noted that the settler frontier in New York was not far enough west of the Hudson to make them lose contact with or feel isolated from the rest of the State. Beside the lack of these usual causes for discontent a potent factor in the situation was the personality of Sir William Johnson, the royal Indian agent for the Northern Department. Sir William had his permanent home at Schenectady and from there he exercised an enormous influence on both the Indians and his white neighbors. His death in 1774 was undoubtedly a severe blow to loyalism in the western part of the State, even though his son Sir John and his nephew Guy Johnson tried to carry on in his place.[3] Albany and Ulster were the only up-state counties in which a majority of the farmers were probably in sympathy with the radical Whig party in 1774. Tryon was actively Tory, but in general the up-state counties simply ignored the city political excitement.[4] This was true to such a degree that a leading Tory propagandist claimed that outside of New York City the delegates to the first Continental Congress represented less than one per cent. of the population.[5]

THE ASSEMBLY AND THE COMMITTEES

The Governor of New York during the period of crisis was William Tryon, a mild and conciliatory individual who had had previous experience as governor of North Carolina. After a few early arguments the Provincial Assembly elected in 1769 became a loyal supporter of the government's policy. The radical opposition charged that this was due to corruption, and the governor's power to make land grants, but it is

[3]M. S. Walker, "Sir John Johnson, Loyalist," *Mississippi Valley Historical Review*, III, no. 3, 318 ff.
[4]Flick, *Loyalism in New York*, pp. 22-24.
[5]Seabury, *The Congress Canvassed*, quoted in Flick, *op. cit.*, p. 24.

equally explicable by the mere fact that the majority mirrored the feeling of the conservative group in the State who felt that there was nothing to be gained by antagonizing the British Government.[6] The radicals in New York City were estranged right at the start by the agreement of the Assembly in 1769 to pay their quota for the quartering of the troops in accordance with the Mutiny Act in exchange for the privilege of issuing £120,000 of paper currency. This meant the abandoning of the principle of withholding appropriations until grievances had been redressed which the radicals had been steadily striving to uphold since the extension of the Mutiny Act to America in 1765. On the other hand, this inflation of the currency in place of taxation not only made its usual appeal to the agricultural debtor class who were more interested in the specific fact of cheaper money than in the theoretical quarrel with Great Britain, but it also relieved an actual shortage of currency that existed as a result of the act of 1764 prohibiting the further issue of paper money.[7]

The line that was to divide the radical from the conservative party up to the beginning of actual hostilities first appeared with the repeal of the Townshend Acts in 1770. Due probably to the money shortage, the merchants of New York had really enforced the non-importation agreement of 1768, whereas those of Boston and Philadelphia had done so only half-heartedly. Therefore the New Yorkers took the repeal of the duties, except that on tea, as a handy excuse to end an inequitable arrangement, and accordingly reduced the restriction on imports to tea alone. The merchants who were fair traders also felt that their hands were tied while the smugglers reaped large profits. In this situation the radicals and the smugglers seized upon complete non-importation as a sound issue upon which to construct a popular party in opposi-

[6]M. L. Booth, *History of New York*, p. 443; Nevins, *American States*, pp. 50-52.

[7]Becker, *Political Parties in State of New York*, pp. 69-71.

tion to the Legislature and the conservative classes.[8] The leadership in this organization was assumed by the "Sons of Liberty," a society formed at the time of the Stamp Act agitation, and composed principally of the small merchants and laborers of the city. While many of these men were able politicians, and some of them wealthy, they had no brilliant leaders. This was one reason why their agitation had so little popular effect outside the city. Although the radicals were decisively outvoted and non-importation was modified, they succeeded in stirring up a good deal of popular feeling and laid the basis for future opposition.[9]

When the news of the coercive acts of 1774 reached New York there was already a standing Committee of Correspondence in the Legislature. The committee being Tory in sentiment, however, took no action in urging retaliatory measures. The Assembly's negative attitude left the leadership of public opinion in the hands of private individuals. The organization of public protest was at once taken up by the Sons of Liberty, but the conservatives, unwilling to see the direction of affairs fall into the hands of an irresponsible minority, soon asserted their power. In general, the wealthy merchants and the landlords were decidedly loyal, but at the same time anxious to uphold the American construction of the Constitution.[10] Only a small group of the followers of Lieutenant Governor Colden, most of them government officials, were thoroughgoing believers in the British policies. The chief difference, therefore, between the radicals and conservatives was the question of the means to be employed in gaining recognition of the American theories by the mother country. The radicals were in favor of coercion, whereas the conservatives held that compromise and conciliation would be more effective. By attending the mass meeting summoned to elect a committee of fifty-

[8]*Ibid.*, p. 83.

[9]Colden, *Letter Books*, II, 221-224, New York Historical Society Collections, 1876-77.

[10]Flick, *Loyalism in New York*, p. 21.

one members to make a reply to the letters from Massachusetts, the conservatives gained control of affairs.[11]

The committee was faced with a difficult problem. If non-importation of tea were going to be maintained in spite of the very low prices, it would almost certainly be necessary to use force; and force was directly contrary to the conservatives' policy. If, however, the committee took no action it would allow the radicals to gain control. Meanwhile the people of Boston and a mechanic's committee representing the Sons of Liberty were demanding complete non-importation. From this dilemma the committee sought escape by proposing a general congress. This recommendation was favorably received by all the groups in the city.[12] Even such an extreme Tory as Colden felt that a congress might do some good.[13]

The Committee of Fifty-one secured the election of Philip Livingston and Isaac Low, moderate Whigs; and James Duane, John Jay, and John Alsop, popularly regarded as Loyalists, as delegates to Congress.[14] The First Continental

[11]They were undoubtedly aided by the growing fear on the part of the men of property lest power should be exercised by the unenfranchised lower class. The committee chosen was decidedly conservative in tone, even though several of the radical leaders were members of it; twenty-one members out of a total of fifty-one took the side of the British when actual warfare commenced. *American Archives*, 4th ser. I, 308 and *Colden Letter Books, N. Y. H. S.*, Col. 1877, pp. 346-348.

[12]T. Jones, *History of New York*, I, 439, 467.

[13]*Colden Papers*, N. Y. H. S. Col. 1923, p. 350.

[14]The farmers could not be made to realize the importance of the issues at stake. As a class they adopted an attitude of complete indifference toward the proceedings. Only Kings, Orange, and Suffolk elected delegates, and they were representative of but a fraction of the population. Albany County held elections but for some reason finally authorized the New York City delegates to act for them. In Ulster, Westchester, and Dutchess small groups of radicals met and also asked the City delegates to represent them. *Am. Arch.*, 4th ser. I, 302, 307, 308. Jones, *History of New York*, I, 34, *New York Colonial Documents*, VIII, 493.

Eleven radical members had already resigned from the committee, and their unsuccessful attempt to have McDougal elected in place of Jay or Alsop proved once more the conservative leanings of a majority of the city voters.

Congress met as a conservative gathering to discuss grievances but, caught in the current of continuously increasing difficulties, it ended as a radical body passing measures that inevitably led to physical conflict. Thus it happened that when the secret sessions were over Congress presented on the one hand a series of mild and conciliatory addresses, and on the other the "Association," a militant agreement in restraint of trade, calling for measures which had been advocated only by the most advanced radicals prior to this time.[15] It left the conservatives without any platform unless they were willing to join hands with the Tories and openly oppose the measures of Congress.

The situation was clearly illustrated when the Association reached New York. A new Committee of Sixty that was organized demonstrated by its personnel the swing toward radicalism. Unable to check the growing control of the radicals in the city, the conservatives still hoped that the counties would assert themselves. In this they were partially disappointed. Only Albany, Suffolk, and Ulster formally agreed to the Association, but the other counties did nothing toward organizing effective conservative protest. In six counties there is no record of any action at all.[16]

From the counties public attention shifted to the Legislature which reassembled in January 1775. The radicals feared, and the conservatives hoped, that if the Assembly endorsed the proceedings of Congress the leadership of affairs would be taken out of the hands of popular committees and irregular congresses. But the Assembly once again refused to assume the responsibility of leading the opposition to the British Acts. They refused to consider the work of the First Continental

[15]The Association provided for: non-importation from England and her colonies after December 1, 1774; non-exportation after September 10, 1775, if the obnoxious acts were still in force at that time; and for the enforcement of its provisions upon all traders by boycotting and confiscation of property.

[16]*Am. Arch.*, 4th ser. I, 328, 399, 1027 ff. Also see: Becker, *Political Parties*, pp. 170-173, and Flick, *Loyalism*, p. 30.

9

Congress or the appointment of delegates to the Second, and ended by sending memorials to the King, Lords, and Commons which substantially represented the moderate Tory viewpoint. This work being finished they appointed a standing Committee of Correspondence composed of Tories and conservative Whigs, and then adjourned. As the time of reconvening was continually postponed, the Colonial Assembly never met again.[17]

In March the Sixty called for the election of a provincial convention for the purpose of selecting delegates to the second Continental Congress. The conservatives still hoped to be able to control this, but the provincial convention because of the irregularity of its election was dominated by the radicals.[18] Hence the delegation chosen for the Continental Congress on April 21st had a decidedly less conservative attitude than the previous one.[19]

The news of Lexington and Concord, arriving the day after the adjournment of the first provincial convention, raised popular excitement to fever heat in the city. The Committee of Sixty, feeling forced to bow before the popular will, called upon the "freemen and freeholders" to elect a new city committee of a hundred members, and twenty delegates to a provincial congress with legislative powers. To justify their position in thus setting up a new state legislature Jay, Duane, and Van Shaak drew up a "New York Association" setting forth the basis of the extra-legal government in the familiar Lockian and "British Constitutional" phrases. The Sixty asked all people to signify their agreement by signing a copy of this

[17]*Am. Arch.*, 4th ser., I, 1302-1324 and II, 461.

[18]Only eight counties beside New York sent delegates, and in three of them there was strong opposition by a majority of the population. In Albany alone there was what we would today consider a "regular" election. Becker, *Political Parties,* pp. 185-192.

[19]To the five delegates who had served in the first Congress were added four more, none of them conservative. This new group plus the moderately radical Philip Livingston could consequently control the vote of the delegation.

document. This expedient was not very successful; only about one-third of the people to whom it was presented ever signed, but at least the revolutionists had eased their conscience.[20] The election of the Committee of One Hundred really marks the final defeat of the old conservative party, and the triumph of a new radical-conservative coalition which had been inevitably developed by recent events. Innately conservative aristocrats like Jay, Duane, and Livingston, having embarked on a thoroughgoing coercive policy, were gradually forced to sponsor the expedients of the group which they had once regarded as dangerously revolutionary.

THE PROVINCIAL CONGRESSES

Three features in particular mark the history of the New York Provincial Congress during the thirteen months between the time of its first assembling and the State declaration of independence: very poor attendance,[21] unusually frequent elections, and slowness in relinquishing the possibility of conciliation.[22]

From the beginning of July 1775 on, the attendance became so small that the expedient of delegating their powers to a Committee of Safety was resorted to again and again.[23] By fixing their quorums at seven or eight members they managed to transact business during months when no meeting of the

[20]Colden, *Letter Books*, II, 400, N. Y. H. S. Col. 1876-1877.

[21]The lack of attendance which frequently made it impossible to maintain any reasonable quorum was probably due both to the divided sentiments of its members, and the little that it could actually hope to accomplish under the existing circumstances.

[22]Deputies to the new provincial legislature were elected in every county, but in at least five out of the fourteen it was by a very small minority of the voters. In general the radicals tried to select men who would conciliate the conservatives, and lend dignity to the new government. Becker, *op. cit.*, pp. 201 ff.

[23]These committees numbered twelve or more delegates, each county having a fixed number of votes, irrespective of how many members it had on the committee.

Legislature would have been sufficiently attended.[24] As the Legislature delegated almost all of its power to the Committee for a specified length of time, the practical government of the State was often carried on by a kind of directory of five or six men.

Public opinion was very slow in crystallizing in New York State, as can be judged from numerous instances already cited. During 1775 and the spring of 1776, however, the process was going on more rapidly than ever before: by October most of the Loyalist members had stopped attending Congress, and by April of 1776 they were no longer allowed to vote. These changes in public opinion necessitated frequent reorganization of the personnel of Congress if it was faithfully to represent the feelings of the voters, and as a result four new legislatures were elected between May 1775 and July 1776.

The Whig coalition group in New York probably clung to the possibility of conciliation longer than the revolutionary party in any other colony. This may have been due somewhat to the difficult position of the Provincial Congress in New York City as well as to the greater loyalty of the voters. The large numbers of Tories in Kings, Queens, and Richmond placed the city in great danger if actual fighting should start, and yet to proceed actively to disarm or imprison them might bring on a bombardment from the fleet. The first Provincial Congress was selected, as has been seen, with the idea of conciliating the Loyalists, and even while they were carrying on their illegal government they were drawing up a plan for conciliation. On July 22d a hastily completed and unworkable plan was agreed to, and copies sent to England and the Continental Congress, in both of which places it received scant attention.

By October 19th Governor Tryon, despite assurances from the Congress, felt it safer to move to a warship in the harbor before Congress or the city committee should take him into

[24] *Am. Arch.*, 4th ser., II, 1242-1328 *passim*.

custody.[25] The Second Provincial Congress elected November 7th was less conciliatory than the first, but it was distrusted nevertheless by the Whig legislatures of the neighboring colonies. It soon demonstrated, however, that it possessed some spirit of resistance by defeating North's Conciliation Plan. Another interesting proof of the general drift of public opinion is shown by the fact that when Governor Tryon called for the election of a new legal Colonial Assembly in February the Whigs were able to swamp the polls, and return a body so entirely useless to the Loyalists that it was immediately prorogued.[26] Finally, in April, intercourse was suspended with the fleet in the harbor, but only after a severe letter from General Washington.[27] This date, April 19th, was later selected as the official beginning of the State. A few days later elections were held for the Third Provincial Congress with the Loyalists barred from the polls.

THE CONSTITUTION AND INDEPENDENCE

By May 1776 the time had arrived when conciliation seemed no longer possible, and a permanent State government must be drawn up. The Congress elected in April, however, refused to undertake the task until specifically authorized to do so by the voters. Hence a new election was held in June and practically the same group of men were reëlected as a combined legislature and constitutional convention.[28] They took no action toward independence or constitution making until after the news of the national declaration reached them, and then they formally accepted it for the State on July 9, 1776.[29]

[25]There were provincial troops under arms and Congress had issued £45000 in paper money. *Journal New York Provincial Congress*, I, 128.

[26]*Am. Arch.*, 4th ser., IV, 1153.

[27]*Jour. N. Y. Prov. Cong.*, I, 411, April 17, 1776.

[28]The radicals had joined with the delegates to the Continental Congress in urging that the question of national independence be submitted to the voters at this same election, but the Provincial Congress had refused for fear of complicating the issues involved in the election.

[29]*Jour. N. Y. Prov. Cong.*, I, p. 518.

This Legislative Convention composed of John Jay, Gouverneur Morris, Philip Schuyler, George Clinton, John Scott, R. R. Livingston, and others, was the ablest assembly that could have been selected in the State.[30] On August 1st a committee was appointed to draw up a constitution. The only fundamental issue was raised by Scott who led a large group in the convention favoring a really democratic constitution. The constitution committee turned out to be decidedly conservative, however, and was easily managed by the aristocratic Jay and Morris group. Thus democracy never came to be a serious issue, and the final draft was reported almost exactly as Jay had written it in the seclusion of his own home.[31] The convention debated the committee report for a month and a half but made no important changes except for the addition of those two political sports, the Councils of Appointment and Revision; not a very remarkable fact inasmuch as the committee represented the brains of the convention.

The New York Constitution of 1777 is well discussed in a number of works so that we need to indicate only a few points that are of interest from the standpoint of this study.[32] No mention of the possibility of a confederation or any external government is included, although the Articles were at this time being debated in Congress. In fact, Article One of the Constitution specifically states "that no authority shall, on any pretence whatever, be exercised over the people or members of this State, but such as shall be derived from and granted by them." The Assembly was to be elected annually on the basis of a county apportionment stipulated in the Constitution. The ratios show clearly that even in such a state as New York the agrarians had a tremendous majority over the mercantile

[30]From New York County there were: Bancker, Van Cortland, Jay, Roosevelt, Beekman, and others.

[31]Alexander, S. de A., *Political History of New York,* I, 13-15.

[32]Flick, *American Revolution in New York* and a number of older constitutional histories of the State contain detailed analyses.

interests. For example, New York County had only nine votes out of a total of seventy, whereas Tryon, the newest and most westerly county, had six. New York, Westchester, Richmond, Kings, and Albany together, the counties that might be considered as partly mercantile in their interests, fell seven votes short of a majority.[33] The Senate was selected by districts made up of several counties. The members were to serve for four years, but a quarter of the first group were to retire annually by lot.[34] All officers other than those specifically provided for were to be appointed by a council composed of the Governor and one Senator from each of the four senatorial districts. Military officers were to be appointed to serve during the pleasure of the council and were to be commissioned by the Governor.[35] The delegates to Congress were to be elected by a joint session of the Senate and Assembly from two complete lists presented by the two houses respectively.[36] The English Common Law and the acts of the royal Assembly up until April 19, 1775, were adopted as the Law of the State. It was provided that sales of lands made by the Indians since October 14, 1775, or to be made in the future should not be valid without the consent of the Legislature, and similarly all land grants made by the King after this date should be null and void.[37] As a whole the constitution compared very favorably

[33]*New York State Constitution*, Art. IV. The number of members from the counties was as follows: New York 9, Albany 10, Dutchess 7, Westchester 6, Ulster 6, Suffolk 5, Queens 4, Orange 4, Kings 2, Richmond 2, Tryon 6, Charlotte 4, Cumberland 3, Gloucester 2.

[34]In the Senate: the Southern district sent nine members, the Middle district six, the Western district six, and the Eastern district three. (See map p. 1 for the district boundaries.) Constitution, Article XII—according to the Constitution the numbers in both houses were not to be changed until seven years after the close of the war. Art. IV.

[35]Arts. XXIII and XXIV.

[36]Art. XXX.

[37]Art. XXXVII.

with those of the other states.[38] It remained in force substantially unchanged until 1821.

A Council of Safety was again resorted to to bridge the gap between the dissolution of the Convention and the inauguration of the new government. The contest for Governor was a portent of the political struggles of the years to come. George Clinton, representing the popular party, defeated the aristocratic Philip Schuyler, who was backed by Jay and Morris. One cause for this, which came as a great surprise, was Clinton's command of the state militia which had made him a well-known figure in the southern counties.[39] The first constitutional Legislature met at Kingston in September, but before they could agree upon a single law the advance of the British from both north and south impelled most of them precipitously to seek a safer locality. The few courageous legislators who remained, prior to the capture and burning of the town by the British, created themselves a convention and then selected seven of their members as a council of safety to govern until the Convention or Legislature should reassemble. This extra-legal body carried on what little government was possible during the fall, until the situation was again taken in hand by the Legislature which reassembled in January 1778. The first official statute of the new state was the one giving its assent to the Articles of Confederation on February 6th.[40] This date properly concludes the introductory history of New York's irregular conventions and congresses.[41]

[38]Hamilton, while he thought the constitution as a whole to be better than that of any other state, wrote G. Morris that the executive was too weak, and the Senate likely to become too aristocratic. *Hamilton's Works*, Const. Ed. IX, 71.

[39]Flick, *American Revolution in New York*, p. 93.

[40]*Laws of New York, 1778-1789*, Chap. I, 1, 1st sess., 1st m.

[41]The fact that the Articles were not legally adopted until 1781 does not prevent our tracing the real history of the Confederation back to the formation of the permanent state governments, and the acceptance of mutual tacit agreements as to the powers of Congress which formed the basis and were in turn legalized by the provisions of the Articles.

POLITICS AND POLITICIANS OF THE NEW STATE

From 1777 until nearly the end of the war it requires close scrutiny to discern any division in New York politics. Of course, the differences between radicalism and conservatism were occasionally in evidence, but the times were so critical that the general atmosphere was one of complete coöperation. Clinton was reëlected governor for additional three-year terms in 1780, 1783, and 1786 without opposition, but by 1783 the beginning of the division that was to produce Federalists and Anti-Federalists was apparent.[42] There has been a great deal of loose generalization regarding the make-up of these two groups, some of it by our leading historians. The usual statement is that the "Manor Lords" were Anti-Federalists and opposed the Federalist merchants for economic reasons.[43] As will be pointed out in Chapters VIII and IX, this statement would appear reasonable from the standpoint of questions bearing on the incidence of taxation, but it is unfortunately not borne out by the facts. The upsetting factor probably is that while the "Manor Lords" feared land taxes they also held public securities to an extent which made many of them favorable to the establishment of an adequate revenue. Thus while the strength of the Anti-Federalists rested on the landed classes, the most powerful of these landlords were often found in the opposition ranks. The principal leaders constantly working for

[42]Schuyler wrote to Hamilton in May, 1783, that the Legislature was still inclined to confer powers on Congress to discharge the debts, but that the contrary view was already taking root. Hammond, *Political Parties,* I, 7. The words "Federalist" and "Anti-Federalist" will be used in an anticipatory sense to denote the distinction between those men who followed the mercantile-creditor-nationalist leadership of Schuyler, and the agrarian-states rights leadership of Clinton. This use of these terms is not unjustifiable in the light of the thought of the period. The word "Anti-Federal" is applied to the followers of Clinton in the *New York Daily Advertiser* of January 31, 1787, that is, prior to the meeting of the Federal Convention.

[43]This theory is advanced in C. A. Beard's *Economic Interpretation of the Constitution,* pp. 38-58, and reiterated in C. E. Miner's *Ratification of the Federal Constitution in New York.,* pp. 13-14.

a stronger central government were: Hamilton, Schuyler, Jay, Duane, Hobart, Duer, L'Hommedieu, Lewis Morris, and Benson. Of this group Duane, Morris, Duer, and Hobart were extensive landowners, and Schuyler was one of the greatest "Manor Lords." Benson and L'Hommedieu were prosperous farmers. This leaves only Hamilton and Jay as men whose chief concerns were in the city. Robert R. Livingston, the greatest "Manor Lord" of the state at this time, was favorable to the Federalist views, although he was not an active leader.

On the opposing side George Clinton was the key figure in New York politics. He was not a member of one of the great families. His ancestors claimed distinction in the dim and safe past of Irish genealogy, but his immediate progenitors were of a middle station in the colony. This built up an intangible, but none the less real, barrier between him and the hereditary aristocracy and made him a queer leader for the "Manor Lords." Schuyler remarked of his election as Governor that his station in the colony scarcely fitted him for such a position.

The late French and Indian war had done much to make the political fortune of the Clintons. George's father had risen to be a colonel, and his brother James to be a general. At the close of the war George began his political career by securing the appointment of clerk of the Court of Common Pleas, etc., in their home county of Ulster. In 1768 he represented the county in the Colonial Assembly. His family war record also paved the way for his appointment as a brigadier general in 1776, and this in turn was a very important factor in his election to the governorship. Clinton was typically Irish in his genial personality, sharp temper, and exasperating obstinacy. He stood midway between the statesman and the demagogue. A Hibernian genius for politics that made him the idol of the lower classes was coupled with an unusual, and at times brilliant, talent for practical administration. A more

18

far-sighted statesman might have preserved the Confederation, but a mere far-sighted statesman might never have remained for six terms the Governor of New York.

The Senate and House usually contained a goodly percentage of the ablest men in the State, together with a large representation of the "great families." The same general group of individuals attended intermittently during the entire decade from 1778 to 1788, and hence it is of interest to discuss briefly the background and personality of some of these legislative leaders. Philip Schuyler of Albany and Saratoga, a typical aristocratic gentleman of the old Patroon nobility, rated by many as the ablest general on the American side, was the leader of the conservative security-holding interests in the Senate. At the same time he took a more active interest in western and Indian affairs than any of the other New York leaders. Opposed to him were two of Clinton's chief lieutenants: Abraham Yates, Jr. and John Haring, both Albany lawyers, and incidentally not "Manor Lords." Yates was the most active and able Anti-Federalist pamphleteer of the post-war period, writing under a series of pseudonyms.[44] Haring, an acute politician and debater, ably coöperated with him as a leader of the Senate.

Some slightly less important Senators deserve our brief attention. John Morin Scott, next to Clinton the most colorful political personality in the early State, would doubtless have been a major factor in post-war politics but for his death in 1784. Although he was a man of great wealth and social prominence, the grandson of Sir John Scott of Ancrum, he became the leading advocate in the Constitutional Convention of real democracy founded on a broad franchise. His popularity throughout the State made him a serious contender for the governorship in 1777. Lewis Morris of Morisania, the brother of Gouverneur Morris and a neighbor of Scott, changed from his advanced radicalism of 1774 to support the

[44] Such as Rough Hewer, Rough Hewer, Jr., Sydney, and probably many others.

conservative Schuyler faction in the later years of the Confederation. William Floyd of Long Island, a hard-working but slightly educated farmer, was thrust by the force of events into politics. It might be presumed that he would be an Anti-Federalist, and it is true that he opposed the adoption of the Constitution, but on the other hand he steadily voted for the impost both in Congress and in the Senate. This may have been a result of the personal influence of Hamilton, or simply the pressure of his constituents in the Southern district. He was one of the first men to make a purchase on the upper Mohawk when the State Land Office was reopened in 1784. Henry Wisner of Orange was one of the few active back-country Whigs from the beginning of the trouble with Great Britain. After attending the First and Second Continental Congresses, he returned to his native town of Goshen and started the manufacture of gunpowder. When the British threatened to invade Orange County he placed cannon along the highlands, hired men, and carried an a private defense of his own. These labors did not keep him from practically continuous service in the Senate as a leading Anti-Federalist.

The changing personnel of the assembly prevented any continuous leadership. Hamilton was too occupied with military affairs, and too young to be a potent influence before 1780. Even after that time his force was usually exerted as a lobbyist rather than as a member of the House. His real strength during these years lay in his personality as a political boss rather than in his official position. One of Hamilton's closest friends was Egbert Benson, who enjoyed the confidence of all the great Federalist leaders including Washington. Benson was Attorney-General from 1777 to 1789, but also served frequently in Congress and the Assembly. Ezra L'Hommedieu, a sound but not brilliant Federalist, was more important than either of these men as a State legislator. He was in office continually from the beginning of the war until the adoption of the Constitution and had a hand in making most of the laws.

His great interest in education led to the establishment of the New York State Agricultural Society, and the University of the State of New York. John Lansing, the most important Anti-Federalist of this group, was one of the great jurists and debaters of the day. His commanding presence and disarmingly logical style of address, which often dignified purely political motives, made him Clinton's ablest supporter. He was among those who left the Federal Convention when he felt they were exceeding their instructions, and helped to lead the State opposition to the Constitution. In 1807 he succeeded the aged Robert R. Livingston as Chancellor. ˙

Of the men who, because of high executive or judicial position, seldom became members of the Legislature, Robert R. Livingston, John S. Hobart, and George Clinton are by far the most important. Of all the great aristocrats Livingston was the greatest in both position and ability. Not even the lordly Van Rensselaers or Van Cortlandts could rival the Livingston's direct descent from the high nobility of the Old World.[45] Nor could they claim a superior record of political distinction in this country. Robert Livingston, however, was of a serious scholarly disposition, more at home on the bench than on the floor of a legislative body. Accordingly as Chancellor he generally remained aloof from petty state politics, only descending occasionally to attend some of the sessions of Congress or the Legislature during the most critical years. His political views were decidedly independent, not adhering steadily to those of either the Clinton or Schuyler factions, but tending toward the latter up until 1789. John S. Hobart was a Yale graduate, the son of a Connecticut minister, who, feeling that New York offered greater opportunities, settled on Long Island. There he gradually increased his fortunes until he became proprietor of Easton Manor, and a power in local politics. He served in the Legislature until 1777 when he was appointed a justice of

[45]The first Lord of the Manor of Livingston was a son of the Fourth Earl of Linlithgow.

the supreme court. Hobart is of particular importance in this study as one of the chief economists of the State, and a delegate to all of the price-fixing conventions at which New York was represented.

James Duane is one of the figures that history has greatly neglected. He was a quiet, hard-working lawyer who saw to it that the business of the Continental Congress was dispatched, advised the high officials at critical times, and could be relied on for sound, if not brilliant, statesmanship.[46] He helped to train the young Hamilton in politics, and although they often differed over minor matters they ably supported each other on every major issue. He served for ten continuous years in Congress, was a member of almost every important committee devoted to economic affairs, was a leading figure in the settlement of all the state boundary disputes, and became the first Mayor of New York City after the British evacuation. We shall hear much more of this man who hewed the wood and drew the water for the Revolution without losing his sense of the larger issues. A more brilliant but lesser figure was Gouverneur Morris. He has been so rewarded by the attentions of the historic muse that there is little more to be said about him here. Morris just failed to be a great statesman. He had the ability but not the persistent concentration necessary. The third and least important of this group of practical economic statesmen was William Duer of New York City, the great speculator of the period. He had a gift of eloquence that served the Federalist cause well in the Legislature and the Continental Congress, but his business interests prevented his devoting his best efforts to politics.

[46]Duane and Boudinot were the chief opponents of the move to hang Cornwallis. Hughes, *Washington*, Vol. III.

CHAPTER II

WARTIME FINANCE

INTRODUCTION

THE study of the financial relations of New York with the Continental Congress may conveniently be divided into three periods: the first extending to the beginning of Morris' labors as Superintendent of Finance, the second from that time until his resignation in 1784, and the third from then until the beginning of the new government in 1789. The first dividing point, 1781, has several things to recommend it: it coincides roughly with the end of actual fighting, the end of emissions of paper money, and the general effort to return to a specie basis.

Before proceeding to study the State relations with Congress it will be well to examine briefly the early evolution of the financial machinery of the latter.[1] Seventeen seventy-five was necessarily a year of experiment in Congress. Although two Treasurers were appointed to take care of the paper-money issues, no permanent organization for financial control was created, and during the course of the year three different five-member committees reported on specific financial questions.[2] These committees had to be chosen more or less at random as there was no general knowledge regarding the ability of the various delegates.[3] By the beginning of 1776 the war seemed likely to last for some time, and permanent arrangements had to be made for army pay. February 17th a standing com-

[1] Bolles, *Financial History of the United States, 1775-1789*, has a good and detailed account of this subject. (Chap. II.)

[2] Michael Hillegas and George Clymer were the Treasurers. *Journal Continental Congress*, II, 79, 192, 221; III, 328.

[3] James Duane of New York and Joseph Hewes of North Carolina were the only members of these finance committees who later became recognized as particularly able in handling financial matters.

mittee of finance was appointed to examine the accounts of the Treasurers and supervise the issue of paper money.[4] February 23rd they were authorized to establish an office.[5] This committee was enlarged from time to time, and replacements made, but without essential change in organization until 1778.[6]

˙ These early Congresses were made up of the ablest men in the country. New York was represented by George Clinton 1775-1777, John Jay 1774-1779, James Duane 1774-1784, Philip Livingston 1774-1778, Lewis Morris 1775-1777, Philip Schuyler 1775-1781, and several others of slightly less prominence. James Duane soon came to be regarded as one of the leaders of Congress in financial matters. Throughout the whole war period New Yorkers played a prominent rôle in financial deliberations.[7]

The year 1777 was largely taken up by the debates on the Articles, but meanwhile increasing financial pressure necessitated drawing bills of exchange upon France. Seventeen seventy-eight opened with finance and foreign affairs as the most pressing questions before Congress. The affairs of the Treasury were badly tangled; reorganization and a larger income were vitally necessary. New York had in Congress the strongest financial delegation of the whole period: Duer, Duane, and Gouverneur Morris. Robert Morris, Roger Sherman, and Elbridge Gerry were in attendance also. These men worked out a plan for a real Treasury Department. The Ordinance passed September 26, 1778, provided for: a Treas-

[4]James Duane, Elbridge Gerry, Thomas Willing, Thomas Nelson, and Richard Smith were the original committee. *Journal Continental Congress,* IV, 156.

[5]*Journal Continental Congress,* IV, 170. April 1st an auditor with assistants was provided for and made responsible to the committee.

[6]By 1777 this standing committee was often referred to as the Board of Treasury.

[7]Duane was joined in 1777 by Gouverneur Morris and William Duer. They left, 1780 and 1778 respectively, and Hamilton served in 1782 and 1783.

ury Building, with separate offices for the Treasurer, Comptroller, and Auditors; two chambers of accounts with three commissioners in each; a Treasurer, Auditor, and Comptroller to be appointed annually by Congress by a vote of nine States; and quarterly reports regarding the condition of the Treasury.[8] This system was still under the supervision of the Congressional "Board" of Treasury.

The worries of the Board increased as time went on. The value of the currency by 1779 was fast approaching zero, the income from the states was wholly inadequate, and the course of the war in the south was far from encouraging.[9] A large number of the ablest men were being actively employed elsewhere, and Congress lacked leaders.[10] Fortunately, Gouverneur Morris, James Duane, and John Jay rose to the occasion, and did much to guide affairs safely through the year.[11]

With the increasing amount of routine business, members of Congress could no longer give sufficient attention to the detailed work of the Treasury. July 30, 1779, therefore, a new general ordinance for the organization of the Treasury was agreed to. The Board was to consist of two members of Congress and three commissioners who were not members. Any three commissioners were to constitute a quorum. The office of Comptroller was discontinued, and the division of

[8]*Journal Continental Congress*, XII, 956 ff. The machinery worked as follows: the auditor received all accounts, then submitted them to one of the chambers, after examination they would be returned to the auditor who would send them to the comptroller, the comptroller would then draw bills on the treasurer for the sums audited, and the treasurer would make payment. Michael Hillegas was elected treasurer under this system, and served continuously in the Treasury Department from this time on.

[9]The problems of the western land and the New Hampshire grants occupied a large part of the time of this session of Congress.

[10]The chief men in Congress during 1779 from States other than New York were: Henry Laurens, Roger Sherman, Elbridge Gerry, and Thomas Burke. Samuel Adams was in attendance, but can hardly be rated as a very valuable constructive worker.

[11]In many respects this was Gouverneur Morris' greatest year of service to his country.

audit greatly expanded. There was to be an Auditor-General, and six Auditors for army accounts. The two chambers of accounts were left unchanged. The Board of Treasury was to supervise the whole system, as before, and was given the right to dismiss auditors, although all appointing power still rested in Congress.[12] This form of organization still retained all the faults of divided responsibility. Hamilton wrote and spoke vigorously in favor of centering responsibility in the hands of one individual, but Congress made no further change until February 1781.[13]

Seventeen hundred and eighty was perhaps the darkest year of the war from the standpoint of Congress. The army was almost destitute. The currency reached a point where no further issue was possible. The French Minister spoke of threatened mediation on the basis of the status quo. In August and September Congress received the news of Gates' defeat at Camden and Arnold's treason.

Madison first took a prominent part in national affairs during this session, and assumed the leadership almost at once. He was assisted by Duane and R. R. Livingston representing New York, but there were few prominent men from the other States.

The affairs of the Treasury Department continued in an unsatisfactory condition despite the reorganization of the year before. In the fall a committee investigated the situation and reported that the office was pervaded by the "Demon of Discord," and that the best solution appeared to be unified control.[14] In February of the following year all the executive departments were reorganized and placed under single responsible officers.

PAPER CURRENCY

The Revolution was after all a revolt against taxation, and the State Assemblies were loath to risk their none too certain

[12]*Journal Continental Congress,* XIV, 903 ff, July 30, 1779.
[13]Hamilton, *History of the Republic,* II, 92 f.
[14]*Journal Continental Congress,* XVIII, 1091 f.

support by any attempts to extract money by force from an unwilling populace. The New York Congress sent an official letter to its delegates in Congress, May 25, 1775, explaining the impossibility of adequate taxation, and a week later dispatched to them a confidential report containing plans for a general currency.[15]

A similar attitude on the part of the other States left Congress with the option of raising money either by currency or loans. To float a loan takes some time even in the case of a government with assured credit, and Congress could scarcely hope to get money with sufficient rapidity by this method. Franklin and John Adams stoutly resisted the issue of paper, but the great majority in Congress saw no other solution.[16] June 22, 1775, a bill was passed providing for the issue of up to two million Spanish milled dollars, pledging the faith of the Confederate Colonies for their redemption. This was the plan favored by the New York Assembly and Delegates.[17] A month later it was provided that each state should be responsible for the redemption of a quota of the currency based upon its *total* population, and temporary quotas were adopted.[18] The basis of assessment was altered in the Articles of Confederation to the value of surveyed property and buildings.

The New York Provincial Congress made no attempt at taxation prior to 1778, and consequently large sums had to

---

[15]*Jour. N. Y. Prov. Cong.*, I, 14, 15, 18-21. An opportunity was afforded the merchants of New York City to attend the Assembly and express their views on paper money, but on the appointed day, May 30, none of them appeared.

Gouverneur Morris was the leading member of the Committee that proposed plans for a general currency. The New York report favored having all the States responsible for the redemption of the money, as they feared the credit of Connecticut and New Jersey.

[16]J. Sparks, *Writings of Franklin*, I, 303; *Works of John Adams*, X, 376.

[17]*Journal Continental Congress*, II, 103.

[18]*Journal Continental Congress*, II, 222. The initial issues were to be repaid in four annual installments starting November 31, 1779.

be raised by either loans or paper.[19] Of the two expedients
the Provincial Congress found the issue of paper both easier
and more popular with the majority of their constituents. The
first issue of £45,000 ($112,500) authorized September 2,
1775, was all gone by the end of the year, and when the Continental Congress quite properly refused to loan money to the
State for the payment of internal expenses further issues were
resorted to.[20] On January 6, 1776, £55,000 was authorized,
and on August 7, the treasury again being empty, £200,300
were added to the fast-swelling total.[21] This new State money,
along with the Continental Currency, was made legal tender for
the payment of both public and private debts.[22] As early as
June 22, 1775, some of the County Committees started issuing
bills on their own account. It is impossible to tell how long
this practice was kept up, but it was obviously discountenanced
by both state and national authorities.[23] The issue of notes
by private individuals which had been going on to some extent
was prohibited by the Council of Safety, June 20, 1776.[24]

Depreciation was from first to last the great evil that the
statesmen feared. For over two years both Congress and the
States tried to fight this evil by legislation, refusing to admit
the inexorable facts. Depreciation was apparent in New York

[19]According to the account books of Treasurer Livingston, N. Y. H. S.,
more than $100,000 was needed. A proposal to levy a tax amounting to
$37,500 was defeated by the back-country representatives in the Legislature
Aug. 30, 1775. The merchants of Albany and New York, being in general
creditors, would have preferred taxation to inflation. *Jour. N. Y. Prov.
Cong.*, I, 128.

[20]The funds for retirement were to be raised by taxation, but no specific
taxes were provided. *Jour. N. Y. Prov. Cong.*, I, 133-134. The refusal of
Congress to lend is recorded. *Ibid.*, p. 239.

[21]The issue of Jan. 6, *Jour. N. Y. Prov. Cong.*, I, 435.
The issue of Aug. 7, *Jour. N. Y. Prov. Cong.*, I, 560.
The account book of P. V. B. Livingston, N. Y. H. S., contains a com-
plete record of expenditures.

[22]*Jour. N. Y. Prov. Cong.*, I, 819.

[23]Flick, *op. cit.*, p. 116.

[24]*Am. Arch.*, 4th ser., VI, 996.

by November 3, 1775, when Peter Curtenius testified before
the Provincial Congress that he had paid 19s. 6d. for blankets
worth not over 12s., and that these same blankets had been
purchased by the retailers about two months before for a
little over 5s.[25] January 11, 1776, the Continental Congress
ordered that any person who refused to receive paper or
obstructed its circulation should be treated as an enemy;[26]
and the States tried to help by similar laws. New York passed
a law March 1, 1776, which made all bills emitted by the Continental Congress, the Provincial Congress or the (constitutional) Convention legal tender, and threatened forfeiture of
a quarter of the debt to the State as the penalty for anybody
refusing the same. The debtor could meanwhile discharge his
obligation by payment to the State Treasurer.[27] The Provincial Congress also appointed an able committee to consider
the question of checking depreciation, but naturally no workable solution was found.[28] At the beginning, and again at the
end of 1777, Congress called upon the States to stop issuing
paper money, and New York outwardly complied with this
policy for the next four years.[29] In reality paper was issued
by New York right along, because in April, 1778, impress of
provision was authorized and the agents paid for the articles
impressed with special promissory notes in lieu of currency.[30]
In February 1780, the tax collectors were authorized to accept
such certificates in payment of taxes, if offered by the original

[25]*Jour. N. Y. Prov. Cong.*, I, 193; Report of P. T. Curtenius and T.
Pearsall.
[26]*Journal Continental Congress*, IV, 49.
[27]*Jour. N. Y. Prov. Cong.*, I, 819.
[28]*Ibid.*, I, p. 775.
[29]*Journal Continental Congress*, VII, 124, and IX, 955-956. J. S. Hobart
gave the following estimate of State issues on Aug. 2, 1777:

Mass.	£470,000	R. I.	£119,000
Conn.	210,000	N. H.	73,568
N. Y.	187,500		

These figures are presumably in Sterling Pounds worth $4.86. *Jour.
Prov. Cong.*, I, 1029-1030.
[30]*Laws of N. Y.*, Chap. XXLX, pp. 28-30, April 2, 1778.

recipient, and they became, to that extent at least, an addition to the circulating medium.[31]

The New England States, particularly, felt that depreciation might be checked by coöperation among neighboring states in the enactment of similar laws. As early as December 25, 1776, these four states met at Providence to consider plans for preventing depreciation. They recommended payment of interest on bills and regulation of prices of goods and labor.[32] Congress approved of these plans, published the report, and sent it to the States. It was resolved to call upon the Middle States, Maryland, and Virginia, to meet at Yorktown, Pennsylvania, and the Southern States at Charleston, South Carolina, on the third Monday in the following March. J. S. Hobart and Robert Yates were appointed by the New York Congress to attend the Yorktown meeting.[33] Delegates from all the states called on assembled, but were unable to agree on any satisfactory plans.

The New England States and New York still felt that they might accomplish something alone. In July 1777 they assembled a convention at Springfield, Massachusetts, at which New York was represented by Hobart.[34] A unanimous sentiment was found to prevail regarding both the cause and effect of the evils of depreciation. The convention proposed to take state currency out of circulation by a loan, and to lay heavy and frequent taxes.

Congress was much impressed by this meeting, and called for a meeting, January 15, 1778, of all the states north of Delaware at New Haven; of Virginia and North Carolina at Fredericksburg; and of South Carolina and Georgia at Charleston. The conventions were advised "to ascertain and regulate the price of labour, manufactures, internal produce [etc.] . . . and also the charges of innholders." The

[31]*Laws of N. Y.*, Chap. XXXV, pp. 102-103, February 12, 1780.
[32]*Journal Continental Congress*, VII, 65.
[33]*Jour. N. Y. Prov. Cong.*, I, 1029.
[34]*Pap. Cont. Cong.*, no. 78, XI, f. 207.

State Legislatures were asked to enact laws to enforce the recommendations of the conventions.[35] This was the most elaborate attempt at uniform price fixing ever authorized by Congress.

The New Haven meeting was assembled as planned, and recommended a detailed system of price-fixing laws. As a result of this Governor Clinton urged some immediate measures in his next message to the State Legislature.[36] March 3, 1778, New York passed a law fixing prices for practically all articles at 25% higher than those of 1774.[37] This law was suspended June 29, however, as Congress decided after reviewing the actions of the various States that it would be better to recommend a uniform Congressional measure.[38]

Feeling throughout the country against the merchants who charged high prices was at its peak in 1779. Washington wrote to Reed regarding engrossers and forestallers: "I would to God that one of the more atrocious in each state was hung from gallows five times as high as those prepared for Haman." He called them the "murderers of our cause."[39]

Congress was so slow in agreeing upon any suitable measures that the New England States again sought to hasten action in the fall of 1779. The representatives from New York and the New England States assembled at Hartford on October 20th.[40] They recommended another detailed plan for the regulation of prices embodying the general principle that they should not exceed twenty times those prevailing in 1774.[41] Congress received the report of the convention, and on November 19 addressed a circular letter to all the States

[35] *Journal Continental Congress*, IX, 956-57.

[36] *Public Papers of George Clinton*, II, 299. The Massachusetts Assembly, however, thought it unwise to fix prices. *Ibid.*, III, 220.

[37] *Laws of N. Y.*, Chap. XXXIV, p. 36.

[38] Suspended until 20 days after the next meeting of the Legislature. Chap. XLII, p. 41. In October the act was repealed altogether. Chap. II, p. 44.

[39] Richard Hildreth, *History of the United States*, III, 272.

[40] Hobart for New York, as usual.

[41] *Pap. Cont. Cong.*, no. 33, f. 369.

urging uniform price-fixing laws "on the following principles, and to commence their operation from the first day of February next [1780] : articles . . . wages . . . water and land carriage, not to exceed twenty fold of the price current through various seasons of the year 1774. Salt and military stores . . . to be excepted." Laws against engrossing and withholding were also recommended.[42]

February 26, 1780, the New York Legislature passed an act complying with these recommendations of Congress. They adopted the twenty fold basis for prices in general, but established specific prices for a large number of articles. The penalty for overcharging was set at treble the value of the article in question.[43]

Men saw, as time went on, the futility of price fixing in a country where governmental authority was weak at best. Duer and Lewis in Congress had urged the removal of all limitations as early as 1778.[44] It was the opinion of the wiser men of the day as well as of later historians that, because of the factor of illicit trading introduced, prices actually tended to be raised by the regulating laws.[45] All New York efforts of this type came to an end in June 1780.[46]

In the face of this decline in governmental credit the merchant or creditor class, in general, urged the correct solution of increased taxation, but the great mass of the farmers refused to admit their ability to pay even the existing taxes, and offered various ingenious schemes instead.[47] This controversy may

[42]*Journal Continental Congress*, XV, 1254 and 1289-1290.

[43]*Laws of N. Y.*, Chap. LIII, p. 106 f.

[44]*Journal Continental Congress*, XII, 990-991.

[45]See letter headed "A Farmer" in *New York Journal and General Advertiser*, January 4, 1779, N. Y. H. S.

[46]In this month, after the repudiation of the continental currency, the act of February 26th was nullified by a law providing that all prices fixed by law should be deemed the prices in gold or silver. *Laws*, Chap. LXXII, p. 142.

[47]The monetary situation in New York was especially bad between 1778 and 1781; the circulating medium was not only depreciating rapidly, but

be followed in any of the newspapers of the day. For example, "A Farmer" in a series of letters to the *New York Journal* said: "There never was a nation who were able to pay such large sums of money in taxes, without being distressed, as we are at present, and it is clearly the duty of the legislature by large and frequent taxes to reduce the circulating medium . . . until the relation of 1775 is restored." He also attacked the price-fixing laws as useless, and oppressive to the honest merchant.[48] He was answered immediately by "A Real Farmer" who claimed that monopolistic trading was to a great extent the cause of high prices. He admitted that "deep" taxes were desirable but claimed the farmer was unable to pay them because of the upset conditions. He proposed a tax on the currency itself. The same writer also had a plan to reduce the domestic debt by calling in all loans and reissuing the certificates at 25% of their original face value.[49] Many county and town meetings were held during 1779, and all kinds of plans other than taxation were proposed to check depreciation.[50]

February 26, 1780, Congress gave up the attempt to keep faith with the holders of the paper currency, and passed an act for the redemption of the old paper by new 5% interest-bearing notes redeemable December 31, 1786, at the ratio of 40 to 1. The Continental Loan Officer in each state was to be given a

appears to have been becoming scarcer at the same time. This situation was claimed to be a result of the large number of quartermasters' certificates taken in return for army supplies. These were not legal tender, and did not circulate readily. On the other hand, there were large amounts of specie gained through trade with the enemy, etc., which were tightly hoarded. Hamilton believed that there was only about $6,000,000 in specie in the country in 1781 as against $30,000,000 before the war. Hamilton, *History of the Republic*, II, p. 230. Two months later, however, he contradicted this by saying "the quantity of our specie has greatly increased" since the beginning of the war. *The Continentalist*, July 12, 1781.

[48]*N. Y. Journal and General Advertiser*, Jan. 4, 1779; see also copies of Dec. 21, 1778 and Jan. 11, 1779.

[49]*Ibid.*, January 18, 1779, January 25, 1779, February 1, 1779 and February 8, 1779.

[50]*Ibid.*, February 15, 1779, July 26, 1779, August 2, 1779, and August 9, 1779.

proportionate quota of six-tenths of the total new bills, and these would be put in circulation as fast as the State Treasurer received old ones to exchange for them. The remaining four-tenths was retained by the Continental Treasury. Accompanying this act was a recommendation to the states to revise their legal-tender laws accordingly.[51]

While this act has been regarded as immoral by many later historians it is hard to see how Congress, once having gotten the currency into such a situation, could have done otherwise. There was no widespread protest against it in the writings of leading New Yorkers of that day; shrewd ones must have undoubtedly realized the course of events and guarded themselves accordingly.[52] The New York Legislature on June 15 agreed to this act of Congress and established the forty-to-one ratio.[53]

On June 27, 1780, Congress established a basis of depreciation in order to reckon justly the specie value of obligations contracted in the old currency at various periods.[54] The New York Legislature felt incapable of doing likewise: "In this state there is no possibility of ascertaining what was the current value of Continental Bills at any period compared with specie, from any actual exchanges of the one for the other, very few having been made, and those few generally in a private way, because of the odium attached to such transactions."[55] In 1781, however, they attempted to deal with the problem in a way that would provide as equitable a solution as possible. By an act passed in February, the act establishing the forty-to-one ratio was repealed and certain officials were constituted

[51]*Journal Continental Congress*, XVI, 261-269. The New York Delegates voted aye. New York made the new bills legal tender June 30, 1780.

[52]Clinton to Duane, April 27, 1780. *Duane Papers*, N. Y. H. S., no. 45.

[53]*Laws of N. Y.*, Chap. LXIV, p. 131, June 15, 1780.

[54]A geometric progression from Sept. 1, 1777 to March 1, 1780 was to form the basis for computation. A table embodying this principle was drawn up by the Treasury on July 29, 1780. *Journal Continental Congress*, XVII, 784-785.

[55]*Pap. Cont. Cong.*, no. 67, II, ff. 322-24.

a standing committee to set the scale of depreciation between the old Continental currency and specie according to their judgment, and until they gave a ruling it was to be regarded as 75-1.[56] State and Colonial paper was to have the same value as the old Continental. March 30, 1781, the Legislature adopted a definite scale for depreciation up to March 15, 1780, giving the ratio between paper and specie at fifteen day intervals.[57]

Although price fixing was now a thing of the past, the New England States still hoped to remedy the general economic situation by conventions. A convention was held at Boston in the summer of 1780. They recommended: A series of measures for better army supply; the repeal of embargo acts; the levying of heavy taxes to sink the new continental bills as fast as possible; and the cessation of state currency issues. A copy of these proceedings was sent to New York with a request for its concurrence.[58] Governor Clinton urged the consideration of these matters in his opening message to the Legislature in August 1780. The houses appointed commissioners who met with those of the Eastern States at Hartford on the second Wednesday in November, and reaffirmed what had been done at Boston.[59] These proceedings were considered by the New

[56]*Laws of N. Y.*, Chap. XIX, February 22, 1781, pp. 166-67.
The Council of Revision tried unsuccessfully to block this legislation on the ground that to delegate such powers to a small group of probably interested men was both unconstitutional and unlikely to work well in actual practice. *Minutes of the Council of Revision*, Feb. 22, 1781.

[57]*Laws of N. Y.*, Chap. L, pp. 191-192. A hundred dollars in specie was worth the following amounts in paper:

Sept. 1, 1777	$100	Jan. 1, 1779	$742
Jan. 1, 1778	146	June 1, 1779	1344
June 1, 1778	265	Jan. 1, 1780	2932
		Mar. 15, 1780	4000

[58]*Proceedings of a Convention of the Delegates of New York and the New England States,* ed. by F. B. Hough, p. 51.

[59]*Journal New York Senate,* p. 17, *House,* p. 65. Philip Schuyler, Egbert Benson, and, as usual, J. S. Hobart, were elected. They recommended a general convention of all states as far south as Virginia. Phillips, *Continental Currency,* p. 149.

York Legislature, but no special action was taken.[60] This put an end to conventions for the alleviation of economic conditions prior to the surrender at Yorktown.

By 1781 the Legislature claimed that the adverse balance of trade in New York, due to selling supplies to the Continental Army and receiving only certificates in return, had drained the State of currency to such an extent that there were probably not enough old Continental bills left in the State to draw into circulation its quota of the new bills at forty-to-one. Accordingly an act was passed to issue State bills of credit in an amount equal to the $411,250 of new bills reposing in the New York Continental Loan Office. Whenever any old bills were brought in to be exchanged, new Continental bills would be given for them and a corresponding amount of the new State paper would be destroyed by the treasurer. The same thing would be done if any new Continental bills should be paid in.[61] Governor Clinton wrote to the Delegates in Congress that in reality this act only furthered the aims of that body to establish a more serviceable circulating medium, because he doubted if there was enough Continental currency in the country to draw out all the new "40 for 1" bills.[62] He assured the Presi-

[60]*Journal New York Senate,* Feb. 1, 1781, p. 37.

[61]*Laws of N. Y.,* Chap. XLVI, 186-188, March 27, 1781. Professor Ralph V. Harlow in an article in the *American Historical Review,* XXXV, no. 1, 50, records on a table of State emissions of paper money that New York voted $487,000 in bills of credit in 1780 and issued $77,750. This is an error. No paper currency was voted or issued under any act of the Legislature during 1780. The confusion probably arises from the wording of section I of the Act of 1781. This reads: " . . . That there shall be emitted on the credit of this state, bills to the amount of $411,250, being the amount of the sum now remaining unissued in the *Continental Loan Office* within this state of the monies allotted to this state for emission and redemption in consequence of the said system recommended by the said act of Congress." These unissued bills here referred to are, of course, the new emission Continental bills, not a State issue of the year before. The $75,750 undoubtedly represents the amount of these Continental bills drawn into circulation by March, 1781.

[62]Clinton to the Delegates in Congress, March 28, 1781. *Duane Papers,* N. Y. H. S., Box II.

dent of the Congress that "we have endeavored to prevent it [the New York system] from clashing with that established by Congress March 18, 1780."[63] This reasoning either shows a remarkable lack of understanding of the aims of Congress, or else it is just a bit of sophistry to cover up the fact that New York was in reality defeating Congress' attempt to return to a specie basis. An issue of still more money without waiting for the old bills to be turned in was simply a continuation of inflation, and tended to depreciate the currency accordingly. Of course, in theory this new State paper would cease to circulate just as soon as all the old Continental bills could be rounded up, but according to the very opinions expressed by the Legislature as an excuse for its issue this would never be likely to happen. Congress apparently felt that the New York pleas of distress had a real basis, for in May 1781 a committee of Congress reported that, realizing the urgency, they could not disapprove of New York's issuing more bills of credit as long as they did not plan to exceed the sum of the new Congress bills assigned to them.[64] Despite the bad conditions in the State and these inflationist views, however, depreciation was less in New York than in the Southern States.[65]

The later history of the old Continental bills should be mentioned before leaving the subject. As the old bills were turned into the State Treasury in exchange for those of the new emission they were sent to the Continental Treasury to be destroyed. Up to January 1, 1786, $3,824,010.45 worth were sent from New York. All the States together sent in $111,406,124.45, which left a balance outstanding in January 1786 of $130,-127,419.45.[66] Of this balance some were redeemed prior to 1788, and a few more after that date in accordance with Hamilton's ratio of 100 to 1, but a great many of them were undoubtedly lost or destroyed.

[63]*Pap. Cont. Cong.*, no. 67, II, f. 372.
[64]*Journal Continental Congress*, XX, 473-473, May 2, 1781.
[65]C. J. Bullock, *Finances of the United States, 1775-1789*, pp. 133 and 166.
[66]*Pap. Cont. Cong.*, no. 139, I, ff. 69-71, 77.

LOANS

New York at the beginning of the war had loan officers left over from the Colonial period. In 1770 the Colony had been given permission to emit £120,000 in bills of credit, as has been mentioned in Chapter I. The act emitting this money February 16, 1771, and a supplementary act passed the same day, provided for the organization of a set of county loan officers, to handle the money. The two officers for each county were to form a corporate body capable of suing or being sued. They were to meet four times a year and keep careful records and minutes of their meetings, and their accounts were to be examined annually by the judges and supervisors.[67]

A marked difference between the Colonial loan officers and the ones established by Congress was that these former officials were lending agents rather than borrowing ones. They took their quotas of the £120,000 and loaned it out in mortgages at 6% interest.[68] Money was collected by the revolutionary State government from some of these Colonial loan officers as late as 1777.[69]

[67]The judges of the inferior courts of each county or any one or more of them together with a majority of the supervisors were to elect two loan officers, except in the counties of New York, Albany, Dutchess, Ulster, and Orange. In Orange, one officer was to be elected in each of the two precincts. The officers for New York, Albany, Dutchess, and Ulster were named in the act, but in case of their death or resignation the vacancies could be filled by election as in the other counties. There were three loan officers for New York County. *Laws of the Colony of New York,* Published by Act of Assembly of New York, 1774, Chaps. 1472 and 1473. (Edition of 1890 same chapters.)

[68]The county quotas were:

New York	£38,000	Ulster	£9,200
Albany	20,000	Suffolk	9,200
Westchester	10,712	Kings	5,168
Queens	10,712	Richmond	3,248
Dutchess	10,560	Orange	3,200

After 1776, the principal would be due at the rate of 10% annually; as this was paid in the officers might reloan it up to 1785. Chap. 1472.

[69]P. V. B. Livingston received £4,640 from the Loan Officers of Albany County in 1777. That was the only large payment made by any of the officials prior to their supercession by the state officers in 1778. *Account Books of P. V. B. Livingston,* N. Y. H. S.

The new Provincial Congress authorized men in specific instances to borrow money for equipping troops and so forth, on its credit, and also received advances from Congress, as did all the other states, amounting to $485,000 by September 1778.[70]

On October 3, 1776, the Continental Congress requested a loan of $5,000,000, and established machinery for its collection. In each State there was to be established a "Continental Loan Office" with an officer appointed by the State to receive the money on loan, answer the drafts of the Continental Treasurer, and pay the annual interest to the individual lenders. He was to keep regular books, and transmit to the Continental Treasurer a monthly account of the cash in his offices. They were to be paid one-eigth of one per cent on the money loaned at their office.[71] Subsequently the Continental Loan Officers were made receivers of monies raised to meet Congressional requisitions, and were allowed an additional two per cent fee on interest payments.[72] H. I. Van Rensselaer, Dirk Ten Broeck, Abraham Yates, Jr., Benjamin Tillotson, and John Cochran served successively in this capacity in New York.

March 30, 1778, the State, in response to request of Congress of the preceding November, provided for the appointment of a Loan Office Commissioner for each county to receive subscriptions to Continental loans, and send the money to the Continental Loan Officer.[73] This plan was quite similar to that by which the Colonial Loan Offices had been established in the larger counties.

[70]*Jour. N. Y. Prov. Cong.*, I, 100.
Clinton Papers, III, Sept. 6, 1778.
[71]*Journal Continental Congress*, V, 845-46.
[72]Jan. 14, 1777 and Sept. 29, 1778, respectively. *Journal Continental Congress*, VII, 37 and XII, 956-967.
[73]*Laws of N. Y.*, Chap. XVIII, p. 22. March 30, 1778. They were also to submit their books to the Continental Loan Officer. Oct. 8, 1779, Chap. VIII, p. 76. The Governor was given the power to appoint commissioners of the Loan Office, with consent of the Council.

This structure had the advantage of reconciling national finance with state sovereignty, but from these same compromises there arose serious defects. The Board of Treasury reported to Congress in 1785 that "the effects which have followed from the establishment of this office [that of Continental Loan Officer] have been such as might be expected from officers not personally responsible for the execution of their trust to those whose interest was confided to them—unsettled accounts, a non-compliance with the resolves of Congress and the instructions of the Treasurer, and in some instances of importance an absolute deviation from them . . . . Without the gift of prophecy it may reasonably be inferred, that the Commissioners of the Treasury will never be able to ascertain what, if any monies are in the hands of the several officers."[74]

The first Continental loan was issued most unwisely at only 4%, the rate used by well-established governments. Money loaned on sound security brought 6% so that naturally the amount subscribed was negligible. The reasoning of Congress appears rather incomprehensible. It may be that the agrarian majority were disinclined to enrich the few commercial capitalists by high interest rates. In January, 1777, Congress provided that loans might be made in State currency, and in February they raised the interest rate to 6%. To the modern observer even this seems entirely too optimistic. For a body with no better security to offer than the Continental Congress to be able to borrow money in large amounts at a rate of less than eight or ten per cent would seem entirely improbable. Not everybody in Congress was blind to the bad psychological effect of unsuccessful loans. John Adams wrote in February 1777: "I fear that for want of wisdom to raise the interest in season, we shall be necessitated within a few months to give eight or ten per cent, and not obtain the money we want after

[74]*Pap. Cont. Cong.*, no. 193, I, ff. 70-81.

all. I have been so often a witness of the miseries of after wisdom that I am wearied to death of it."[75]

Congress asked for $15,000,000 in loans in 1777, and $10,000,000 in 1778, but as these loans could be made in paper the specie value received rapidly became very small. $65,558,-454 was borrowed in all and netted a specie equivalent of $11,391,554.[76] These certificates were of two types, one bearing interest in specie and the other in paper. As a result of a motion of Gouverneur Morris, interest paid on money loaned after 1778 was increased in proportion to the total circulation of Continental Currency.[77] By 1779 it was clear to most men that the further issue of loan office certificates was no better than printing paper money.[78] The two and three hundred dollar certificates were, owing to the depreciation of the currency and non-payment of interest, a handy circulating medium, and hence tended to increase depreciation just the same as any increase in the amount of currency would. As a result no further loans receivable in paper at its face value were issued after 1780.[79] The nominal sums advanced by the States give only a very rough indication of the actual specie value loaned unless we take into consideration the period at which the money was paid.[80] In general the New England States and New York loaned the largest percentages of their total when Continental money was valuable. This contrast between the Northern and Southern States comes out more forcibly when we compare the $7,050,000 loaned by the former prior to March 1, 1778, as against about $300,000 for the latter.[81]

[75]Adams, *Works*, IX, 452.
[76]*Journal Continental Congress*, XIX, 160-172. An estimate made in February, 1781.
[77]*Ibid.*, XIV, 760-762.
[78]*Ibid.*, XV, 83. Also Bolles, p. 260.
[79]*Ibid.*, XVII, 804, 5th Sept. Also Bolles, p. 103.
[80]For a statement of the sums lent by the States see Appendix F.
[81]*Pap. Cont. Cong.*, no. 12, ff. 90-91. Delaware is excluded from both these estimates—her contributions being negligible and her status as much Southern as Northern. Pennsylvania paid in only $18,000,000 prior to 1780,

New York loaned $495,833 between the opening of the Loan Office in November 1776 and September 10, 1777; $354,167 between then and March 1, 1778; and $2,226,074 between this date and March 18, 1780—making a total specie value $949,729,575.[82] As the total specie value for all the loans was only $11,391,563 New York's real contribution was very large in proportion to her effective population and resources.

The above figures represent only money recorded as paid into the Continental Treasury. Exactly what the receipts of the Loan Officers were it is impossible to tell with exactness. An investigating committee in 1788 reported that only in New Hampshire and Massachusetts had the Loan Office accounts been adjusted. In Virginia the accounts of the first Loan Officer had been lost, in Rhode Island, North Carolina, South Carolina, and Georgia no records were in shape to examine. "In New York . . . there having been two Loan Officers, the accounts of the first were settled by the commissioners of accounts for the Northern Department in 1780, but not having been approved by the Board of Treasury, or the Auditor General, the same has not been entered on the books, but remains in the state they were returned to the Treasury. The accounts for the other Loan Officer have been settled by the late Commissioner, but no order has been given for their entry."[83] This is a typical example of the ineffiency with which all government affairs were administered.

so that approximately $10,000,000 of her large total of $28,522,500 represents paper scarcely worth $100,000.

The following table may be of interest to the reader:

Date Received	Nominal Sum	Specie Sum
Prior to Sept. 10, '77	$3,868,466	$3,868,466
Sept. 10, '77 to Mar. 1, '78	3,444,480	2,560,926
Mar. 31, '78 to Mar. 31, '80	43,939,765	4,729,505
Mar. 31, '80 to Feb. 16, '81	9,305,373	232,667*

*Reckoned at forty to one, which is of course a large over-valuation. *Pap. Cont. Cong.*, no. 12, f. 76.

[82] *Ibid.*, f. 58.

[83] *Pap. Cont. Cong.*, no. 26, III, f. 707.

Chapter III

WARTIME FINANCE
(Continued)

REQUISITIONS AND TAXES, 1775-1781

THE cost of the war had to be borne, in the end, by the tax-payers. The problem was what percentage should be apportioned to the taxpayers at the time, and what percentage left as a debt for future payment. This country was more than normally prosperous during the greater part of the war and could easily have stood taxation that would have made it unnecessary to borrow or issue paper money in any large amounts.[1] But the war was being fought over the question of taxation, and the people were no more anxious to pay money to the agents of the Legislature than to those of the Crown. This deficiency in revenue from taxation was the fundamental cause for all the devious expedients resorted to by Congress.

Since the close of the French and Indian war in 1763 there had been aside from quit rents no direct taxes levied by the New York Colonial Government either on land or personal property, the necessary sums being provided by indirect revenues totaling about £17,000 ($42,500) a year.[2] Freedom from direct taxes for so long a period prior to the Revolution made it exceedingly difficult to collect taxes when the war commenced.

[1] See Channing, *History of the United States,* III, Chap. XIII, for a very good discussion of this wartime prosperity.

[2] In 1774 Governor Tryon reported that the annual revenue from import duties and certain minor items averaged about £5,000 ($12,500 in New York currency). The State in 1771 had taken advantage of a special permission granted by Parliament, and had loaned £120,000 in paper to its citizens which would bring in $5,602 a year interest, and after 1776 10% of the principal would also be repaid annually. *Colonial Laws of New York,* V, chap. 1472. See also *supra* chap. I, p. 3 for a discussion of the political aspects of this loan. A new excise on liquor was calculated to produce £1,450. *N. Y. Colonial Documents,* VIII, 452-454, Tryon to Dartmouth.

From the beginning the new government of the state placed no reliance on such revenues.[3] The political leaders were undoubtedly afraid of the effect that taxation would have upon the loyalty of the people. The Tory party was too strong for the Whigs to risk any measures that might increase its size. While the Provincial Congress realized the necessity of laying a tax on the Colony, prudence made it imperative to proceed with caution so as not to incite popular opposition.[4] August 30 the Provincial Committee on Ways and Means suggested that £15,000 ought to be raised by taxes, but instead the act was amended, as we have seen previously, to provide for the issue of £45,000 in paper, despite the opposition of the merchants and creditors.[5]

The actual transfer of financial control from the Colonial Treasury to the new State Treasury in New York was gradual.[6] The irregular authorities, we cannot as yet call them revolutionary, were given courage to contract debts by the Continental Congress's promise of May 24th to repay all monies advanced in the public cause. Old Peter van Brugh Livingston, who was nearly seventy, was made a special treasurer by the Provincial Assembly, July 8, 1775, to handle such funds.[7] At the same time the working of the existing treasury system and the collection of Colonial taxes was not interferred with. Although efforts were made to bring this dual system to an end as soon as the break with England appeared inevitable, it was

[3]Letter to Continental Congress, May 21, 1775. *Jour. N. Y. Prov. Cong.*, I, 12.

[4]*Ibid.*, I, p. 20. A tea tax was suggested in a letter to the Delegates as safer than a land tax, and they were asked to get the opinion of Congress.

[5]*Jour. N. Y. Prov. Cong.*, I, 128. Albany, Ulster, and Richmond Counties voted against the amendment, and New York County was evenly divided. (It should be remembered, however, that some of the largest property interests in this latter county were not represented in this Congress; the delegation was more radical than usual.)

[6]This is described in some detail in A. C. Flick, *The American Revolution in New York*, pp. 105-110.

[7]*Jour. N. Y. Prov. Cong.*, I, 69.

not until the fall of 1776 that Livingston completely super-
seded the Colonial Treasurer, Abraham Lott. No attempt was
made by these revolutionary officers to collect such unpopular
taxes as quit rents, and the loss of New York City in July 1776
deprived them of the impost and tonnage duties which had
formed the chief permanent income of the Colonial Government.[8]

Peter Livingston, grandson of the first lord of the manor,
was not without business experience, and in his younger days
might have made a good treasurer. As it was, his infirmities
prevented him from assuming the full burdens of his office,
and the real direction of affairs was taken over by the Vice-
Treasurer, an experienced middle-aged merchant, Gerard
Bancker, who replaced Livingston at the latter's request early
in 1778.[9] Bancker came from an upper-middle-class merchant
family. He had been made a city surveyor in 1763, and master
of the military barracks in 1769. He was a man of considerable
culture who made a large collection of revolutionary broad-
sides.[10] Politics were of no particular interest to him, and he
seldom went beyond the confines of his own treasury affairs
to voice an opinion on any subject. His task as treasurer was
peculiarly arduous during the war. The whole equipment of
the office was contained in an iron chest which, like the Legislature, had to be moved up and down the state to avoid the
British. It is not surprising therefore that the records were
often lost or confused. From the end of the war, however, the
accounts were well and efficiently kept. Bancker retained his
post, despite changes of administration, until his death in 1798.

January 14, 1777, the Continental Congress asked the several
states to raise as much money by taxation during the year as
their conditions would permit, and pay it into the Continental

[8]See note p. 57.

[9]*New York in the Revolution, from Documents in the Controller's Office*,
ed. by E. C. Knight, I, 193.

Laws of N. Y., chap. XXVI, p. 25. April 1, 1778.

[10]I. N. P. Stokes, *Iconography of Manhattan*, VI, 606.

Treasury. The final basis of apportionment was left for the future, but the sums paid in would be credited to the individual states.[11] The response to this first summons was very slight, and therefore in November Congress appealed to the States to raise $5,000,000 in taxes the following year.[12] Five days later the States were advised to confiscate enemy property and loan the proceeds to Congress.[13]

When these appeals reached New York the first Legislature had been forced to dissolve hastily by the advance of the British army on Kingston, but upon their meeting again in February they took up the question of taxation and passed the first state tax law. It provided for a levy of 3 pence per pound on land, and 1½ on personal property. An added tax of 50 pounds per 1,000 was laid on money gained by trade since September 12, 1776. The assessors and collectors were to be paid a commission on the amounts collected. The bill passed the House and Senate, but as might be expected the surtax on mercantile profits was rejected by the conservative financiers such as Robert R. Livingston and Lewis Morris in the Council of Revision.[14] The Legislature had the necessary two-thirds majority in both houses to overrule the objections, and the bill became law May 28, 1778.[15] The policy of specific assessment inaugurated in this first law was abandoned late in 1779 in favor of a county quota system. The quotas were regarded

[11] *Journal Continental Congress*, VII, 37.

[12] The New York temporary quota of this $5,000,000 requisition was relatively low, amounting to only $200,000 or four per cent of the total. The sums advanced were to be regarded as a six per cent loan to Congress until a final reckoning could be made. *Ibid.*, IX, 971.

[13] This second recommendation was acted on by the New York Legislature the following year, and will be discussed in Chapter IV. *Ibid.*, IX, 955.

[14] They claimed: That it was unequal and hence unjust and unconstitutional taxation; that commerce and trade should be encouraged; that no valid excuse for any such discrimination existed; and that the method of collection was unconstitutional. MSS. *Minutes of the Council of Revision*, March 25, 1778.

[15] *Laws of N. Y.*, Chap. XVII, pp. 19-20.

as temporary, and surpluses and deficiencies were ultimately to be adjusted with six per cent interest.[16]

Neither of these systems provided an adequate revenue. Both the assessors and collectors were locally elected officers. Their unwillingness to incur popular disfavor often led to a non-performance of their duties.[17] Four months after the first state tax law had been passed Governor Clinton wrote: "My anxiety for the public welfare is very much increased by the unexpected Neglect of the assessors to make the assessments without which the Supervisors cannot rate the Tax . . . it is obvious that had the County done their Duty as effectually as the Legislature have made provision, the whole Tax might before this Time have been deposited in the Treasury for public Use."[18]

Another difficulty, both in New York and many other states, was that the Continental and State taxes were assessed together on one tax list.[19] The result of this procedure is well described in a letter to Robert Morris.

The Assembly when they grant a tax for continental purposes direct the Collection through the same channels in which State Taxes are collected. This in most instances makes the same Person Collector both of the State and Continental Tax and the Executions to inforce both the one and the other issue from the same person, Viz. the Treasurer of the State. The Consequence is that a preference will be given to taxes for State Purposes and if no urgent Necessity requires issuing Executions for State Taxes, there will be danger of delaying execution for Continental Taxes, and the more popular the Government is, the greater will their danger be increased, and whenever the same Person is in Arrears on different Taxes, he will apply all his Collections to that which will give him the longest time to collect in.

[16]The County Supervisors were to apportion the county quota among the various wards. *Laws of N. Y.*, Chap. XXVII, October 23, 1779.

[17]See letter of Wolvert Ecker, *Clinton Papers*, IV, 794, as a typical protest against taxation.

[18]*Ibid.*, III, 662.

[19]Sowers, D. C., *Financial History of New York*, p. 117.

I should not have troubled you on this subject, but I see the Collectors in this State of the Continental Taxes are in general in Arrears on every State Tax granted since 1776, and to my full satisfaction are applying the Monies collected on the Continental taxes to paying the Arrears of their old State Tax. . . . [20]

During the fifteen months from January 1779 to March 1780, Congress made desperate efforts to raise money to preserve the value of the declining paper. The states were asked for: $66,000,000 prior to January 1, 1780; $15,000,000 a month from February 1780 on; and an additional $10,000,000 by the act of March 18, 1780.[21]

Internal conditions in New York had been growing steadily worse as the war progressed. Early in 1778 Clinton had written in response to the appeal of Congress for assistance at Valley Forge:

New York is practically powerless to do anything, but is sending 100 head of cattle and 150 bbls of potatoes. The interest that this state has in the success of the American Cause, and may I add the attachment the People have for the Commander in Chief, will excite them to the most vigorous exertions for the relief of the Army. I wish I could send you assurance of further supplies, but I fear the exhausted state of the country will not admit of them.[22]

At the beginning of 1780 Clinton wrote to the President of Congress:

The supplies furnished by this state for the army have been at a much lower rate than those procured from neighboring states, it is with great difficulty that we can collect the monthly supplies for the Continental Treasury. . . . The support of our civil establishment has been almost totally neglected, and large arrears remain due to the militia who have been from time to time drawn into the field.[23]

[20]*Clinton Papers,* VIII, 20.
[21]See Appendix A.
[22]*Pap. Cont. Cong.,* no. 67, II, ff. 110-112.
[23]*Ibid.,* ff. 238-240; see also ff. 314-317.

A little later Clinton reviewed the whole history of the situation in a letter to Congress. He pointed out that the five lower counties then occupied by the British had borne three-fifths of the Colonial burdens prior to 1776. Not only had their support been lost, but they had become an actual liability because refugees from them had to be cared for by the State. The year of the Burgoyne expedition the State was ravaged from end to end except for a radius of about thirty miles around Albany. In 1778 there had been terrible Indian raids that laid waste all of Tryon County south of the Mohawk, one of the most fertile parts of the State. While 1779 was quiet from a military standpoint, the crops were blighted and the harvest very poor. In 1780 the enemy laid waste Tryon County as far east as Stone Arabia and captured all the northern forts except Edward.[24]

New York had also borne a heavy burden for extra troops. Every State was expected to supply a quota of troops to the Continental Line which would then be supported at the expense of Congress. But if special emergencies called for the raising of additional troops to defend their own borders these men might not be included immediately, or at all, in the Continental establishment, and therefore had to be paid and provisioned by the State. New York in reply to Continental requisitions continually pointed out that it had a larger number of state militia in the field than other States, and hence had to bear a larger proportion of the expense of the war. Clinton wrote to the Delegates in Congress in March, 1781:

We should be justified in not furnishing any supplies of any kind, as we have heretofore made advances ruinous to the state and greatly distressing to individuals, and much beyond our quota; as we are now raising for the defense of our frontiers a number of men equal to 1/20 part of all the male persons of the age of 16 and upward within the state. . . . [25]

[24]*Pap. Cont. Cong.*, no. 67, II, ff. 344-361.
[25]Clinton to the Delegates in Congress March 28, 1781, *Duane Papers*, N. Y. H. S., Box 2.

In spite of these bad conditions, and a minority group who felt that the State should be relieved temporarily from taxation, the New York Legislature passed tax laws totaling $10,000,000 between October 1779, and July 1780.[26] The percentage of collection was low, however, and the continued invasion made it necessary to spend the money for defense of the State.[27] Nevertheless the $277,500 in old bills which New York paid into the Continental Treasury during the fiscal year 1780 was the largest sum received from any northern State.[28]

From August 1780 on Congress made requisitions payable only in specie or new bills, but New York took no effective action toward meeting these demands during 1780 or 1781.[29] It was probably impossible to collect taxes in specie in the State during these years, and comparatively few of the new bills had found their way into circulation.[30]

When Congress reached the arbitrary limit of $200,000,000 which it placed on the issue of bills of credit at the end of 1779, it became impossible for Congressional purchasing agents to find money to pay for provisions, and some new means of supply had to be found. December 17, 1779, a committee was appointed by Congress to estimate the quantity of supplies nec-

[26]See Appendix A; and *Journal of the New York Assembly*, 3d sess., 2d meeting, pp. 107-108. The State also pledged: Certain forfeited estates as security for the redemption of its quota of the new "40 for 1" Congressional notes; and an annual tax for redemption purposes after April 1, 1781. *Laws of N. Y.*, Chap. XLIV, pp. 131-133, June 15, 1780.

[27]June 29, 1780 Congress sent a circular letter to the States imploring them in the strongest terms to make payments. *Journal Continental Congress*, XVII, 576 f. The New York Legislature cited the hard conditions in the State in reply. *Journal of New York Senate*, p. 133, *Assembly*, p. 190; July 1, 1780. In fact the New York Treasury was in such bad shape in the fall of 1780 that instead of paying money to Congress they unsuccessfully sought a loan from that body. *Journal Continental Congress*, XVIII, 929; *Papers*, no. 20, I, 363.

[28]*Journal Continental Congress*, XVIII, 1223. For specific amounts and dates see XVI-XVIII, 161, 208, 275, 370, 402, 552, 574, 993 and 995.

[29]See Appendices A and B.

[30]See p. 45.

essary for the ensuing year and to report quantities and kinds of goods that each State should furnish.[31] February 25, 1780, the system of specific supply by the States was inaugurated. Under this system the states were called upon for specific quotas of provisions to be turned over directly to the Quartermaster's Department. The price of these supplies was fixed by acts of Congress, and their value was placed as a credit on the State's account with Congress, just as if a cash requisition of the same amount had been met.[32]

Specific supply had been used by the States for their own militia since the beginning of the war. New York had started it at the first session of the Legislature. As a preliminary, an adequate supply of wheat, the basic necessity, was insured by placing an embargo on its export in March, 1778, and this restriction was made more stringent by the laws of November 10, 1779, and March 10, 1781.[33] The first law giving State agents the authority to impress provisions at set prices was passed April 2, 1778. It was a very detailed act enumerating all types of provisions and the prices to be paid for them.[34] Soon all wheat and peas purchased with the intention of resale or storage were made subject to seizure at a fixed price.[35] In March 1779, the Governor, with the consent of any six legislators, was given power to seize all wheat necessary, fix the price of it, and dispose of it in any way.[36] February 12, 1780,

[31] *Journal Continental Congress*, XV, 1391.

[32] *Ibid.*, XVI, 196-201.

[33] *Laws of N. Y.*, Chap. X, p. 10, Chap. XXI, p. 82, Chap. XXIV, p. 173, respectively.

[34] *Ibid.*, Chap. XXIX, pp. 28-30. This and later laws worked a hardship on many producers due to the fact that the State agents did not pay in cash, but in 6% promissory notes which did not pass as regular currency; although February, 1780, they were made receivable for taxes when offered by the original payee. *Ibid.*, Chap. XXXV, p. 102 f., Feb. 12, 1780.

[35] *Ibid.*, Chap. V, pp. 45-46, Oct. 30, 1778, for wheat; Chap. I, p. 73, Oct. 4, 1779, for peas. Oct. 13, 1779 the fixed prices were removed and the current prices substituted.

[36] *Ibid.*, Chap. XXI, p. 57, March 5, 1779, extended by Chap. IV, p. 74, Oct. 4, 1779.

the final step was taken: The people of the state were placed on a wheat ration of one bushel per head per month, and all surplus was made subject to impress.[37] Thus we see that New York had perfected the machinery of specific supply before the adoption of the system by Congress.

The State responded to its first Congressional quota by an act of June 24, 1780. It agreed to raise the whole quota, valued at $171,605, and a surplus toward the next quota at the prices fixed by Congress. These supplies were ultimately to be paid for in the new "40-1" bills, but for the time being the old system of certificates was necessarily continued.[38] In order to facilitate the raising of these supplies within the State a specific tax of 5,800 barrels of flour was apportioned among the counties on September 22, 1780.[39] November 4th, Congress passed a second quota act calling upon the State for approximately $208,000 worth of specific supplies, and $89,295 in specie, its quota of a requisition totaling $6,000,000. New York did not act upon this requisition until March 27, 1781, when the act of the preceding June was superceded by a law increasing the size of the levy and making it payable in the more easily collectable commodity, wheat. Any payments made on the previous flour tax would be credited on this tax.[40]

The system of Continental specific supply worked reasonably well in New York because there were always enough Continental troops there to consume the supplies at hand; but taken over the country as a whole it worked badly because of inade-

[37]*Ibid.*, Chap. XXXIV, p. 101. These strict impressment laws may have had a considerable bearing on the eagerness with which the farmers disposed of their grain to the enemy. A barn full of wheat became a very doubtful asset when it was subject to seizure by State agents in return for paper that would only have a value sometime in the dim and uncertain future.

[38]*Laws of N. Y.*, Chap. LXIX, p. 135, June 24, 1780. Quota assigned by Congress, Feb. 25, 1780.

[39]*Ibid.*, Chap. II, p. 149.

[40]If a person taxed less than a bushel did not possess sufficient wheat to pay the tax he might get an abatement, and then pay the balance in the money equivalents. *Ibid.*, Chap. XIV, p. 185.

quate facilities for storage and transportation. According to the account of Undy Hay, the New York State purchasing agent, he supplied between December 1779, and June 24, 1781, provisions worth $83,642 more that the State's first quota, but had not as yet considered the second quota. As Hay estimated the returns for the first 243 days of the above period, the accounts not having been adjusted, we cannot place any great reliance on these figures.[41] They only prove that New York at least made a real effort to comply with the specific requisitions.

An accurate summary of the financial relations between the State and Congress up until the middle of 1781, when Robert Morris took control, is impossible. The sums mentioned on the various accounts are all stated in currencies of different value, and it is necessary to make very rough approximations in seeking a common measure. Nevertheless we can at least get a general idea of the situation in 1781 from the data at hand.

Gerard Bancker, the State Treasurer, reported on October 1, 1781, that New York had paid to Congress a total of $6,813,-482.50 in old bills.[42] Up until June 1, 1781, New York's quota of Congressional requisitions amounted to $15,400,000 in old

[41]*Clinton Papers,* VII, 44.

[42]*Clinton Papers,* VII, 366-367. According to the Auditor-General, New York paid into the Continental treasury between 1777, the beginning of requisitions, and July 19, 1781, $3,796,400 in old bills and $24,825 in specie. During the same period Congress advanced to the State cash and goods valued at $652,980. The account of the State against Congress had not been submitted. *Clinton Papers,* VII, p. 99. New York also furnished specific supplies worth perhaps, $250,000, but as these are not included in either the Auditor-General's or the State Treasurer's statements they may be omitted temporarily. *Clinton Papers,* VII, p. 44 f. The difference between the Treasurer's figure and that quoted by the Auditor-General is probably due to the fact that certain drafts by the President of Congress upon the State treasury, totaling $2,657,100, are not included in the former account. When these are added the two statements come as near to agreeing as can be expected under the circumstances.

bills and $243,642 in specie.[43] The State's payment of $6,813,-482 in bills therefore amounted to about 40% of its assessed paper quota during the period of actual fighting, and the specie payments of $24,825 to about 10% of the specie quota. The total value of the tax laws discussed previously, plus the law of June 30, 1781, converted into old bills at 40 to 1, is approximately $21,100,000. $7,521,200 was paid in to the State treasurer, or about 35% of the amounts levied.[44]

It is interesting to note from these figures that the State Government had an income from this source of only $707,718 in six years, or, in other words, over 90% of the money raised by county taxes went to Congress. This, of course, represents only a part of the State's actual revenue during these years. Paper money was issued and not redeemed, forfeited property was sold, loans negotiated, license fees and harbor dues col-

[43]See Appendix A; also *Clinton Papers*, VII, 99 and 365-6. The requisition of $77,589, Jan. 15, 1781, in specie or new bills to pay the troops is not included in the Auditor-General's statement, neither are the requisitions for specific supplies.

[44]*Clinton Papers*, VII, 365. The $250,000 worth of specific supplies furnished has been left out of all the above discussion, in accordance with Robert Morris' policy (*Diplomatic Correspondence*, XI, 451), that is, included neither in the requisitions or the state responses. The reason for this is that it is impossible to reckon this sum in any proper currency equivalent. It was levied by Congress on the basis of new bills. It represented, however, neither the actual value of the goods in specie or in old bills at 40 to 1, but the sum of the prices that Congress considered fair to offer for the specified commodities. Hence it would only confuse our above summary to include it. If the two specific quotas called for were included together with New York's response up until June 24, 1781, and converted into old bills at 40 to 1, the figures would be:

1, and in specifics to the/above
Total state responses, in cash to Oct.
1781 .... (approx.) $41,500,000
Total requisitions, payable by June 24,
date .... (approx.) $16,800,000, or 39%.

It is impossible to get an exact correspondence of dates but as the specifics totalled much more than the cash payments during this period I have taken the date at which we have an accounting of these goods.

lected, and sundry small amounts raised by lotteries, etc.[45] The equivalent of fairly large sums was also raised by impressing provisions and merchandise for the use of the *State* troops, and giving only promissory notes in payment. A complete statement of the revenues of the State government is not, and very likely never was, available. The counties, of course, raised the usual sums for local government, and often extra amounts to pay for wartime replacements and so forth, but that does not directly concern our study of the relations of the State and Congress except as these activities may have led to the withholding of payments to the State treasury.[46]

To form any idea of the aid really received from or the burdens imposed by requisitions and taxes in paper currency we should need to know the exact rate of depreciation when each amount was received and when each was spent. This knowledge is definitely unavailable in the case of New York, and probably so in the case of any other State.[47] It must inevitably have been true, however, that the State returns represented money at a lower value than at the time when the requisition was made, and hence as representations of real purchasing power our percentages given above are too high, perhaps as much as thirty or forty per cent if we consider the long periods of time lost in collection.

After thus reviewing the history of these six years we see that the real cause of financial impotency in New York was not the unwillingness of the Legislators to vote taxes or turn the proceeds over to Congress, but to the inability of the county collectors to get the money. It forms a striking example of the weakness of the *State* governmental machinery during the

[45]See Chap. II and Chap. IV.

[46]Flick, *op. cit.*, 125-126, has a brief discussion of some typical county expenditures.

[47]A large part of the New York State records were destroyed by fire in 1911, but as both State and Continental accounts were very laxly kept during the war period it is doubtful if sufficient data to base an estimate of "real" taxes on ever existed.

Revolution, a point often overlooked because of the more obvious weakness of Congress. It leads us to some rather interesting speculations as to whether Congress might not have been able to govern tolerably well had the States been able to perform their part equally well. To put it still another way, the financial expedients of the Revolution may have failed not because of unwillingness of the State Legislatures to coöperate in a reasonably liberal spirit with Congress, but primarily because of the basic weakness of the whole new structure of civil authority. This gives us the clue also to why Congress during the following years laid such stress on appointing their own collectors for the proposed impost. An examination of later United States history, however, makes it appear doubtful whether Congressional collectors of direct property or excise taxes could have done much in the face of the deep-seated feeling of the American farmers against taxation. Internal Revenue taxes were never agreeably received in this country prior to the Civil War, as instanced by the Whiskey Rebellion and the withdrawal of such taxes by Jefferson and his successors.

CHAPTER IV

LAND AS A FACTOR IN ECONOMIC RELATIONS

THE LOYALIST ESTATES

L AND was a major factor in the economic relations between New York and the Continental Congress in two respects. First, through the revenue supplied to the State government from the sale of confiscated estates which helped it to meet requisitions; and second, through the cession of New York's far western claim which helped create the national public domain. The Vermont dispute, which involved Congress, and the Northern States; and the relations of Congress and the State with the Indians in New York, are next in importance, although they were not major economic issues in the life of the confederation. The settlement of the Massachusetts-New York boundary dispute involved a major economic adjustment in State relations, but affected Congress only indirectly. The State land system, except for the sale of forfeited estates, was not productive of any considerable revenue or settlement prior to 1788. These various topics will be taken up in this order, which is roughly chronological.

The outbreak of hostilities at the beginning of 1776 in both northern and western New York, together with the Vermont dispute, made the sale of wild lands impossible for the time being. It may be said that the State land system, in regard to both sales and the collection of quit rents, was in abeyance from 1776 to 1783. But, during this period the State sold hundreds of thousands of dollars' worth of property belonging to loyalists.

As long as the possibility of conciliation existed, the New York Congress proceeded with caution in the matter of Tory property. They ordered it seized, but kept in trust for its owners.[1] As the probability of a general war increased the various local committees in the counties interpreted the act in a broader and broader sense. The possessions of Tories who fled or refused to enlist in the militia were often sold without waiting for any general State law.[2] These local seizures proceeded at such a rate during 1776 that the Provincial Convention decided to take the matter in hand early in 1777 and create State Commissioners.[3] The act passed March 6 provided that three Commissioners of Sequestration, appointed for each county by the Convention, should take into custody all the personal property of persons who had joined the enemy, and cause it to be sold at public auction. The net proceeds were to be turned in to the State Treasurer and disposed of as the Legislature saw fit. Men on parole who failed to report to the Commissioners for Detecting Conspiracies would be regarded as having joined the enemy.[4]

It must be noted that only *personal property,* not *real estate,* was to be sold under this act. May 13th the Convention decided that the lands seized should be leased by the Commissioners at moderate rates to patriots, giving first option to those driven from their homes by the Tories. The destitute families of escaped Tories were to be cared for also.[5] These Commissioners of Sequestration were kept busy until well after the close of the war, their office being terminated by an act of May 12, 1784.[6] Flick estimates that comparatively little con-

---

[1]Act of Sept. 1, 1775. *Jour. Prov. Cong.,* I, 132. A. C. Flick in his *Loyalism in New York* treats the whole matter of confiscation, forfeiture, and sale exhaustively. The following discussion is necessarily only an abridgement of his long chapter, plus some important additional facts regarding the actual treasury receipts.

[2]Flick, *op. cit.,* 137.

[3]The local committee did not turn the money collected into the State Treasury. *Account Books of P. V. B. Livingston,* pp. 12, 38 and 57-58.

[4]*Jour. Prov. Cong.,* I, 826-827. The Commissioners for Charlotte and Gloucester were not appointed until April 2 and May 2, respectively.

[5]*Jour. Prov. Cong.,* I, 930-931.

[6]*Laws of N. Y.,* Chap. XLIV, pp. 102 ff. See *infra* p. 81.

fiscated *personal* property remained unsold at this time.[7] The total sales from 1777 to 1784 were close to $400,000 in hard money or its equivalent.[8] It is worth noting that during the two worst years of the State finance, 1780 and 1781, this source of revenue was not of any real help, yielding only $8,000 in specie value. Nor is there any complete record of when the sums were turned over to the State Treasurer.

As stated above, the real estate of the Loyalists was at first held in trust, and leased to deserving patriots by the Commissioners of Sequestration. In the spring of 1779 both Congress and the public were demanding that these valuable properties be converted into a source of revenue. A majority of the Legislature was equally desirous of reducing taxes for personal reasons. A bill was passed early in March providing machinery for sale, but received a crushing veto by the conservative Council of Revision. They felt that some of the confiscations (the property-holders were named in the act) were "repugnant to the plain laws of justice;" that the act was badly worded; and that it would not render the forfeitures beneficial to the community. The sales would be made in return for depreciated currency, the price in specie value would be much less than could be secured in normal times, and the whole process

[7]Flick, *op. cit.*, 145. Hamilton in his *History of the Republic* claims the Commissioners carried on many harsh and oppressive proceedings. III, 27.

[8]At the time Flick wrote, all of the records of the counties were still available, and the exact figure could be stated if it were not for the factor of depreciation. Many of these records were destroyed in the fire of 1911, however, and therefore his analysis has to take the place of the sources. The sales year by year and the estimated real money value were as follows:

	Nominal Sum	Specie Equivalent
1777	£27,757 at par — approx.	$68,700
1778	(not given) at 2.6 to 1 "	56,350
1779	(" ") at 13 to 1 "	2,060
1780 1781 }	£315,000 at 40 to 1 "	8,000
1781 on	£ 61,338 in specie "	153,300
Total		$390,000 (*op. cit.*, 141-144)

would further depreciate the currency.[9] This whole policy of selling the forfeited estates instead of levying higher taxes was opposed by many of the mercantile class as a gigantic land grab on the part of the speculators in the Legislature who would despoil the State for their own private benefit.[10] It has been estimated that the State received scarcely half the real value of the lands in normal times.[11]

Despite these objections the Legislature was able to put through a slightly amended act which became law October 22, 1779.[12] Sales were to be at public auction after eight weeks' notice, and in plots of no more than five hundred acres, but no auctions were to be held before October 1, 1780. The Governor was authorized to appoint the Commissioners of Forfeiture for the great districts of the State, seven men in all. In February, 1780, the Legislature passed an act repealing the suspending clause, and providing for immediate sale. Again the Council of Revision rejected the bill, on the same grounds as before, and again the Legislature had a sufficient majority to repass it.[13] June 15, 1780, certain specified properties were reserved as security for the new Congressional bills of March 18, and the Commissioners were forbidden to dispose of these until further orders.[14]

Although sales now proceeded, and by the late spring of 1781 had totaled over £800,000 in currency, the objections of the Council were rather well founded. Payments were not made when due, and the State received comparatively little

[9]*Journal of the New York Assembly*, 1779, pp. 83, 85, 98. *Mss. Minutes of the Council of Revision*, March 14, 1779.

[10]See *infra*, Chap. IX, p. 178. R. R. Livingston thought the estates should be preserved intact as a fund for the redemption of the paper money. *Clinton Papers*, IV, 717.

[11]Flick, *op. cit.*, 143, note 4.

[12]*Laws of N. Y.*, Chap. XXV, p. 95.

[13]*MSS. Min. Council of Revision*, I, March 4, 1780: *Laws of N. Y.*, Chap. LI, p. 116, March 10, 1780, L. Morris, Hobart, and R. R. Livingston could be relied on to oppose all such measures.

[14]*Laws of N. Y.*, Chap. LXIV, p. 132 f. Some of the Sir John Johnson, Butler, Skeene, Philipse, Bayard and DeLancey properties.

in hard money.[15] It was necessary from time to time to extend the period of payment. In March, 1781 a new law was passed providing for a scale of depreciation on payments of principal and interest, extending the time of payment indefinitely, and making New York Treasury Certificates or soldiers' certificates for depreciation in pay acceptable in payment.[16]

The evacuation of the Southern District by the British opened up the most valuable Tory lands for sale. Despite the obligations under the Peace Treaty to restore confiscated property, an act of April 8, 1784, authorized the immediate sale of £20,000 worth of estates in that District while a new general act was being formulated.[17] A comprehensive act was agreed to May 12. The Commissioners of Sequestration were discharged and their duties taken over by the seven Commissioners of Forfeiture who were to sell *all* forfeited property either by private sale or public auction as they judged best.[18]

The party lines in the Senate and Assembly did not hold in quite their usual form in the passage of these acts. Schuyler, for example, had been urging the immediate sale policy, against a group of city merchants and up-state men.[19] The criterion

[15]*Clinton Papers,* VI, 56. Clinton orders the Attorney-General to start prosecutions to collect.

[16]*Laws of N. Y.,* Chap. LI, p. 192, March 31, 1781.

[17]*Laws of N. Y.,* Chap. XX, p. 26. These laws were directly contrary to Article V of the treaty of Paris.

[18]In either case one-third of the price had to be paid down and the residue before June 1, 1785. Practically every form of currency was made receivable except that the total sum in Continentals could not exceed $5,000,-000. Mortgage claims were to be adjusted by the Chancellor. The following spring the period for residual payments was set at nine months from the time of sale, and preëmption rights were extended to settlers on the basis of an appraisal that must be met in gold or silver only. *Laws of N. Y.,* Chap. XLIV, pp. 102-117, Chap. XLIX, p. 42, March 31, 1785. This amounted to a repudiation of the State's guarantee of the Continental bills of 1780.

[19]For example, in March, 1783, a bill of Schuyler's for the immediate sale of all forfeited estates not in the possession of the enemy had passed the Senate 10 to 5, and had been decisively beaten in the House. *Journals,* 1783, *Senate,* p. 155, *Assembly,* p. 176.

was very likely the ability of a member to profit by buying up the estates.

The ratification of the treaty and the return of peace brought up the question of how the Loyalists should be treated who desired to return to their old neighborhoods. In the early months of 1783 the feeling was so strong that one town after another passed resolutions against permitting any Loyalists to settle among them.[20] Articles appeared in the newspapers urging the election of legislators who would deal harshly with those who had adhered to the enemy. Exclusion laws and special fines and taxes were proposed.[21] The Legislature in the heat of this excitement mirrored the feelings of the populace. The up-state majority put through an act giving the original owners the right to start action for trespass against all persons, whether Tory or not, who had occupied the property of refugee Whigs. No enemy military order could be urged in defense, nor could the action be appealed to a higher court.[22] This act contravened the spirit of the Treaty of Peace, and, as ineffectually pointed out in the Council of Revision, the spirit of the common law as well.[23] In rebuttal the radicals argued that Great Britian was not living up to the treaty

[20]See Loudon's *New York Packet*, March 17, May 15, May 22, May 29, and June 12, 1783.

[21]The entire issue of the *N. Y. Packet* for March 17, 1783, is given up to these letters.

The question of the collection of pre-war mercantile debts does not seem to have been an important issue in New York.

[22]*Laws of N. Y.*, Chap. XX, p. 283, 1783. The Legislature of 1783 contained a specially radical anti-Tory group from New York City, elected at the height of post-war feeling. Isaac Lamb from the city became the leader of this group which was spurred on by Governor Clinton's unconciliatory message. Hamilton, *History of the Republic*, III, 29 f.

[23]*MSS. Minutes of the Council of Revision*, I, March 16, 1783. It was not vetoed by the Council. During this spring the only officers in attendance at the meetings were Hobart, Clinton, and Robert Yates, and the latter two were in sympathy with the public demands. They did, however, veto an act which would have permanently disfranchised all Tories, and had their veto sustained by the Senate. Street, *Council of Revision*, p. 246, Jan. 15, 1784.

either, and hence we were justified in reprisals.[24] A large number of actions were at once started under this law, and in some cases damages were awarded beyond the value of the property.[25]

Fortunately the Mayor's Court of New York City presided over by the able James Duane was so impressed by the argument of Alexander Hamilton in the case of Rutgers v. Waddington that it held the act unconstitutional and refused to render a judgment.[26] The legislators were furious. The Clerk of the Court was commanded to appear before the bar of the House with the records of the case, and a vote of censure against the Court was passed by a large majority.[27] A resolution to recommend to the Council the appointment of a new Mayor of New York was defeated only because of the distinguished career and great popularity of Duane.[28] By this time, however, the moderate group had gained in strength, and the Whig newspapers were printing articles against the extreme radicals.[29] April 5, 1787, the Legislature repealed that part of the act which disallowed enemy military orders as a valid

[24]*N. Y. Packet,* July 17, 1783.

[25]Chief Justice Richard Morris received a judgment of £5000 against Governor Tryon for damages to a farm worth only one-third that much. Smith to Sydney, April 18, 1785, Bancroft Transcripts America and England, 1783-86, New York Public Library.

[26]The case of Rutgers v. Waddington has been so often discussed at length, because of its importance as a precedent for the doctrine of judicial review, that it is useless to go over the ground again at this time. See E. S. Corwin, *The Doctrine of Judicial Supremacy.* Hamilton also wrote an article, under the title Phocion, against the disfranchisement of Loyalists. He was answered by I. Ledyard, under the title of Mentor. Hamilton, *Hist. of the Rep.,* III, 33 ff.

[27]*Jour. N. Y. Ass.,* p. 33, November 2, 1784. It is interesting to notice that this vote illustrated no sectional alignment. Apparently many Legislators who had opposed the original act doubted the right of the Court to set it aside.

[28]*Jour. N. Y. Ass.,* p. 34.

[29]N. Y. Packet, April 8, and May 10, 1784, *New York General Advertiser,* April-June, 1784, *passim.*

plea, and in 1788 formally repealed all laws contrary to the Treaty of Peace.[30]

This sale of the large Loyalist estates led to a certain advance in political and economic democracy within the State, but not as great a one as might be assumed from the fact that a dozen great holdings were sold off in some 500 parcels. In New York City, for example, the James DeLancey estate was disposed of by some 250 separate sales, yet eighty-seven of these, involving over half the total property, were to leading merchants and landowners and involved no democratic readjustment.[31] It must also be born in mind that while some old families such as the DeLanceys, Phillipses, and Robinsons lost their power, the Schuylers, Clintons, Sands, and many other families gained greatly through the overturn. The land acquired from the Indians in the western part of the State and sold by the government was also gobbled up by the speculators in large tracts, as we will show in Chapter V.

By September 1, 1788, the sale of Loyalist property was so far completed that the Commissioners of Forfeiture were done away with, and their powers lodged in the Surveyor-General.[32] Flick estimates the total sales in the various districts as follows:[33]

Middle District..........	$575,000	in specie	
Western "	1,250,000	"	"
Eastern "	100,000	"	"
Southern "	1,160,000	"	"
Total	$3,085,000	"	"

These figures represent the total in most cases up to 1808. For the period up to 1788, only, we should probably deduct several hundred thousand dollars. It must not be supposed,

---

[30]The courts were requested to interpret all cases "according to the tenor, true intent, and meaning" of the treaty. *Laws,* Chap. XLI, p. 78 f.

[31]Flick, *op. cit.,* 216 ff.

[32]*Laws of N. Y.,* Chap. XC, p. 195 f.

[33]Flick, *op. cit.,* 150-157.

however, that any such large sums were actually paid into the Treasury prior to 1788. Both the Commissioners and the purchasers were far in arrears. The actual receipts of the Treasurer from the Commissioners from 1784 on were as follows :[34]

Year	Approximate Amount
Jan. 1, 1784 to Sept. 20, 1784	$25,080
Sept. 21, 1784 to Dec. 31, 1785	34,925
Jan. 1, 1786 to " " 1786	93
Jan. 1, 1787 to " " 1787	14,118
Total	$75,116

From the above tables it appears that while the proceeds of the confiscated estates formed a large potential resource of the State, their net aid in paying Congressional requisitions or in other financing was not great prior to 1788. The same laxness of accounting and collection that cursed every part of the Revolutionary financial administration seems to have shown itself in this case to a marked degree.

THE WESTERN CESSION

A consoling fact to the hard-pressed financiers in Congress was the thought that if the United States could make good their claim to the vast territory between the Appalachian Mountains and the Mississippi River a potential fund of national wealth would be created beside which the national debt would appear insignificant. This was based on a general feeling of extreme optimism in regard to the immediate value of western lands, and it is only by keeping this fact in mind that we can understand the bitterness of the controversies over the state claims.[35]

During the war there were several obstacles in the way of gaining credit from the wild lands. First, the English, French,

[34]Report of the Auditor, *Jour. N. Y. Ass.*, 1788, pp. 16 ff.

[35]Testified to by the fact that there were five commercial companies seeking grants from the British government when the Revolution commenced.

and Spanish all wished to confine the colonies to the Atlantic seaboard; second, the land was claimed by several States which would have to be persuaded to make over their rights to Congress; and third, the whole problem of profitable administration would have to be solved after Congress secured the land. The first and third difficulties lay necessarily in the future; it was the second one that concerned Congress immediately. As a result, the cession of the State claims to western lands became one of the most important financial questions of the Revolution. If this could be obtained limitless vistas opened before the eyes of the politicians. The paper currency and the funded debt could be paid off, a great land bank organized, and taxes dispensed with altogether.

The general question of the soundness of the claims of the various States to the western territory is unanswerable in any satisfactory fashion, and possibly unimportant, but a rapid survey of what they were is necessary.

Virginia based her claims on a Royal Charter of 1609, the territorial provisions of which had never been replaced by any others, although the Charter itself had been twice modified and then rescinded in 1624. The significant clause of 1609 read, "from the point of land called Cape or Point Comfort, all along the sea coast to the northward two hundred miles, and . . . to the southward two hundred miles, and all that space and circuit of land . . . from sea to sea west and northwest . . . "[36] A line northwest from the 40th degree of latitude where it touches the Atlantic coast would include part of the present state of New Jersey, almost all of Pennsylvania, all of Maryland, a little of New York and all of the later Northwest Territory. Virginia, of course, admitted the superior title derived from the later grants of the King, but claimed that wherever no such grants had been made the land still belonged to her.

[36]Henry, *Patrick Henry,* II, 99. A complete brief for Virginia's claim is given II, 97-109.

Connecticut and Massachusetts had also been granted sea-to-sea charters, but considerable doubt was cast upon them by the later grant of New York which cut directly across their claims. At all events they were only narrow strips running across the Great Lakes, the northern part of the Northwest Territory, and some of Canada, none of which was then regarded as useful for immediate settlement.

The other really comprehensive claim to the Northwest Territory was that of New York. This claim rested upon a general protectorate established by the early Colonial Governors over the Six Nations of Indians.[37] These tribes claimed all the hinterland south of the Great Lakes, north of the Ohio, and east of the Mississippi, as well as extensive tracts both north and south of these boundaries. As Indians west of the Proclamation Line of 1763 had been dealt with only through the royal Indian Agents, and as Sir William Johnson's residence in New York was in no essential way connected with the State government, some doubt might be entertained as to the strict legality of this claim by 1776.[38] Legal correctness, however, was of minor importance in the case of all the State claims; the important point was how strongly the citizens of the particular State were willing to back them up and insist

[37]Board of Trade to Queen Anne, June 2, 1709: ". . . We have likewise added a copy of a memorial . . . proving the constant subjection and dependence of the said five Nations upon the government of New York, ever since the first settlement of the Colony by the Dutch." *New York Colonial Documents,* V, 74-75. By treaty of 1701 they made the protectorate specific. Tryon to Dartmouth, *Ibid.,* VIII, 436-437.

That this relation was retained is shown by a letter from Governor Hardy to the Lords of Trade, January 18, 1756, in which he says that the Governor of New York "has always directed transactions with them [Six Nations] . . . and . . . it is through him that his Majesty's commands have always been conveyed to them." *Ibid.,* VII, 3. And similarly, Tryon to Dartmouth, *Ibid.,* VIII, 436.

[38]It is interesting to note that Congress paid for the presents, etc., given to the friendly tribes of the Six Nations during the war. *Pap. Cont. Cong.,* instructions to New York Delegates, March, 1781, no. 67, II, 369.

upon their recognition, for after all, Congress, the only arbiter, had no real power to decide the matter.

New York's claim received particularly violent abuse from its opponents in Virginia.[39] But according to their correspondence the leading New Yorkers felt sure of their rights and had no particular antagonism in this respect toward Virginia or any other state. R. R. Livingston wrote to Richard Morris: "You know my sentiments about restricting our western boundaries . . . an ill-judged wish of Mr. Duane to go hand in hand with Virginia kept us while I was in Congress (contrary to my sentiments) from pressing some determination thereon."[40] Duane wrote to Schuyler in March 1778, in a letter that had no connection with the land argument, "Our state extends from Lake Nipissin to the source of the Mississippi or at least along the 45th parallel of north latitude from Connecticut to the Mississippi."[41] Jay wrote to Clinton October 7, 1779, "The country west of Niagara on the present ideas which prevail and by the Articles of the Confederation belongs to New York."[42]

Beside the conflicting State claims there were also private ones to ownership in this territory beyond the Proclamation line of 1763. At least five great land companies, the Indiana, Vandalia, Transylvania, Illinois and Wabash, had claims resting on purchases from the Indians, or uncompleted grants from the British government. A resolution of the Virginia Convention invalidating all land purchases from Indians within her borders convinced these companies that the State would probably not confirm their grants.[43] Accordingly they threw their lot in with those which favored a cession of all western

[39]It was trumped up for the purpose of embarrassing Virginia, claimed Patrick Henry. Henry, *Patrick Henry*, II, 80.

[40]*Livingston Papers*, 1777-1799, N. Y. P. L., p. 227.

[41]*Schuyler Papers. Letters*, 1778-1779, N. Y. P. L., no. 553.

[42]*Clinton Papers*, V, 314 f.

[43]June 24, 1776, Hening, *Statutes at Large of Virginia*, IX, Chap. II, p. 119.

claims to the Congress in the hope that they would fare better at the hands of that body [44]

Virginia first laid down the gage of battle by reaffirming all her land claims in the Constitution of 1776.[45] The Convention of the "landless" State of Maryland replied with a resolution against extensive claims by any one state to the "common lands."[46] The controversy was inflamed by Congress' proposal to pay the soldiers a bounty in the form of western lands. Maryland at once saw the danger of the landed States, especially Virginia, forcing the government to pay a fancy price for the promised lands when the time came for settlement.[47] She passed a resolution inquiring of Congress the location of the proposed lands, and offering to substitute a commutation of $10 cash for each hundred acres promised.[48]

While this controversy was going on the Articles of Confederation were being prepared in Congress. The Maryland delegates were defeated on a motion to give Congress power to ascertain the western boundary of those States claiming to the Mississippi.[49] Then Virginia succeeded in passing the famous amendment to Article IX; that no State shall be deprived of territory for the benefit of the United States.

The Articles were completed and adopted by Congress on November 15, 1777. A month later Maryland refused to ratify them, although she made it clear that her refusal implied no lack of willingness to do her share in prosecuting the war.[50]

[44]*Etting Papers,* Ohio Company, I. See *Letter Book* of Thomas Wharton in Pennsylvania Historical Society for a lengthy discussion of the Indiana Company position.

[45]Hening, *Statutes of Virginia,* IX, 118.

[46]October 30, 1776; *Maryland Archives, Convention of Maryland,* p. 272.

[47]S. Sato, *History of the Land Question,* pp. 28-29. Scharf, *History of Maryland,* p. 290.

[48]*Convention of Maryland,* pp. 370-372.

[49]*Journal Continental Congress,* IX, 806-808.

[50]B. Bond, *State Government in Maryland,* p. 26. She reaffirmed this stand by resolutions of June 20, 1778. Affirmed by Jay in a letter to Count Florida Blanca, *Correspondence of Jay,* I, 284-85.

Her main reason for this decisive and somewhat heroic action was the needless fear that western lands would be an immense source of profit to their owners. Virginia was envisioned as becoming so wealthy from land sales that she would be able to abolish taxes and thereby either lure away the population of Maryland or financially ruin those who remained by underselling them.[51]

Rhode Island and New Jersey soon demonstrated that Maryland did not stand alone. They developed a different plan of action, however. Rhode Island moved on June 23, 1778, that the "lands within those states [the claimant states] . . . which . . . before the present war were vested in the Crown of Great Britain or [for which] quit rents arise payable to the said Crown, shall be considered as the property of these United States, and be disposed of . . . by Congress for the benefit of the whole Confederacy, reserving however, to the States, within whose limits such crown lands may be the entire and complete jurisdiction thereof." [52] The motion was lost six to three. Two days later the New Jersey delegation presented a long "representation" which called for the same thing and met a like fate.[53] Such a plan was obviously more distasteful to the claimant States than absolute cession, for it would leave them with all the expenses of an extended government and no profit in return.[54] It strongly suggests the

[51]For a much fuller discussion of Maryland's views see S. Sato, *History of the Land Question,* Johns Hopkins Studies, IV, 27-30. In June the Maryland Delegates had attempted to force amendments in regard to the land claims that would make the Articles acceptable to her, but they had been overridden by the nervous majority which feared the delay that would ensue if amendments were considered. *Journal Continental Congress,* IX, 631, 636, 637. See also Hinsdale, *Old Northwest,* p. 207.

[52]*Journal Continental Congress,* XI, 639.

[53]*Ibid.,* XI, 649-50.

[54]See R. H. Lee to Governor Henry, Nov. 15, 1778: Burnett, *Letters of the Members of the Continental Congress,* III, 495-496. Also the opinion of Governor Clinton on the impracticality of extended State government. Clinton to Livingston, Jan. 7, 1780; *Clinton Papers,* V, 445-446.

connection of the small-state politicians with the land companies.[55]

Despite her objections Rhode Island ratified under protest on June 2. Congress now sent a circular letter to Maryland, Delaware, Georgia, and New Jersey, the four States who had not yet acted. Georgia had no real excuse for her delay and ratified immediately, New Jersey and Delaware gave in the following winter, although they both accompanied their action by resolutions calling for a moderation of the territorial claims of certain States.[56]

Maryland was not dismayed by this apparent isolation. May 31, 1779, her Delegates in Congress announced that they were instructed not to ratify the Confederation until an amendment for the limitation of territory was added in accordance with the Maryland proposal of 1777.[57] Both the States with definite limits and the great land companies approved of Maryland's course although the former were unwilling to defeat the Confederation for this cause.[58] In fact within Maryland the men interested in western land speculation undoubtedly did much to strengthen those opposed to ratification.[59] The two sets of interests, local patriotism and self-interest, necessarily went hand in hand, as is so often the case.

[55]There is, however, so far as I can find out, no direct proof of such influence.

[56]*Journal Continental Congress*, XII, 1162, and XIII, 236.

[57]*Ibid.*, XIV, 619-622.

[58]*Writings of Madison*, I, 482; Henry, *Patrick Henry*, II, 83, Bland to Jefferson, Nov. 22, 1779.

[59]Henry, Madison, Pendleton, Mason, and R. H. Lee all made this accusation in letters to their friends, and the Virginia Assembly drew up a formal protest. Hening, *Statutes of Virginia*, X, 557-559. Private Letters in: Henry, *Patrick Henry*, II, 120; Writings of Madison, I, 115; *Pendleton Letters*, Massachusetts Historical Society Collection, XIX, 114; *Bland Papers*, Mason to Jones, July 27, 1780; Burnett, *Letters of Members of Continental Congress*, III, 495-96.

Additional proof of this influence can be found in: *Letters of Members of the Old Congress*, MSS., III, Pa. H. S.; Jenifer to Christie, March, 1779; *Letters of Members of the Federal Convention*, MSS., Pa. H. S., Fitzsimmons to Christie, March 16, 1779.

Virginia committed a tactical blunder at this time which suddenly shifted the onus of the situation from Maryland's shoulders to hers. On May 18, 1779, she followed the lead of North Carolina and opened an office for the sale of her western lands.[60] The Indiana and Vandalia Companies at once petitioned Congress to suspend the action of the Virginia land office.[61] Congress was now favorable to the companies,[62] or at any rate thoroughly opposed to such State disposal of the lands.[63] A Congressional resolution was sent to the States October 30, asking them to refrain from making land grants until after the War, and Virginia was asked to reconsider her actions.[64]

The resolution was warmly received in Maryland, and engrossed on the Senate journal. Virginia replied by drawing up a formal remonstrance on December 14, addressed to the Delegates of the United States in Congress assembled. The leading points of this document were: (1) that Virginia had already enacted a law preventing further settlements on the northwest banks of the Ohio River; (2) that Virginia learned with surprise and concern that Congress had received and countenanced petitions from the Indiana and Vandalia Companies asserting claims to lands within her limits; and that for Congress to assume a jurisdiction such as granting these petitions would imply would be contrary to the fundamental law of the Confederation; (3) that Congress had stated in their ultimatum as to boundaries in their instructions to Mr. Adams that the "United States holds no territory but in right

[60] Hening, *Statutes of Virginia*, X, 50.

[61] *Etting Papers*, Ohio Company, II, Sept. 14, 1779, Pa. H. S.; Indiana petition was signed by George Morgan, Vandalia by Major William Trent.

[62] The Companies had distributed handbills and other literature to members of Congress explaining their claims prior to this occurrence. Morgan to Trent 1778. *Etting Papers*, Ohio Company, II, 30-31, P. A. H. S.

[63] There were really sound arguments against encouraging land speculations at this time. Washington, for example, opposed opening the land office because speculation would divert troops from the line. Ford, *Washington*, VIII, 97.

[64] *Journal Continental Congress*, XV, 1226.

of some one individual state . . . fixed and determined by their respective charters . . ." Hence any territory claimed not to be part of some States must also not be a part of the United States; (4) Virginia was willing to listen to any just and reasonable proposition for removing the ostensible cause of delay to the complete ratification of the Confederation.[65] This last clause distinctly held out hope for a solution, and as an actual fact the leading men of the Virginia Legislature were already in favor of a cession.[66]

During the fall of 1779 the matter of claims to territory based on Indian Grants again became the subject of debate by Congress. Forbes of Maryland introduced a motion on November 27 that read, in part: "Congress are willing to accept any cession of territory which the said Indians may be inclined to make to the United States reserving to any particular state their right to a prior claim to the territory."[67] This motion, if carried and acted on by the Six Nations, might have involved New York in a very nasty argument with Congress as to whether the former protectorate would invalidate such action. Although it was defeated, Marchand of Rhode Island immediately introduced a motion which was even more obnoxious to New York's pretentions. It read: ". . . that it be one condition of the peace, that no land be sold or ceded by any of the said Indians, either as individuals or as a nation, unless to the United States of America or by the consent of Congress."[68] This motion, striking directly at the basis of the New York claim, was not acted upon, but it probably had its effect on the view which New Yorkers took of their situation.

[65]Hening, *Statutes of Virginia*, X, 557-559. See also Hinsdale, *Old Northwest*, pp. 214-215; and S. Sato, *American Land System*, pp. 32-33.

[66]Henry, *Patrick Henry*, II, 85, mentions Henry and Mason as particularly favorable. Mason was the one who drew up the remonstrance and is probably responsible for the conciliatory ending.

[67]*Journal Continental Congress*, XV, 1321.

[68]*Ibid.*, XV, 1322.

Leading New Yorkers had been impressed for some time with the advantage of fixing a definite western boundary, and ceding to Congress that land which was too remote to be readily governed. Jay suggested to Clinton on October 7, 1779, that the western territory was too extensive to govern and might readily become an inconvenience.[69] R. R. Livingston wrote later that he had early urged the cession in a conversation with Jay and Gouverneur Morris at Kingston, but that Morris had opposed it, likening such action to that of the small boy who lets a valuable bird fly away because it pecks at his fingers.[70] Philip Schuyler claimed that he always favored a relinquishment of States' rights and greater consolidation.[71]

Because of her great and unprotected frontier and the almost continual fighting going on within her borders, New York felt more keenly than almost any other State the need for coöperation between the members of the Congress. The Vermont difficulty made an additional reason for desiring the support of her neighboring States. Morris illustrated this feeling when he wrote to Livingston advising New York to declare Vermont independent and in return get Congress to guarantee lakes Erie and Ontario to New York; then "amalgamate" her politics with the Eastern States and laugh at those seeking extensive territory.[72]

By the end of 1779 the men in control of affairs in New York had definitely decided to make a cession and thereby

[69]Jay to Clinton, October 7, 1779, *Clinton Papers*, V, 314.

[70]Livingston to Morris, Jan. 18, 1781, *Livingston Papers*, 1777 to 1799, N. Y. P. L., p. 227. It was reported in France in 1778 that Jay and Morris dreamed of a North Western Commercial republic centering in New York and including Canada; guarded by France in New Foundland and Spain in the South West. Etats Unis, V, no. 47, in Phillips, *Opinions Regarding the West*, p. 299.

[71]Lossing, *Life and Times of Philip Schuyler*, II, p. 436.

[72]Gouverneur Morris to Livingston, January 2, 1781, *Livingston Papers*, 1777-1799, N. Y. P. L. While written after New York's offer of cession, the outlook on this particular situation is essentially unchanged. It does represent a marked change from Morris attitude cited in the last paragraph.

gain the good feeling of all the elements in Congress except
Virginia and North Carolina, the two great land claiming
states.[73] On October 7, 1779, before either the Forbes or
Marchand motions had been introduced in Congress Jay wrote
to Clinton: "The country west of Niagara on the present ideas
which prevail and by the Articles of Confederation, belongs
to New York, as it lies beyond the convenient reach of government it would rather incommode than benefit us. I would
be for ceding it to the Continent at a proper season, or otherwise disposing of it *in a way that would conduce to the credit
and interest of the State. To this way you can be no
stranger.*"[74] Livingston, who had a large part in securing the
cession,[75] wrote on November 30, 1779, that the weight of taxation would force the states to demand the western lands, and
that New York would do well to cede some in order to preserve
the rest. "This I think we may do to advantage now, while
they treat our title with some respect." He proposed almost
the same boundary as was later adopted, to wit, the north-
western corner of Pennsylvania to Lake Ontario and then
across the 45th degree of latitude. "It will put our claim out
of dispute," he continued, "and enable Congress and us to
apply our lands to counter secure our money. We have already
had one attack which we . . . warded, although Virginia
is unrepresented.[76] The attempt convinces me of the risk we
run by being too insatiable in our demands."[77] Clinton replied
to Livingston January 7, 1780:

I have long suspected from hints which have fallen from individuals, an intention of some of the states to claim not only our
Western Lands, but the forfeited estates [Loyalist] also as a

[73]Georgia was not a factor to reckon with at this time due to the British
control of the South.

[74]Jay to Clinton, October 7, 1779, *Clinton Papers,* V, 314. This letter
has been quoted from twice before.

[75]Livingston wrote Morris January 18, 1781, that the New York Act
of Cession was passed at his suggestion.

[76]Probably referring to the Marchand motion of three days before.

[77]Livingston to Clinton, November 30, 1779, *Clinton Papers,* V, 381-384.

common interest. . . . . I would for my part, be contented
with the boundary described in your letter, as it would leave us
territory nearly as extensive as the influence of Government could
reach. . . . . The Legislature were to have met at Albany the
4th instant but . . . the Roads [are] impassable; *as soon as
they are convened, I will communicate to them your sentiments
and endeavor to procure the necessary instructions to the Delegates on this subject.*[78]

A letter from General Schuyler to the Legislature seems
to have been used as the occasion for action. He wrote January
29, 1780, of Marchand's motion aimed, he claims, to acquire
the lands of the Six Nations for Congress, directly neglecting
the New York title. He felt that many who opposed the motion
only did so from their desire to conciliate the Indians. More
recently, he says, "a member afforded us . . . a resolution which he intended to move the house . . . that all
the lands within the limits of any states, heretofore grantable
by the King of Great Britian . . . should be considered
as the joint property of the U. S. . . . " The arrangement
was supported even by "Gentlemen who represented states
in circumstances seemingly similar to ours." It was contended
that if the States claiming to the South Sea or having indefinite
bounds would consent to a limitation it would remove the
obstacle which prevented the completion of the Confederation.
"They" showed what the boundary of New York should be on
a map (approximately the present boundary). "We found
this matter had been in contemplation some time, the delegates
from North Carolina having then already requested instructions."[79] The Delegates referred to as "they" in this letter
were undoubtedly those of Maryland.

Whether this letter was written at the suggestion of Governor Clinton in order to hasten the action of the Legislature,

[78]Clinton to Livingston, January 7, 1780, *Clinton Papers*, V, 445-446.
[79]*Report of the Regents of the University of the State of New York*,
1883, pp. 136-141.

because of General Schuyler's own restrictionist feelings,[80] at
the instigation of the Maryland delegation, or because of all
three, it has not the predominant importance hitherto accorded
it.[81] Governor Clinton had probably already communicated
his wishes on this matter to some of the members of the Legislature,[82] and the fact that the conditional act of cession passed
both readings in the Assembly with practically no debate just
nine days after the letter was first received argues that the
members must have been already informed on this subject and
ready to act.[83] The exact influence of the Maryland Delegates
in Congress is hard to determine, but certain facts do stand
out: First, it was not the motion of Forbes of Maryland that
excited Schuyler's and Livingston's fears, but that of Marchand
of Rhode Island; second, Clinton, Jay, and Livingston had
desired a cession before these motions were made; third, no
record has so far been found of the proposed motion to deprive
the States of the lands formerly vested in the Crown which
Schuyler mentions; fourth, Robert Livingston claims direct
responsibility for the act (see above); and fifth, to most New
Yorkers the Vermont situation, which will be discussed later,
was a more important reason for conciliating Congress than
was the pressure of Maryland.[84]

The New York act which received the Governors' approval
on February 19, 1780, was entitled an "Act for facilitating the
completion of the Articles of Confederation and perpetual
Union among the United States of America." It provided:

[80]Lossing, op. cit., II, 436.

[81]Professor H. B. Adams in his monograph on *Maryland's Influence*
. . . gives the impression that Schuyler's letter was the primary factor
in producing the New York cession, pp. 39-42.

[82]See letter to Livingston quoted above. *Clinton Papers*, V, 446.

[83]*Report of the Regents of the University of the State of New York*,
1883, pp. 141-142, and *Jours. N. Y. Sen. and Ass.*, Spring Session, 1780.

[84]See numerous letters on the subject of Vermont and New York's position in Congress; *Clinton Papers*, IV, V, VI, and VII; *Livingston Papers*,
N. Y. P. L.; *Duane Papers*, Box 6, N. Y. H. S. Also a very good discussion in Hinsdale's *Old Northwest*.

First, "that the delegates of the state in Congress, or a majority of them are authorized and empowered, in behalf of the state to limit . . . its boundaries in the western parts by such . . . lines, and in such manner and form, as they shall judge to be expedient, with respect either to the jurisdiction or the right of soil or both;" second, "that the territory so ceded shall be and inure for the use and benefit of . . . the Federal alliance of the said States, and for no other use or purpose whatever;" third, "that such of the lands, so ceded, as shall remain within the jurisdiction of the State, shall be surveyed, laid out, and disposed of only as Congress may direct."[85] The act was laid before Congress March 17, 1780. It effected a complete change in the situation. From now on the claimant States had to justify themselves for not following the example of New York.[86]

On September 6 a committee to which all the papers relating to the western claims had been committed recommended to Congress that they issue a call asking the other claimant States to follow the example of New York. This document also included a new request for Maryland to ratify. It was sent to all the States, together with copies of the New York act of cession, the Virginia Remonstrance of 1779, and the Maryland "Instructions."[87] A resolution passed by Congress October 10 assured the States of the good faith of Congress in regard to the disposal of the lands. It read, in part:

Resolved, that the unappropriated lands that may be ceded or relinquished to the United States, by any particular state, . . . shall be disposed of for the common benefit of the United States and be settled and formed into distinct Republican states, which shall become members of the federal union. . . . That each state which shall be so formed shall have . . . terri-

[85]*Laws of N. Y.*, 3d sess., 2d meeting, p. 205.
[86]Hinsdale, *Old Northwest*, p. 216.
[87]*Journal Continental Congress*, XVII, 806-7. See also Hinsdale, p. 218, for a discussion of the wisdom of Congress' policy of neutrality and moderation.

tory not less than one hundred or more than one hundred and fifty miles square. That the necessary and reasonable expenses which any particular state shall have incurred . . . in acquiring any part of the territory that may be ceded . . . shall be reimbursed.[88]

This resolution was designed to meet all of the possible objections of Virginia, particularly those based on the expense she had gone to for the George Rogers Clarke expedition. On the same day Connecticut offered a conditional cession of her claims, but under such conditions that Congress subsequently rejected it.[89]

The general Assembly of Virginia, anxious over the "happiness, strength and safety" of the United States, passed an act ceding their land northwest of the Ohio on January 2, 1781, but attached, among others, the condition that the remaining territory of Virginia between the Atlantic Ocean and the southeast side of the Ohio should be guaranteed to the commonwealth by the United States.[90] The Virginia Legislature reversed its former stand as the result of a number of causes. The men in the State who dominated politics had begun to see that Virginia was endangering the common cause for something of very doubtful value.[91] The French were bringing pressure to have the Confederation completed and lands placed in the hands of Congress.[92] The pro-Spanish faction in Congress threatened to offer our western territory in return for Spain's active support in the war.[93] Virginia was invaded by

[88]*Journal Continental Congress*, XVIII, 915-916.

[89]*Ibid.*, 917-918.

[90]Hening, *Statutes at Large*, X, 564-567.

[91]See: *Bland Papers*, Mason to Jones, July 27, 1780; *Letters of R. H. Lee*, II, 20; Hunt, *Writings of Madison*, I, 67, 97-99; *Pendleton Letters, Mass. H. S. Col.*, XIX, 114; Henry, *Patrick Henry*, II, 85.

[92]*Letters of Colonel Armand, N. Y. H. S.*, and Phillips, *West in the Revolution*, pp. 169-170.

[93]Phillips, *op. cit.*, 300-01, and *West in the Diplomacy of the Revolution*, pp. 163-168; 181-184.

British armies and Kentucky was threatening revolt, so that the friendship of Congress seemed very valuable at this time.[94]

Virginia's offer of cession persuaded the Maryland Legislature, after some hesitation, to ratify the Articles.[95] The official act of ratification was passed on February 2, 1781. The preamble declared, however, that the State did not, by acceding to the Confederation, relinquish any right or interest that she had with other States in the back country; that she still stood by her declaration of 1778, but relied on the justice of the States hereafter in regard to their claims; and that no article of the Confederation could bind her to guarantee any exclusive claim of any particular State to the soil of the back lands. This last clause was, of course, aimed at the guarantee of Kentucky asked for by Virginia. The Maryland delegates executed their orders on March 1, 1781, and the Confederation was completed.[96]

The same day that the Confederation came into existence the New York Delegates framed a definite proposal for a cession of the New York claim and laid it before Congress. By this instrument New York proposed to "relinquish all right, title, and interest, jurisdiction, and claim" to all lands and territories southward of the forty-fifth parallel of North Latitude and westward of a meridian line drawn through the western bend or inclination of Lake Ontario, or westward of a meridian line twenty miles west of the most westerly bend of the Niagara River, provided the former meridian should not be found to fall that distance beyond said river. The delegates added a "declaration" to the effect that this cession should be

[94]Hildreth, *History of the United States,* III, 339. Luzerne wrote that Kentucky would throw in her lot with any nation that would protect her if Virginia did not grant her statehood at once. *Report of the Canadian Archives,* 1913, p. 161.

[95]Luzerne, the French Minister, addressed a letter to the Legislature urging them in the name of the King to cease obstructing the completion of the Union. *Report of the Canadian Archives,* 1913, pp. 175-176. Edward S. Delaplaine in his *Life of Thomas Johnson,* says that the Legislature were induced to change their attitude by the eloquent pleadings of Johnson as a leader of the Assembly, pp. 367-370.

[96]*Journal Continental Congress,* XIX, 208.

subject to the approval of the State Legislature unless New York's remaining lands were guaranteed similarly to those of Virginia.[97] Duane apologized to Governor Clinton in behalf of himself and his colleagues for attaching this declaration to their act, but felt it only fair in order to offset the Virginia guarantee.[98] From this we see that the New York guarantee was merely a diplomatic "make weight" whereas that of Virginia was looked upon as a fundamental part of the act of cession.

During the spring and summer of 1781 all matters concerning western lands were in the hands of a Congressional committee made up of Boudinot of New Jersey, Varnum of Rhode Island, Jenifer of Maryland, Smith of Pennsylvania, and Livermore of New Hampshire.[99] All of these men except Livermore were from States naturally jealous of the claims of Virginia. In addition to this natural bias they were probably subject to great pressure by the agents of the land companies and other speculators in Congress. The committee called upon the Connecticut, New York, and Virginia Delegates and agents of the four land companies to present their respective claims with the proofs on which they rested. The Virginia delegation responded by submitting a representation to Congress which urged that any inquiry into the validity of the claims of the States was beyond the committee's jurisdiction and that it was derogatory to the sovereignty of a State to be drawn into a contest with a land company.[100]

The evidence of the leading men of the day makes it appear reasonably certain that there was a great amount of land speculating going on in Congress. Duane of New York wrote that many members of Congress were land jobbing[101] Lee

[97]*Journal Continental Congress*, XIX, 210-214.

[98]*Duane Papers*, N. Y. H. S., Box 5, no. 75, p. 277.

[99]*Journal Continental Congress*, XXII, 223.

[100]*Journal Continental Congress*, XXI, 1057 f., Oct. 16, 1781.

[101]*Duane Papers*, Box 5, no. 117, p. 427. He was doing it himself, according to the *Peters Papers*, Pa. H. S., and Jones, *History of the Revolution in New York*.

wrote to Adams, February 5, 1781, that the land jobbers desired to prevent any action, hoping in the resulting uncertainty to substantiate their Indian purchases. He prophesied that they would seek some means of defeating the cession under the cloak of patriotism.[102] Jay also indicated the same opinion by writing to Schuyler, April 1781, that he hoped their State would not permit the public peace and interest to be hereafter endangered by the partial politics of self-interested and unfeeling land jobbers.[103]

Congress considered the report of the committee on May 1, 1782. First, it was recommended that the New York cession be accepted as it then stood; second, Massachusetts and Connecticut were urged to make unconditional cessions, but there was no mention of the one already made by Connecticut; third, the Virginia cession was claimed to be inconsistent with the interests of the United States, or the rights of Congress or its constituents for the following reasons: (1) "All the lands ceded, or pretended to be ceded" by Virginia were within the claims of New York, Connecticut, or Massachusetts; (2) the greater part of the lands claimed by Virginia were part of the country of the Six Nations and their tributaries; (3) the lands were beyond the proclamation line of 1763 which the King had made the western boundary of the Colony of Virginia; (4) a large tract of the said lands had been conveyed by the King to private persons prior to the Declaration of Independence; (5) the conditions attached to the grant were altogether inadmissible.[104]

The New Jersey influence was being continually exerted for the land companies. Former Chief Justice Stockton of that state had assured George Morgan of the validity of the com-

[102]Ballagh, *Letters of R. H. Lee,* II, 214-15.

[103]*Jay Correspondence,* II, 14.

[104]*Journal Continental Congress,* XXII, 223-232, May 1, 1782. This report was violently denounced by all Virginians. Madison wrote to Jefferson telling him of the action of the committee and asking him to try and prevent the Legislature from doing anything intemperate. Hunt, *Writings of Madison,* I, 162 f.

pany titles.[105] Madison wrote in a paper of observation, dated May 1, 1782, that Maryland, Pennsylvania, Delaware, and New Jersey were principally influenced against the Virginia claims by the intrigues of their citizens interested in the land companies.[106] William Wirt Henry remarks: "Had this report been written by the agents of the Indiana Company, it could not have been more entirely in their interests."[107] Beside any possibly illegal pressure brought to bear by the land companies there was also some moral pressure by prominent men who were interested in them. Benjamin Franklin sent a memorial from Passy, France, in favor of the claims of the companies which was read to Congress on March 16, 1781, together with one from William Morgan as agent for the Indiana Proprietors.[108] Thomas Wharton distributed a propagandist booklet entitled, "Plain Facts," a strong statement of the companies' case, to the members of Congress.[109] Thomas Paine's "Public Good," an argument for unconditional cession which appeared in 1780, may also have had some weight. The manner in which the report of this committee was treated is strong evidence against it. Bland moved that each member of Congress should take an oath that he was not connected with any of the land companies. The motion was parried and on May 6 the consideration of the report was dropped by a motion of Pennsylvania.[110]

On October 29, 1782, the New York cession was formally accepted. Virginia and Massachusetts voted against acceptance, the Carolinas were divided and Georgia was not represented; the remaining States voted favorably.[111] Nothing more was

[105]Morgan to Rev. Dr. Smith, *Etting, Ohio Company Papers*, II, October 19, 1779, Pa. H. S.

[106]Rives, *Life of Madison*, p. 457. See also Hinsdale, *Old Northwest*, pp. 231-234 for many extracts from Madison's letters on this subject.

[107]Henry, *Patrick Henry*, II, 92.

[108]*Pap. Cont. Cong.*, no. 77, ff. 167-206; A. F. Volwiler, *George Croghan and the Westward Movement;* also *Journal Continental Congress*, XIX, 264.

[109]*Gratz Papers*, 2d ser., I, 105, Pa. H. S. and also the volume itself.

[110]*Journal Continental Congress*, XXII, 240.

[111]*Ibid.*, XXIII, 694.

done about the land question until the 18th of the following April, when a new call was sent out to the States to cede their lands in accordance with the resolutions of September 6 and October 10, 1780.[112]

The leaders in Congress had become weary of the whole controversy by this time.[113] In June 1783 a new and favorable committee was appointed to consider the Virginia cession.[114] This committee made a very clever and conciliatory report which took up the eight conditions attached to the Virginia cession and disposed of them one by one. Some were conceded as reasonable and should be met, others were unnecessary, and some had been complied with already. The report closed with a recommendation that Congress accept any cession made by Virginia conformable to these views.[115]

The adoption of this report by Congress on September 13, 1783, made the ultimate settlement only a matter of time. It appeared to Patrick Henry and other Virginians that the report did not really change Virginia's conditions, and the Legislature on October 20th authorized their Delegates to present a deed for the acceptance of Congress.[116]

So ended the vital land cessions to the Confederation. The fact that Connecticut, Massachusetts, and the Southern States had not as yet acted was not so important. The New York and Virginia cessions gave to Congress all the land it could possibly expect to sell for the time being.

[112]*Ibid.*, XXIV, 191.

[113]Madison probably voiced the general sentiment when he wrote to Randolph, August 13, 1782: "Every review I take of the western territory produces fresh conviction that it is the true policy of Virginia, as well as of the United States to bring the dispute to a friendly compromise. A separate government cannot be distant, and will be an insuperable barrier to subsequent profits. If, therefore, the decision of the state on the claims of companies can be saved, I hope her other conditions will be relaxed." Hunt, *Writings of Madison*, I, p. 233; Jay had written to Gerry, Jan. 9, 1781, urging that all questions of disputed boundary be settled before the end of the war, wh'le a "sense of common danger guarantees our union."

[114]*Journal Continental Congress*, XXIV, 384, June 5, 1783.

[115]*Journal Continental Congress*, XXV, 559 f., Sept. 13, 1783.

[116]Henry, *Patrick Henry*, II, 94.

CHAPTER V

LAND AS A FACTOR IN ECONOMIC RELATIONS
(Continued)

THE VERMONT QUESTION

THE Vermont dispute dates from the grant of the township of Bennington, twenty miles east of the Hudson River, by Governor Benning Wentworth of New Hampshire in 1749.[1] Governor George Clinton, the elder, appealed to the Crown on the ground that the territory belonged to New York. The King in Council in 1764 decided that the west bank of the Connecticut River north of the Massachusetts line was the boundary of New York, but meanwhile Governor Wentworth had made over a hundred additional township grants. New York declared these null and void, and started dispossession proceedings. As might be expected the New Hampshire grantees resisted, and led by Ethan Allen and Seth Warner called a convention, and dispatched an agent to the King who temporarily interdicted the making of further grants by New York. The Governor of New York, however, paid no more attention to the royal order than had the Governor of New Hampshire.

By 1774 the inhabitants of the New Hampshire Grants were armed to defend themselves against New York interference, and the New York Assembly called out the militia and authorized the Governor to place a price on the heads of the rebel leaders.[2] It is hard to say what would have happened had war with Great Britain not commenced. Fortunately, Allen

---

[1]Volumes I and II of the *Proceedings of the Vermont Historical Society* contain a documentary account of this controversy. There is a concise discussion of it in Street, *The Council of Revision and Its Vetoes*, p. 94 ff.

[2]*Colonial Laws of New York*, Chap. 1660, p. 647 f., March 9, 1774, ed. of 1890 (Chapter numbers were as provided for in 1773, however).

and Warner were both anxious to coöperate with New York against the British, and so, on July 4, 1775, they were permitted to attend the New York Provincial Congress to formulate plans for a northern expedition.[3] This spirit of coöperation was short lived. January 1776 a convention met at Dorset in the Grants, and unsuccessfully petitioned Congress to accept their services in the war independently of New York.[4] A year later a convention at Westminster declared the Grants to be an independent State, adopted the name of New Connecticut, alias Vermont, and dispatched delegates to the Continental Congress.[5]

Several interests were involved in this Vermont situation. A minority of the population had received land on bona fide New York grants, and now demanded that they be protected in their ownership by the State. There was a feeling of indignation on the part of the men in the New York government because of their undoubted legal rights to the territory when under the British Crown. Probably more important than this, however, was the fact that a group of the most powerful politicians in the State held large New York grants in the disputed region.[6] As a result formal State protests demanding some action were sent to Congress at frequent intervals.

James Duane, one of the large grantees who kept in close touch with the situation, felt optimistic in the middle of 1777. He thought that Congress would soon aid New York in putting an end to the revolt.[7] Duane brought about the dismissal of the question of recognizing the Westminster Government with-

[3] *Jour. N. Y. Prov., Cong.*, I, 65.

[4] *Journal Continental Congress*, IV, 334-335. Petition dismissed, IV, 405.

[5] *Ibid.*, VII, 239, and *Papers*, no. 40, I, 135.

[6] According to Thomas Jones, *History of New York During the Revolution*, p. 212, this list included: William Livingston, James Duane, R. R. Livingston, Robert Livingston, J. M. Scott and Richard Morris; a most imposing group, practically sufficient to control State politics by themselves.

[7] Duane to Colonel (William?) Livingston, June 16, 1777. *Duane Papers*, N. Y. H. S., p. 8.

out difficulty on June 30, 1777.[8] Just three days later the Vermont Convention adopted a State Constitution. Congress might have taken some decided action had the Vermonters not won the Battle of Bennington, but this important victory made it difficult for Congress to pass a vote of censure.[9]

At the beginning of 1778, in accordance with resolutions of the Legislature, Clinton issued a proclamation which opened the door for a compromise. New York was ready to confirm all New Hampshire or Massachusetts grants which had been occupied and improved, to confirm land to squatters up to 300 acres apiece, and to annul all posterior New York regrants. The grievance that New York's quit rents had been higher than New Hampshire's at the time of granting was to be cared for by reducing the former in that area to the level of that written in the original grants.[10] This proclamation gave new life to the New York settlers in the Grants. They held a convention at Brattleboro and sent a circular letter to the towns in the territory, and also to "the Gentlemen convened at Windsor under the stile of the general assembly of the State of Vermont," setting forth the desirability of New York allegiance.[11] This effort had no result, however; the Vermonters had gone too far to want to turn back.

During this same spring New Hampshire was drawn actively into the dispute by the adhesion of sixteen towns east of the Connecticut River to the Vermont government. In retaliation New Hampshire reasserted her claim to the entire area.[12] Massachusetts, not to be outdone, also resurrected a colonial claim to the southern section of the Grants.[13] All three States now joined in demanding that Congress adjust

[8]*Journal Continental Congress,* VIII, 509.

[9]Hughes, *Washington,* III, 148.

[10]*Pap. Cont. Cong.,* no. 40, I, 73.

[11]April 15, 1778, copies in the *Duane Papers,* N. Y. H. S.

[12]*Journal Continental Congress,* XI, 916-17.

[13]This claim had been decided against her by the Privy Council in a dispute with New Hampshire.

the matter, Clinton threatening to use force if they did not act quickly.[14]

During the spring of 1779 a mild civil war actually broke out in the Grants. When New York officials were imprisoned by the rebels, Clinton complained of this matter to Congress with increasing emphasis. On May 27, 1779 he wrote the Delegates that the matter had reached a crisis, and that he was about to issue orders to the militia, as well as to 1,000 men raised to complete the Continental Battalions, to march to Brattleboro unless the immediate interposition of Congress should render this unnecessary.[15] This spurred Congress to action, and a five-member committee was appointed to proceed to Vermont and investigate; a resolution of apology was also sent to Governor Clinton for their slowness in acting.[16] Congress further resolved that the imprisoned officials should be released at once, and then suspended all action to wait the report of the committee.[17] The committee, however, never managed to assemble in Vermont, although two of the members went there and reported that the people were willing to abide by the decision of Congress.[18] September 24, Congress by unanimous resolution asked Massachusetts, New York, and New Hampshire to vest them with full power to settle the disputed points on the first of February next.[19] This resolution was agreeable to the States, but they did not have the necessary evidence prepared by February 1780 and the hearing was postponed to June.[20]

[14]Clinton to the President of Congress (Laurens). He says that the people of the Grants gather from the attitude of Congress that their activities are not altogether unwelcome. April 7, 1778. And again in the same tenor December 17, 1778, *Duane Papers*, N. Y. H. S.

[15]*Duane Papers*, no. 95, N. Y. H. S.

[16]*Journal Continental Congress*, XIV, 673-675.

[17]*Ibid.*, XIV, 741-742.

[18]*Ibid.*, XIV, 823-824.

[19]*Ibid.*, XV, 1095-1099 (Resolution quoted in full in the Journals).

[20]*Ibid.*, XVII, 499. It is interesting to note that this made New York favorable to Burke of North Carolina's motion that the lands within the limits of the United States are under the jurisdiction of one or the other

The hearing, after being again postponed because the New Hampshire delegates were not present in June,[21] finally opened September 19 with the New York testimony.[22] The New York case was a good one legally, especially as Duane had found that the boundary of New York had been reaffirmed in the instruction to two of the early Governors.[23] After a few sessions of the hearing, however, it developed that there were forces at work in Congress that made the decision of the case on its legal merits very unlikely. Duane wrote to Clinton early in October:[24]

. . . The Debates took a turn which could not have been looked for and clearly satisfied me that several states were disposed to support the independence of our revolted citizens. The delegates of Pennsylvania act under the influence of instructions from their legislature requiring them to consent to no act of Congress against any people friendly to the Revolution. . . . The Delegates from Rhode Island have declared that many of the principal people of that state have accepted grants under the assumed state . . . the governor is one and that he has desired the delegates to take care of his interest. The delegates from Delaware felt that Congress could not interfere. A delegate from Virginia moved that Vermont should be declared independent. This was not seconded, however, and the other delegates did not agree with him. The use made by Vermont of public land grants to gain a party in some of the states have in my judgment no inconsiderable weight.

of the thirteen states. *Ibid.*, XVII, 452. Thus at the time of the New York Western Land Cession, February, 1780, the Vermont situation seemed to demand the most careful cultivation of the friendship of the other states. That New Yorkers were fully conscious of this is illustrated by a letter from John Morin Scott to James Duane, a Delegate to Congress, written February 2, which says: "It is wise to conciliate our Judges—many of the states you know are interested against our Western Claim." Duane and Benson replied to Scott on the 8th that they agreed with him. *Duane Papers*, N. Y. H. S.

[21] *Journal Continental Congress*, XVII, 499, June 9, 1780.
[22] *Ibid.*, XVIII, 840 ff.
[23] Duane and Benson to Scott Feb. 2, 1780. *Duane Papers*, N. Y. H. S.
[24] *Duane Papers*, N. Y. H. S.

I am of the opinion that our Legislature must depend on their own wisdom to manage this unhappy business.

This letter really marks and explains the turning point in the Vermont affair. Up until the hearing began the New Yorkers had felt they were going to win back the jurisdiction of the territory. From this time on the wiser ones must have realized that they were going to fail. October 6, Congress adjourned consideration of the matter after pretty well demonstrating that New York would not be able to secure a majority in favor of its stand.[25]

Clinton upon receipt of this news wrote to Duane that there was universal disgust among all ranks of people, and that the best informed felt that there was a premeditated intention to make a political sacrifice of New York to the interest of individuals in other States. The next meeting of the Legislature might very likely withdraw the New York Delegates and support from Congress.[26] Duane replied that he believed the Governor's remarks well founded, but that to press for a decision on the Vermont question would appear selfish at a time when so much was at stake. As soon as this "great business is dispatched" they could seek a settlement.[27]

Any remaining hopes as to the chances of regaining Vermont were dispelled by the attitude of the session of Congress of 1781.[28] In May Vermont, very likely to gain bargaining power, extended her claims to the Hudson River, and got twelve towns from that section to send delegates to a conven-

[25] *Journal Continental Congress,* XVIII, 908-909.

[26] Clinton to Duane, Oct. 29, 1780. *Duane Papers,* N. Y. H. S.

[27] Duane to Clinton, Nov. 14, 1780. *Duane Papers,* N. Y. H. S. These letters illustrate well the difference of opinion between a future Anti-Federalist, and a future Federalist.

[28] Clinton wrote to Duane on April 6, "I most sincerely wish a speedy decision of our controversy with these people . . . I am persuaded . . . that any decision that can be made, not extending their original claims will be preferable to delay. They now daily gain strength at our expense, and while the matter hangs in suspense it excites divisions, on the subject, among ourselves; which I am apprehensive will have an unhappy influence on our own public affairs." *Duane Papers,* N. Y. H. S.

tion at Cambridge which pledged allegiance to the new government. In Congress a series of motions were made during the summer tending to deny New York's contentions.[29] August 7th Congress, by a vote of all the States except New York, resolved to appoint a committee of five to confer with representatives of the Grants as to terms on which they might be admitted into the Union. The agents of New York and New Hampshire could attend the meeting. These two States were asked to free Vermont from all claims of jurisdiction, and leave it to Congress as to when the concessions would take effect.[30] Clinton wrote the Delegates that he questioned Congress' power to settle the dispute under the Articles.[31] Hawley of Georgia in Congress had struck the real note when he said the whole question was one of expediency, not legality.[32] Duane had assured Clinton that there was no hope now of preventing recognition of the independence of Vermont. The best they could expect was to get satisfactory boundaries. New York must give way to the common good.[33]

Vermont showed its assurance by holding up the negotiations until April 1, 1782, before relinquishing an extravagant western claim, and agreeing to join the Confederation with its present boundary.[34] After the reception of this resolution the only thing that held up the admission of Vermont was the inability of Congress to muster a vote of nine States. The New England States, wishing to add to the weight of their section in Congress, plus the landed interests in Vermont of members from other States, made a fairly consistent vote of seven or

[29]*Journal Continental Congress*, XX, 770-71, 923-25, 829, 830-31.

[30]*Ibid.*, 838 f.

[31]Clinton to Delegates, August 27, 1781, *Duane Papers*.

[32]Notes on debate, *Duane Papers*.

[33]Duane to Clinton, August 9, 1781, *Duane Papers*.

[34]*Journal Continental Congress*, XXII, 157. Resolution of Aug. 20, 1781, fixing acceptable boundaries; *Ibid.*, XXI, 887, was passed nine to one, only New York voted against it.

eight States against New York.[35] Virginia, however, fearful of back-country rebellions herself, sided steadily with New York, and as only ten States were usually represented a deadlock was created.

For another year or so the situation produced some excitement, but nothing was accomplished. The Governor of New Hampshire suggested to Clinton at one time that they divide the territory forcibly between them,[36] but political opinion was by now so divided in regard to what ought to be done that all action was impossible. Meanwhile rumors were rife that Vermont intended to ally itself with Great Britain. Sufficient proof of these negotiations was secured to prejudice some of the members of Congress against Vermont.[37] The tone of communications from Vermont was sharp and unconciliatory in many instances. The net result was that by the end of 1783 the whole affair was at a standstill and Vermont had little to hope from Congress until New York should agree to give them their independence.[38]

From 1783 on, the Vermont situation received little attention from the politicians.[39] The Legislature of New York was afraid to grant independence for fear of public disapproval, and therefore the anomalous situation went on year after year. Finally a commission was appointed by the Legislature in 1789 which arranged terms for independence. In 1790 this

[35]New York Delegates in Congress (Scott and Floyd) to Clinton, March 15, 1782, *Duane Papers.*

[36]Clinton to Duane, August 8, 1782, *Duane Papers.*

[37]These rumors were true in so far as negotiations went. Lieut. Governor Haldinand of Quebec was in touch with the Vermont leaders from 1780 to 1782, but the best opinion is that the Vermonters were merely playing him off against Congress to secure the State from invasion. The Haldinand correspondence is in Vol. II of the *Proceedings of the Vermont Historical Society.*

[38]*Journal Continental Congress,* XXV, 888. Discussion in Madison's notes of general attitude toward Vermont.

[39]From the beginning of 1784 on there are no important references to Vermont in the *Duane* or *Clinton Papers,* and very little in the *Journals of Congress.* See statement to same effect in Street, *Council of Revision,* p. 105.

was granted in return for a payment of $30,000 to satisfy New York land titles.[40]

THE MASSACHUSETTS BOUNDARY DISPUTE

The Massachusetts boundary dispute never aroused the passions, or received the attention from the politicians or people that the Vermont question did.[41] There are several obvious reasons for this difference. No land grants had been made in the area in dispute. The territory was occupied by the partly hostile Six Nations who were apparently not anxious to part with land at this time.[42] The whole affair was handled as a legal case, and the public knew very little about the matter.

The dispute, as in all these cases, resulted from the loose way in which the early Colonial charters had defined boundaries. The Charter of 1629 had given Massachusetts all lands to the west, included within its parallels of latitude, not inhabited by any Christian Prince or State. The Charter of 1691 had said nothing further about the boundary, except that Massachusetts extended to the western boundary of Connecticut. As Connecticut also had a sea-to-sea charter, this was no restriction.[43] The New York Charter of 1664 merely specified the boundaries of New York as the Connecticut River, and the east shore of Delaware Bay.[44] In 1701 the treaty with the Iroquois, mentioned in the previous chapter, was negotiated, giving New York a protectorate over the Indian lands stretching indefinitely westward.[45]

[40]There were seventy-six claimants under these titles, and they were all taken care of by 1799. Street, *Council of Revision*, p. 105.

[41]Paul Evans in his *Poultney Purchase*. *N. Y. S. H. A. Proc.*, XX takes the same view.

[42]See *infra* p. 100f. for difficulty in negotiating treaties.

[43]*Report of the Regents of the University of the State of New York on the Boundaries of the State*, Senate Document, no. 71, Albany 1883, p. 403 f. This voluminous report contains all the essential documentary information regarding this question. The only major additions made in the following discussion are from the *Duane Papers* in the New York Historical Society.

[44]*Ibid.*, p. 404.

[45]*New York Colonial Documents*, VIII, 436-437.

The western boundary question was not brought forward until 1768, and the New York governors exercised unquestioned jurisdiction over this region prior to the Proclamation of 1763.[46] In 1768 the Massachusetts General Court gave the first hint of trouble when they affirmed the Massachusetts title west of New York.[47] The New York Assembly promptly protested, but the war prevented any settlement.[48]

The matter had been allowed to lapse entirely when early in 1784 Massachusetts reaffirmed its right to a continuous strip between 42°.02' and 44°.15' westward from the western boundary of New York, and petitioned Congress to determine where that boundary lay. Congress replied on June 3 by calling upon the two States to send their agents to a Federal Court to be appointed by Congress in accordance with Article IX the first Monday in the next December.[49]

Clinton informed the Legislature of this action of Congress in his fall message, and on November 12th they appointed Duane, Jay, R. R. Livingston, Walter Livingston, and Egbert Benson as agents for the State.[50] Although the calibre of this delegation testifies to the seriousness with which the Legislature regarded the question, involving as it did millions of acres of fertile land, yet there was no indication of political or popular excitement either in private letters or the newspapers.

The two sets of agents reported to Congress as scheduled on December 10th and prepared a list of judges as provided for in Article IX of the Confederation.[51] It was impossible, how-

[46]*New York Colonial Documents*, VII, 3. Governor Hardy to the Lords of Trade. *Ibid.*, VIII, 436. Tryon to Dartmouth.

[47]This was in connection with a minor uncertainty regarding the eastern boundary.

[48]*Report on the Boundaries of the State*, p. 407 f.

[49]*Journal Continental Congress*, 1823 ed., IV, 444.

[50]*Jour. N. Y. Senate*, 1784, p. 20, *Laws of N. Y.*, Chap. II, p. 3.

[51]*Journal Continental Congress*, 1823 ed., p. 453.

ever, to get satisfactory judges to serve.[52] The agents themselves were not averse to delay. As late as April 1785 Duane had no copies of the English records.[53] He also had heard that the cause was not a popular one in Massachusetts, and that delay might work in New York's favor and lead to a dropping of the claim altogether.[54] Meanwhile, Alexander Hamilton and Samuel Jones had been retained as attorneys for the State.[55]

The necessary papers for the New York side were finally secured early in 1786.[56] By this time the agents had despaired of finding satisfactory judges, and had decided that the matter could be more readily settled by direct negotiations. On April 28, 1786 the New York Legislature empowered the agents to settle the controversy otherwise than in a Federal Court, and in such a way as seemed most efficacious.[57] The Massachusetts General Court agreed and the agents met at Hartford, Connecticut, the sixteenth of the following December.[58]

The problem was quickly disposed of by a compromise agreement. New York granted to Massachusetts full right of preemption from the native Indians to 230,400 acres to be located northward of certain specified grants between the Owego and Chenango Rivers, and from a north and south meridian drawn eighty-two miles west of the northeast corner of the Pennsylvania boundary practically to the western limits of the State.[59] New York was to retain full sovereignty over this territory

[52]*Report on Boundaries of the State*, p. 410. See *Duane Papers, passim,* for lists of judges decided upon, and letters from the same declining the honor, usually because of difficulty in selecting a convenient location for the Court.

[53]Duane to R. R. Livingston, April 8, 1785, *Duane Papers.*

[54]*Ibid.,* Sept. 25, 1785.

[55]Resolution of the New York Agents, June 9, 1785, *Duane Papers.*

[56]As late as Jan. 1, 1786, however, W. L. Smith, the New York attorney in London, had still three papers to find copies of. *Duane Papers,* Smith to Jay, Jan. 1, 1786.

[57]*Laws of N. Y.,* Chap. XLIX, p. 95.

[58]*Report on the Boundaries of the State,* p. 411.

[59]New York retained a mile wide strip along the Niagara River.

as far as jurisdiction was concerned. Massachusetts grants would be exempted from quit rents for fifteen years from the time of granting. Massachusetts could negotiate the necessary Indian treaties, and might if necessary employ troops to safeguard its agents. Copies of all treaties were to be filed within six months with the New York Secretary of State. Massachusetts might delegate this treaty-making power to private individuals providing a state commissioner was present, and the State ratified the treaties so made. Massachusetts grants had to be filed with the New York Secretary of State, and new patents issued by the latter, but without fee or reward.[60] February 19, 1787, the New York Legislature agreed to this decision, and resolved to have the Governor explain the conditions to the Indians.[61]

April, 1788, the Massachusetts General Court sold their preëmption right to all their New York land to Oliver Phelps and Nathaniel Gorham for the sum of $1,000,000 payable in Massachusetts Consolidated Securities (a scrip worth about 20% of its face value). Phelps and Gorham were the representatives of a large group of speculators. In July they assembled the Indians and purchased the rights to 2,600,000 acres of this land which Massachusetts gave them quit claims for on November 21.[62] This was the only part ever actually acquired by the Phelps and Gorham group. The residue of the tract reverted again to Massachusetts and was sold to an agent of Robert Morrison March 12, 1791.[63] How a New York State land company figured in these western dealings will be discussed in the following section.[64]

[60] *Report on the Boundaries of the State*, pp. 411-414.

[61] *Jour. N. Y. Sen.*, 10th sess., p. 33, Feb. 17; *Assembly*, p. 57, Feb. 19.

[62] O. Turner, *History of Phelps' and Gorham's Purchase*, and *History of the Holland Purchase*, p. 325 ff.

[63] O. Turner, *History of the Holland Purchase*, p. 396 f.

[64] The New York Genesee Land Company, see *infra*, p. 103f.

LAND IN ECONOMIC RELATIONS

ACQUISITION OF THE INDIAN TITLES

New York embraced the most important sphere of Indian relations in the United States during the Revolution. In fact it is but a small exaggeration to say that New York was the whole Northern Department. These important relations were almost entirely of a military character during the war and consequently must be omitted here. It will be necessary, however, to say a little about the machinery of Indian relations.

There had been, since 1756, two royal Indian agents, one for the Southern Department and another for the Northern. Sir William Johnson, the agent for the Northern Department during the entire period until his death in 1774, lived at Schenectady, New York. The Iroquois or Six Nations were his principal charges, and these in turn constituted, as we have seen, a protectorate of the Government of New York. We have also seen that Sir William Johnson's nephew Guy Johnson, who succeeded him as Agent for the Northern Department, became a Loyalist and was forced to flee to Canada at the beginning of the war.[65] This left no official intermediary between the Iroquois and the new Congress. All of the Six Nations except the Oneidas, and the smallest tribe, the Tuscaroras, took the British side in the war. These two tribes tried at first to preserve neutrality.[66]

As soon as war appeared inevitable a committee of Congress was appointed to draw up plans for dealing with the Indians. July 12, 1775, the resolutions of this committee were adopted. Three departments, Northern, Middle, and Southern, were created. There were to be five Commissioners for the Southern

[65]For an account of all this see W. C. Griffis, *Sir William Johnson and the Six Nations,* and M. G. Walker, *Sir John Johnson, Loyalist, Mississippi Valley Historical Review,* III, no. 3, 318 ff.

[66]All of the Iroquois at the treaty of Albany in August 1775 had expressed a willingness to keep peace, and Congress had appropriated money to start Indian trade at Schenectady. *Journal Continental Congress,* III, 365 f. The Senecas, Cayugas, Onondagas and Mohawks soon actively joined the British, however.

Department, and three each for the others. The Northern Department included the Six Nations and all other Indians to the north and east. The Commissioners could appoint agents to assist them. They were to see that the friendly Indians were supplied with arms, ammunition, and clothing.[67] The following day one more Commissioner was provided for the Northern Department, and Joseph Hawley, Turbot Francis, Oliver Woolcot, and Philip Schuyler were elected Commissioners.[68] Schuyler was by far the most important Commissioner.[69] He conducted the affairs almost single handed. He alone of the four was known to almost all the Iroquois chiefs, because of his long residence at Saratoga and his interest in Indian affairs during the Colonial period. His command of the Northern army also kept him in close contact with the situation.

Schuyler arranged to hold a treaty with as many of the Iroquois nations as would attend at Johnstown early in 1778.[70] At this meeting the Oneidas and Tuscaroras were won over to active coöperation on the American side [71] Having acquired these Indians as allies, Congress had to pay the usual price for keeping them. $10,000 was apportioned to start Indian trade at Fort Schuyler, and General Gates was directed to afford all the protection to the friendly tribes that the Commissioners had promised them.[72] All of this concerned New York only indirectly. Although Schuyler was a citizen of New York and the operations were entirely on New York territory, the complete responsibility rested on Congress. Governor Clinton,

[67]*Journal Continental Congress*, II, 174-177.

[68]*Ibid.*, II, 183.

[69]Schuyler's personal wealth and credit were also great assets. Aug. 30, 1781, Schuyler asked Morris if he might take care of the Oneidas and Tuscaroras on his own resources until contracts could be arranged. Schuyler to Morris, *Schuyler Letters*, New York State Library.

[70]Congress appointed a group of Commissioners to attend this treaty and gave them elaborate instructions. *Journal Continental Congress*, VI, 105 ff.

[71]*Pap. Cont. Cong.* no. 153, III, f. 286.

[72]*Journal Continental Congress*, VI, 456.

however, was often consulted: for example, he was asked to select one of the Commissioners to represent Congress at the Johnstown treaty.[73]

On May 4, 1776, a standing committee on Indian affairs was appointed by Congress, composed of James Duane, John Armstrong, Thomas Burke, Henry Laurens, and Roger Sherman.[74] During this entire period supplies were continually sent to the Oneidas and Tuscaroras, who were driven from their lands by the more powerful hostile tribes, and forced to seek the shelter of the New York forts.[75] The chiefs of these two tribes were given commissions in the Continental Line, and put on the Continental pay roll.[76] The Indian Commissioners were directed to keep in close touch with Washington, and direct their policy accordingly.[77]

By the fall of 1779 it was hoped that a general pacification of the Northern Indian tribes might be brought about. October 23, the New York Legislature appointed four Indian Commissioners, who, together with the Governor, should represent the State at any treaty of pacification that might be held, and to enter into any formal document that might be drawn up as a separate party.[78]

October 15, 1783, Congress adopted a long report regarding Indian pacification. The sixth article stipulated that the Oneidas and Tuscaroras should be reassured that they could rely upon keeping their inherited lands for their exclusive use until it should be to their own interest to dispose of the same.[79]

[73]*Ibid.*, VI, 110-111. Occasionally the State advanced money to Schuyler, and then collected it from Congress. *Pap. Cont. Cong.*, no. 67, II, f. 369.

[74]*Journal Continental Congress*, X, 544 f.

[75]*Ibid.*, IX, 335, 363, etc. In fact toward the close of the war Congress thought it wise to make a point of dealing liberally with the Oneidas and Tuscaroras so as to show the other tribes the value of American friendship. *Ibid.*, XXIII, 603.

[76]*Journal Continental Congress*, IX, 411; X, 693.

[77]*Ibid.*, X, 600.

[78]*Laws of N. Y.*, Chap. 1779, XXIX, 97.

[79]*Journal Continental Congress*, XXV, 687.

The articles of the report regarding the detailed financing, etc., of these general treaties were amended and recommitted from time to time until March 19, 1784,[80] on which date $15,000 was appropriated for the use of the Commissioners in drawing up the treaty with the Six Nations.[81]

Meanwhile the New York Government, impatient with the long delay of Congress, decided to act for itself. The Legislature by Act of March 3, 1784, directed the Council of Appointment to designate three Commissioners who, acting with the Governor, should settle the Indian boundaries. The Oneidas and Tuscaroras were to be secured in their rights, and the Acts of the Commissioners were to be passed on by the Legislature.[82] The Commissioners immediately got in touch with the Iroquois chiefs, and on June 6th received a reply from Joseph Brant, the greatest chieftain, that all the Six Nations would meet with them at Fort Stanwix in September.[83]

The British had acted with more dispatch than either the Continental or New York governments. The Canadian authorities were in a very embarrassing situation. The loss of the war had injured their prestige, and made it impossible to fulfill their promises to the Six Nations.[84] Sir John Johnson assembled the tribes, sixteen hundred strong, at Niagara July 22 to 31, 1783, and partially succeeded in reconciling them to the situation. It was not difficult for the Indians to realize that they had little to fear from British encroachment, and a great deal from American.[85] Therefore the three western tribes of the Six Nations became natural allies of the British,

[80] *Journal Continental Congress,* XXV, 747 and note 2 on same.

[81] *Pap. Cont. Cong.,* no. 30, II, f. 213.

[82] *Laws of N. Y.,* 6th sess., p. 290.

[83] *Proceedings of the Commissioners of Indian Affairs of the State of New York,* ed. by F. B. Hough, pp. 10-15.

[84] "The Indians feel they have been abandoned to an ungenerous and implacable enemy." Haldimand to Lord Townshend, May 7, 1783. *Report of Canadian Archives,* 1885, p. 350 and 1886, pp. 31-35 (Haldimand Correspondence Calendar).

[85] *Ibid.,* 1887, pp. 153-154, and 198 (Haldimand Cor. Calendar).

and led by the great chieftain Joseph Brant did all they could to impede American progress westward.[86]

When the Congressional Commission heard of the plans of New York they decided to meet with the Indians at the same place. The New York treaty was concluded, however, before the Congressional Commissioners arrived.[87] This latter group entered into an exactly similar agreement, in so far as it concerned New York, on October 22, 1784. This treaty of Fort Stanwix is not properly speaking a treaty of cession, but merely a pacification by which each party recognized the legal boundaries of the others territory. The eastern boundary of the Six Nations was to be the old "Line of Property" established at Fort Stanwix in 1768.[88] The western boundary was to be, roughly speaking, four miles east of the western boundary of the State. In the intervening space they held all the land from Lake Ontario to the Pennsylvania boundary.[89]

This treaty of 1784 marks the end of intimate dealings between the Congressional Commissioners and those of the State. Congress had acquired a quit claim from the New York Indians for the Ohio territory, which was their main concern. The future dealings with the Six Nations, who, south of the Great Lakes, were now entirely confined to New York State, became a local matter with which Congress had no immediate concern, so long as peace was preserved.[90]

[86]In September 1783 the Six Nations held a conference with the southern and western Indians at Sandusky, and formed an offensive and defensive league. They agreed to keep peace with the U. S., however, unless attacked. *Rep. of Canadian Archives,* 1887, p. 40.

[87]*Proc. N. Y. Indian Comms.,* pp. 56-62. The treaty was concluded September 10, 1784.

[88]This went from where the Mohawk Branch of the Delaware intersects the Pennsylvania boundary, northward to where the Unadilla branches from the East Branch of the Susquehanna, north along the Unadilla to its source, and then northwest to a point seven miles west of Fort Stanwix on Wood Creek. See map, p. 102.

[89]*Proc. N. Y. Ind. Comms.,* pp. 64-65.

[90]A large Congressional Indian Commission was retained until July 12, 1786, when they surrendered their powers to a Superintendent of the

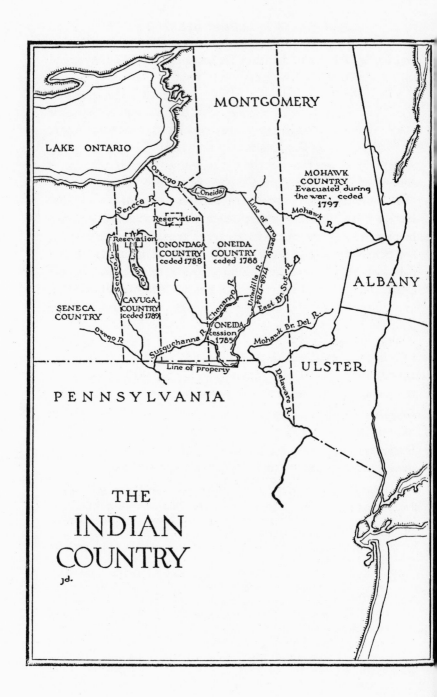

MONTGOMERY

LAKE ONTARIO

Oswego R.

L. Oneida

MOHAWK
COUNTRY
Evacuated during
the war, ceded
1797

Mohawk R.

Seneca R.

Reservation

Reservation

Line of property

ONONDAGA
COUNTRY
ceded 1788

ONEIDA
COUNTRY
ceded 1788

ALBANY

Seneca R.

Cayuga L.

Chenango R.

Unadilla R.

East Br. Sus. R.

1768—1784

SENECA
COUNTRY

CAYUGA
COUNTRY
ceded 1789

ONEIDA
cession
1785

Mohawk Br. Del. R.

Owego R.

Susquehanna

Line of property

ULSTER

Delaware R.

PENNSYLVANIA

THE
INDIAN
COUNTRY

jd.

As a glance at the map on p. 102 will show, this treaty did not clear the military tract, or in fact provide a boundary much beyond the existing limits of western settlement. The following year, as a part of the act establishing a system for State land sale, the New York Commissioners were instructed to obtain before October 1, 1785, a grant of as much land as the Indians would dispose of on reasonable terms.[91] The Commissioners assembled the Oneidas and Tuscaroras at Fort Herkimer in June, and after some controversy persuaded them to part with a substantial block of land between the Unadilla and Chenango Rivers in return for $11,500, in money and goods.[92] By this treaty salable land was released along the Pennsylvania boundary.

Before another State treaty could be negotiated a gigantic land grab was attempted by a New York company. The State Constitution prohibited the private purchase of land from the Indians, but said nothing about leases. On the basis of this technicality John Livingston, Peter Schuyler, Caleb Benton, Ezekiel Gilbert and others organized a large company of wealthy New York landlords to seek a lease from the Six Nations. They very shrewdly established a subsidiary company in Canada in which John Butler and Sir John Johnson took stock.[93] Through the influence of these Canadians the Iroquois tribes were induced at the close of 1787 to sign 999-

Northern and Southern Department, respectively. *Pap. Cont. Cong.*, no. 30, II, ff. 291-293, 297 and 315. July 26, 1787, the Superintendents asked the states to be more careful about citizens wrongfully invading the rights of the Indians. *Ibid.*, f. 319.

[91]See *infra*, p. 110.

[92]*Proc. N. Y. Ind. Comms.*, pp. 102-108.

[93]The organization of this "Genesee company" is given in detail in *Proc. N. Y. Ind. Comms.*, pp. 120 ff. A good general account of the whole incident is in O. Turner's *History of Phelps' and Gorham's Purchase*, pp. 107 ff.

year leases turning practically all of their lands in New York State over to the company.[94]

When news of this deal reached Governor Clinton he at once informed the Indians that such action was illegal.[95] February 19 the Legislature passed an act stating that anybody offering lands for sale acquired under *any* Indian title without the consent of the State should be punishable by fine and imprisonment at the discretion of the court.[96] This act placed the company in a very difficult position as they had already sent some hundred and sixty settlers into the new territory. The State militia was dispatched to the aid of the sheriff of Montgomery County, and one settler was actually placed under arrest as a squatter.[97] John Livingston now offered to turn the land over to the State if it would assume the Indian lease, and grant the company 1,000,000 acres of land.[98] This proposal was laid before the Indian Commissioners who promptly turned it down. The lessees kept up an agitation for the next five years, impeding State Indian relations in every way possible, and trying to start a movement for independent statehood in western New York. In 1793, however, the Legislature put an end to the trouble by granting the company township Number Three in the military tract.[99]

[94]The three western tribes were to receive $20,000 as a bonus and $2,000 annually. The Oneidas $1,000 annually for the first ten years, one hundred dollars more for each of the next five years, and then $1,500 for the remainder of the time. *Proc. N. Y. Ind. Comms.*, pp. 121-123 (Main lease Nov. 30, 1787, Oneida lease Jan. 15, 1788). The Iroquois could afford to part with their New York land as the Canadian government had given them large tracts in Canada in reward for their loyalty during the war.

[95]*Proc. N. Y. Ind. Comms.*, p. 133 f.

[96]*Laws of N. Y.*, Chap. XLVII, p. 100 f. February 16 the Legislature had declared the leases illegal by a concurrent resolution. *Jour. N. Y. Assembly*, p. 80. A few days later the fine for illegal dealings with the Indians was placed at £100. *Laws*, Chap. LXXXV, p. 188 f. March 18, 1788.

[97]Turner, *History of Phelps' and Gorham's Purchase*, p. 108.

[98]*Proc. N. Y. Ind. Comms.*, p. 138.

[99]Turner, *History of Phelps' and Gorham's Purchase*, pp. 109 ff. This agitation may not have been as important as Turner makes it appear. A

Spurred on by these illegal activities and the pressure of military warrant holders, the State concluded further treaties in 1788. At Fort Stanwix, September 12, the Onondagas' ceded all their lands except a reservation around their chief village, in return for about $12,000 and a $500 perpetual annuity.[100] Ten days later the Oneidas ceded their remaining lands on approximately the same conditions.[101]

These treaties, plus one concluded with the Senecas by Oliver Phelps, for the Massachusetts purchasers, on July 4, 1788, and one concluded with the Cayugas at Albany the following year, practically cleared the central and western part of the State of Indian titles.[102]

THE STATE LAND SYSTEM

The New York Colonial land system prior to the orders of 1774 was an extremely loose one. There had been no fixed policy as to price, quantity, or quit rents for the last hundred years. Land had been given liberally by Governors to their friends, or in return for debts or political support. Only small quit rents were reserved on most of this land. There were strong suspicions of fraud in the purchases made from the Indians.[103] In fact the Government in London had very little idea as to what the situation was in New York.[104] Large grants were made after 1763 to officers and others who claimed to have aided during the war. These grants were reviewed by the Board of Trade and the Privy Council, but

circular signed by Livingston and Benton was sent around urging the people to hold town meetings and petition for statehood. A thorough study of the Canadian Archives would likely throw much light on this subject.

[100]*Proc. N. Y. Ind. Comms.*, pp. 198 ff.

[101]*Ibid.*, pp. 210 ff.

[102]There is a good brief discussion of all these treaties up through the final Mohawk treaty of 1797 in Turner's *Phelps' and Gorham's Purchase*, pp. 306-307. *Proc. N. Y. Indian Comms.*, contains the complete details.

[103]*New York Colonial Documents*, Colden to the Board of Trade, Dec. 6, 1765, VII, 795-800.

[104]*New York Colonial Documents*, VIII, 77.

as these bodies knew very little about the merits of the case they adopted a uniform policy of allowing half the request.[105]

Governor Moore (1765-1769) pointed out repeatedly the bad effects of this whole system. The annual quit rent received was £1,806, and the annual arrears £18,888, despite the fact that no rent had ever been assessed on many of the older grants. The Assembly would not pass a bill to complete the rent roll because too many members would be affected thereby. The system of large grants with vague boundaries discouraged the small farmer as it led to continuous litigation, and often ruined him even if he won out in the end. These injustices practised by the great landlords often led to riots, and the imprisonment of tenants and small farmers.[106] Governor Tryon (1771-76) on the other hand regarded the system of granting large tracts "to gentlemen of weight and consideration," as stimulating to the settlement and cultivation of the lands, and valuable in gaining the support of the influential classes in the Colony.[107]

In 1773, after long deliberation, the British government prepared a completely new set of instructions to the Governors for the disposal of land. All previous instructions were declared null. All lands to be granted were to be previously surveyed in lots of 100 to 1,000 acres and recorded on maps. Copies of such maps were to be sent to Lord Dartmouth, the Colonial Secretary. Land was to be sold from time to time at public auction on a specified date after four months public notice. The officials were to establish the minimum prices which must not be less than 6 pence per acre. Quit rents were uniformly fixed at one half-penny per acre. The only persons who could acquire land in any other way, from the Colonial authorities, were ex-soldiers, seeking to satisfy bounty war-

[105]*Acts of the Privy Council;* (Col. Series) VI, 390.
[106]*New York Colonial Documents,* VII, 900-902, 795; VIII, 12.
[107]*Ibid.,* VIII, 293.

rants in accordance with the proclamation of 1763.[108] These regulations meant that the British government was going to try and make a profit from land sales, and possibly to pay the cost of Colonial administration from quit rents.[109] They produced widespread protest throughout the Colonies. Tryon wrote: "The new instruction for granting lands I look upon as a mere nullity in affect, to say no worse of it; and I took the liberty to assure Lord Dartmouth I did not believe it could have any operation."[110]

Just how the regulations would have worked in practice cannot be told. The period between their promulgation and the outbreak of hostilities was mainly occupied by the Colonial officials in asking questions as to their precise meaning. Dartmouth did agree to approve certain grants purchased from the Indians under licenses from Governors Dunmore and Tryon providing the grantees would abstain from the Association to obstruct trade.[111] Outside of these western grants, however, the land system came to a standstill in 1775. The danger from the Indians and British on the one side, and the Vermont trouble on the other made further settlement too dangerous.[112]

August 2, 1776, the New York Convention resolved that quit rents formerly due the Crown were now due to the government of New York.[113] No effort was made to collect

[108]*New York Colonial Documents*, VIII, 410-412. This did not mean, however, that the British officials in London bound themselves not to make large grants.

[109]B. Bond, *Quit Rent System in the American Colonies*, p. 438.

[110]*Colden Papers*, N. Y. H. S. Col., 1923, pp. 226-227.

[111]*New York Colonial Documents*, VIII, 569, 570. John, Earl of Dunmore, had been Governor of New York for a few months between the death of Moore, and the appointment of Tryon. Dunmore had then been switched to Virginia.

[112]"The desolation of the frontiers has driven the inhabitants to the interior." Haldimand to Lord Germaine, Oct. 22, 1781. *Rep. of Canadian Archives*, 1885, p. 340.

[113]*Jour. N. Y. Prov. Cong.*, I, 554. Books relating to them were to be seized by the Provincial Officials.

them, however, and the Colonial Land Office records were not collected from Alexander Colden, the Surveyor-General of the Colony.[114] No act for the sale of land, other than confiscated property, was passed by the Legislature until 1784.[115] The fact that a State land office would compete with the sales of the Commissioners of Forfeiture, and possibly result in a net loss in revenue, was very likely one cause for this inaction.

Wild land did occupy the attention of the Legislature during the war, however, in the form of military bounty grants. Congress had led the way on September 16, 1776, by promising land bounties to the Continental Line.[116] This promise was renewed from time to time as new battalions were raised. In 1781 and 1782 New York also promised bounties in order to raise regiments for the defense of the frontiers.[117] In July of this latter year the Legislature established a military tract to take care of the State grants and its share of the Congressional grants. The boundaries were: Lake Ontario, the Onondaga river, and Oneida Lake on the north; a line drawn from the mouth of the Great Sodus or Aforodus Creek through the most westerly inclination of Seneca lake on the west; a line from the most westerly boundary of the Oneida country on Oneida Lake, through the most westerly inclination of the

[114]Mentioned in *Laws of N. Y.*, April 1, 1786, Chap. XXIII, p. 24 f. and March 2, 1784, Chap. XVI, p. 20, respectively.

[115]May 10, 1784, *Laws of N. Y.*, Chap. LX, p. 91 f.

[116]*Journal Continental Congress*, V, 762. The expenses necessary to procure such lands were to be borne by the States in the same proportion as the other expenses of the war. We have already referred to the effect of this act on Maryland in the last chapter.

[117]March 20, 1781, *Laws*, Chap. XXXII, p. 178.

March 23, 1782, *Ibid.*, Chap. XXII, p. 220.

These men were to form part of the Continental Line, and be paid and subsisted by Congress. The first act provided bounties of from 500 acres to a private to 2,000 acres to a lieutenant colonel. It was promised that the State in erecting townships from these grants would reserve 500 acres per township for religious purposes, and 360 acres for education. The second act increased the bounty to 600 acres, and provided several subsidiary types of bounties. All these lands were to be surveyed and granted as soon as possible after the close of the war.

Oneida country in the east; and by the Pennsylvania boundary on the south.[118] No Indian titles to this land except those of the friendly Oneidas and Tuscaroras were to be respected.[119]

March 27, 1783, the Senate and Assembly by concurrent resolutions fixed the amount of bounty land due each type of soldier. The grants ranged from 5,500 acres to a Major General down to 500 acres for a private.[120] The following year the necessary machinery for satisfying the warrants was established. The Governor, Lieutenant Governor, Speaker, Secretary of State, Attorney General, Treasurer and Auditor were made Commissioners for granting bounty lands. The surveys were not made until 1788 and no ex-soldiers moved into the military tract prior to 1789.[121] In fact only a few or the original grantees ever settled there as their warrants were the subject of widespread speculation right after the war.[122]

With the close of the war there was a popular demand for the establishment of a general State Land Office for the sale of the vacant back lands.[123] As we have seen, even after the

[118]This tract constituted 1,680,000 acres.

[119]*Laws of N. Y.*, 1782, Chap. XI, p. 267 ff. This meant that unfriendly Senecas, Cayugas, and Onondagas would be driven out, as none of this land was clear of Indian titles.

[120]*Jour. N. Y. Sen.*, p. 164. *Ass.*, p. 178 f., 1783.

[121]The Governor and any two of the others could act. The claimant, under any of the bounty acts had to get a certificate from the Surveyor-General giving the location and size of the tract, and then the Commissioners would issue a patent. The grantees had to pay survey costs, and improve their lands within three years. The Commissioners could lay out townships in whatever manner seemed most beneficial. *Laws of N. Y.*, May 11, 1784, Chap. LXIII, p. 98 ff.

[122]J. B. Sherwood, *The New York Military Tract, New York State Historical Association Journal*, XXIV, 175. The Indian titles were not disregarded after the treaty of peace, and it took until 1788 to open the tract up. See *supra*, p. 105. 600 acre warrants sold for from 8 to 30 dollars each as late as ten years after the war. Turner, *Phelps' and Gorham's Purchases*, p. 309.

[123]As early as February 1780 General Parsons of Connecticut had urged Clinton to open a land office for western New York. *Clinton Papers*, V, 505 and 519.

treaty of Fort Stanwix in 1784 the western part of the State still belonged to the Indians, but in the north and northwest particularly there were vacant lands already owned by the State.[124] The initial step was taken in March of this same year when the executors of Alexander Colden, the late Surveyor-General of the Colony, were ordered by the Legislature to turn over the records of the office to the Surveyor-General of the State.[125] On May 10 a seven-member commission similar to the one discussed above was created with power to run the Land Office and dispose of any land not already set aside by law for other purposes.[126] Townships six miles square were to be surveyed and settled by groups of forty-two or more proprietors at a price of one shilling per acre. Certain portions of each township were to be reserved for education and literature.[127] Sales under this act were negligible and in May, 1786, the system was radically altered. The townships were made ten miles square, and divided into lots one mile square. Every fourth township was to be sold by single lots. Sales were to be at public auction, after proper notice, with a minimum price of one shilling per acre, a quarter down and the residue within sixty days. The Surveyor-General and Secretary of State were both to display maps of the lands for sale. Preëmption rights up to 200 acres at the minimum price were accorded to squatters. Practically all forms of public securities were receivable in payment. The Governor

[124]F. B. Hough, *Proc. N. Y. Ind. Comms.*, pp. 10-60 (Main Negotiations, pp. 48-60) and *supra*, p. 138 f.

[125]*Laws of N. Y.*, Chap. XVI, p. 20, March 2, 1874.

[126]Composed of the Governor, Lieutenant Governor, Speaker, Secretary of State, Attorney-General, Treasurer, and Auditor.

[127]*Laws of N. Y.*, Chap. LX, pp. 91-95, May 10, 1784. It is interesting to note that the Council of Revision unsuccessfully vetoed this act on the ground that certificates from the Continental Loan Officer were made receivable in payment for land. They felt the State should not give up its lands to help pay off the national debt, while a large State debt still existed. Street, *Council of Revision*, p. 253.

and any two Commissioners were given the right to direct survey and sale of any lands in any quantities they saw fit.[128]

This act, or rather the administration of this act, was bitterly criticized. The Commissioners put the land up for sale in large parcels which excluded the small buyer, and allowed certain speculators to bid in the land unopposed.

Many felt that the details were arranged with the speculators in advance. In this way the western lands came to be held by just a few individuals who were not willing to sell until they obtained a high price.[129] Regardless of whether or not this criticism is well founded, the fact remains that by 1791 the area east of the Indian line was held in very large tracts.[130] Only a handful of settlers went into the public lands prior to 1788.[131] From then on settlement speeded up some-

[128]*Laws of N. Y.*, Chap. LXVII, pp. 129-137, May 5, 1786. The question of the collection of quit rents is discussed in Chap. VIII, p. 157 below.

[129]James Macauley, *History of New York*, III, 43-52.

[130]O'Callaghan, *Documentary History of New York*, III, 645 f. The list of holders with 25,000 acres or more is as follows:

Alex. Macomb	3,635,200 acres
L. M. Cutting	75,000 "
M. Meyers J. Sanger J. J. Morgan	67,000 "
J. Tallmadge Ezra Thompson	25,000 "
John Taylor	43,000 "
W. S. Smith	270,000 "
T. Ludlow J. Shippey	50,000 "
R. C. Livingston	25,000 "
Wm. Henderson	64,000 "
John & N. I. Roosevelt	500,000 "
James Watson	60,000 "
J. W. Watkins Royal Flint	341,000 "
Mathew Agate	85,000 "
James Caldwell	128,000 "
Col. McGregor	64,000 "

[131]Macauley, *op. cit.*, III, 421-422. Judge White was the first man to settle on the western lands. He bought under the act of 1784 and settled

what, but mainly in the Phelps and Gorham tract.[132] The New York Genesee land company has already been discussed in relation to the Indians, and the Phelps and Gorham purchase in connection with the Massachusetts settlement. Combining these descriptions gives a fair picture of what was happening regarding the lands in the western part of the State up to 1789. How much the Treasury ultimately received from sales during this whole period cannot be ascertained, but up to the beginning of 1788, at least, the Commissioners had made no payments.[133]

a few miles beyond the old settlement at German Flats. 1785, Horatio Jones and Lawrence Smith settled at Seneca Falls. 1786, Webster, an interpreter, settled on land given him by the Onandagas at Onandaga Hollow. 1787, James Bennett settled at West Cayuga. In 1788, Whitestown, where White had originally settled had a population of about 200 people. It embraced an enormous area, however.

[132]*Ibid.*, p. 427.
[133]Report of the Auditor, *Jour. N. Y. Ass.*, 1788, p. 14 ff.

Chapter VI

THE ADMINISTRATION OF ROBERT MORRIS
1781-1784

INTRODUCTION

IN the summer of 1780 James Duane asked Hamilton to send him his ideas on the defects of the financial system and the steps that should be taken to remedy them. Hamilton replied with a voluminous letter discussing all the weaknesses of the Confederation and proposing that a general convention with plenary powers be called to form plans for a new Confederation. He suggested the establishment of Secretaryships; named Robert Morris as the man who should be given the Treasury; and proposed a National Bank.[1] When in February 1781 Congress had acted on the plan for Secretaryships, William Floyd of New York nominated Morris for Superintendent of Finance.[2]

Morris took the office in May 1781, and held it, more or less against his own wishes, until November 1784. While he was prevented from actually stabilizing the finances by lack of State coöperation he probably kept the government from going into complete bankruptcy. In the Spring of 1781 Congressional finance was on the point of disintegration. The total debt was estimated in February at $26,617,812 specie,[3]

[1] Hamilton, *History of the Republic*, II, 86-109.

[2] *Ibid.*, II, 202. The establishment of unified executive authority was greatly feared by some. Dr. Rush wrote to Gates on this score: "There is a greater crime in the eyes of some than treason—it is Republicanism. It will take half a century to cure us of our monarchial habits and prejudices." *Ibid.*, II, 205.

[3]

Item	Face value	Specie value
Domestic debt	$65,558,454	$11,391,554
French debt		7,331,306
Other foreign loans		3,128,743
Currency	200,000,000	5,000,000
Arrears of army pay		1,000,000
Notes issued by Q.M.G. and Commissary depts.	63,966,156	852,822

and the probable cost of the war for 1781 at an additional $20,000,000.[4]

The old system of requisitions had been demonstrated to be wholly unreliable. Further issue of paper was to be avoided at all costs; it would depreciate the existing currency to such an extent that the damage done would exceed the small additional income gained by the government. Therefore new financial expedients had to be found. A Congressional committee appointed for this purpose advised: the levying of impost duties; the retirement of the old bills from circulation; the establishment of State funds for the redemption of new bills; the giving of the power to lay embargoes to Congress in time of war; the raising of $6,000,000 in specie by a domestic loan to increase the circulating medium; and the establishment of a Central Bank.[5] It is readily seen that these plans, except for the impost and the bank, involved no new solution. Despite of the fact that Congress considered the question of finance every day from April 6 on, nothing was accomplished during the spring.[6] A special committee chairmanned by James Duane could only suggest a further issue of paper.[7] Meanwhile the monthly reports of the Board of Treasury on State payments indicated no improvement.[8]

Such, then, was the condition of the finances when Morris accepted the post of Superintendent on May 14, 1781.[9] He felt that the first need was for order and system. He planned:

[4] *Journal Continental Congress*, XIX, 160-172, Feb. 19, 1781. The statement of the debt in April 1781 that was mailed to the States placed the total at $24,057,157 2/3 in specie, and interest at $1,096,528 6/9 annually. The difference in these figures is due to the fact that in the earlier estimate the old bills of credit are carried at their theoretical value, whereas in this second estimate they are reduced to their actual specie value at the time.

[5] *Journal Continental Congress*, VXIII, 1157-1164 and 1164 n.

[6] *Ibid.*, XIX, 358.

[7] *Ibid.*, XIX, 432. Apr. 21, 1781, see also: *Ibid.*, XIX, 402-420. Apr. 18, 1781; and *Ibid.*, XVIII, 1223 for other actions taken by Congress.

[8] *Ibid.*, XIX, 135. Prepared in accordance with an act of February 9, 1781.

[9] *Diplomatic Correspondence*, XI, 350 and *Journal Continental Congress*, XIX, 433.

to receive requisitions in specie only; to try and get the States to supply enough money for current expenditures; to secure the adoption of an act giving Congress at least a limited power to levy impost duties; to reach a basis for the settlement of the proportions of the public expenditures to be borne by the individual States; to find a better system for maintaining the army than that of specific supply; and to establish a Central Bank to facilitate government borrowing.

"The President, Directors, and Company of the Bank of North America" received a formal act of incorporation from Congress on December 31, 1781.[10] Its initial capital was only $400,000, but Morris regarded a small beginning as the safest.[11] Its paper was to be acceptable for taxes and the States were asked to pass laws giving it a monopolistic position until the close of the war; which New York did April 11, 1782.[12] Despite the fact that it started with only $40,000 in specie in its vault, it was firmly established inside of a year and rendered an important service in stabilizing the finances.[13]

The system of supplying the army had been unsatisfactory from the first. Although from the spring of 1777 on there had been an elaborate Quartermaster's Department with a Director of Clothing, and Commissaries of Purchases and Issues, with an appropriate number of deputies, the whole system had failed to function properly from lack of funds.[14] As we have seen, specific supply by the States was attempted at the end of 1779, and worked badly from the start. From the summer of 1780 on everybody recognized its great weaknesses, but without money Congress could devise nothing to take its place.

[10]For the documentary history of the formation of the Bank see: *Diplomatic Correspondence*, XI, 365 and 462; *Journal Continental Congress*, XX, 545-548, May 26, 1781; and XXI, 1187-1189.

[11]*Dip. Cor.*, XI, 365.

[12]*Laws of N. Y.*, Chap. XXXV, p. 236.

[13]Bolles, *op. cit.*, pp. 273-275.

[14]L. C. Hatch, *The Administration of the American Revolutionary Army*, p. 89.

It was the personal credit of Morris, his most valuable contribution to the cause, that made it possible for him to introduce the system of private contract. He first entered into arrangements with Comfort Sands and others of New York City on December 6, 1781. This group agreed to supply as many rations as were called for at specific places during the following year.[15] Sands was stingy in his carrying out of the contract, and generally unsatisfactory, so that when he demanded payment in specie only in the fall of 1782 he was released.[16]

Other interests came forward ready to assume the work, but at a considerably higher rate, which the Treasury was forced to grant.[17] Chief among these new contractors was the New York firm of Parker & Duer who carried on the business until the close of the war. While the service was not faultless it was apparently satisfactory on the whole, for both Duer and the system of contract were again employed by the government in connection with the Ohio Indian troubles in the late eighties and early nineties.[18]

THE SETTLEMENT OF STATE ACCOUNTS

A prime object of Morris' policy was to have the State quotas definitely decided on, so that the entire account between Congress and the States might be adjusted. July 25, 1781, he wrote a circular letter to the Governors pointing out that the idea that the accounts are not to be adjusted spreads a "listless languor over all our operations." Each State claimed that

[15]Disputes as to quality and quantity were to be decided by three commissioners, one appointed by the Continental Congress, one by the contractors, and the third by the other two.

[16]Hatch, *op. cit.*, 115.

[17]Sumner, *op. cit.*, II, 61-63.

[18]S. J. Davis, *Essays on the Earlier History of American Corporations*, I, no. 2, 120-121, p. 259 ff. for the later period. The contractors had the same difficulty in obtaining payments as everybody else who had dealings with the Continental Congress. In 1785 the Treasury was still in arrears for services rendered during the war. *Pap. Cont. Cong.*, no. 18, f. 105, Letters from the Contractors to Robert Morris.

it had done more than its share, and until its real share was determined on these claims could be proved neither true nor false.[19] He submitted to Congress on November 23 an ordinance for the settlement of the public accounts which, after reference to several committees, was finally adopted on February 20, 1782.

The States were asked to authorize Congress in the final settlement of accounts to January 1, 1780, to partially disregard the rule laid down in Article VIII, and to adopt such principles as would appear equitable in view of the circumstances of the several States at different periods. Money loaned to the United States was not to be included in this settlement. The States were asked to send, as soon as possible, all information that would assist Congress in forming just estimates of the resources of each State at the end of every year. After the annual proportions were fixed, six per cent would be allowed or charged on surpluses or deficiencies respectively. A Commissioner for each State was to be appointed by the Superintendent and approved by the State Legislature or Executive as the particular State should direct. He was to have full power and authority finally to settle the accounts between the State for which he was nominated and the United States, in accordance with the table of depreciation framed by the Board of Treasury July 29, 1780, and the various price regulations incorporated in the acts for specific supplies. The States were further asked to give the Commissioners the power to summon witnesses.[20] On February 27th Congress gave the Superintendent power to appoint a Commissioner to adjust the accounts of each of the five principal departments of government, and the States were requested to give these Commissioners also the right to call for and examine witnesses under oath.[21] On July 20th and 22d the New York Legisla-

[19]*Dip. Cor.*, XI, 400-405.

[20]*Journal Continental Congress*, XXII, 12-14, 36, 83-86.

[21]*Ibid.*, 102-104.

ture agreed to these arrangements. The Governor was given the power to approve the Commissioners, and Congress was authorized to adjust the proportions of the State on whatever basis they thought just.[22]

The completion of these arrangements, however, made only the first step in the matter. Hamilton, as a Delegate to Congress, tried to see that the information asked for by the Superintendent was secured, but from the correspondence available it does not appear that he was successful.[23] The reader can by this time surmise how much possibility there was of ever getting an orderly statement of the resources of the State at the end of each year. As 1782 drew to a close without substantial progress on the settlement, some observers even doubted that all of the States would agree to the above acts of Congress.[24]

Debate on the subject of ways for making an estimate began early in January 1783.[25] The principal question was: whether the States could be trusted to make their own estimates, or whether some kind of an estimate by impartial Congressional Commissioners would be necessary. Most of the members of Congress seemed to feel that the method of apportionment provided for in the Articles was a bad one anyway, and that population with some allowance for slaves would be a much better basis. But only a few of them, including Hamilton and Madison, wanted to submit a change in the Articles to the States.[26] Hamilton thought that a solution might be to classify various types of land and then place a uniform value on each type, but the southern States because of their large uncultivated areas objected to this or any other

[22]Laws of N. Y., Chap. IV, p. 259, July 20, 1782; and Chap. V, p. 259, July 22, 1782.

[23]Clinton Papers, VIII, 23-33.

[24]Ibid., 37-38; L'Hommedieu to Clinton.

[25]Journal Continental Congress, XXV, 847-850; 854, 855, 886-896.

[26]Ibid., 854, 895.

mode involving comparative quantity of land.[27] The period during which any valuation should remain in force was also the subject of long debates.

It soon became apparent to both Madison and Hamilton that this matter of valuation would have to be settled before any plans for a permanent revenue could be agreed upon.[28] On February 17, 1783, it was moved: That the States be required to submit the necessary information for an accurate account of the surveyed land and buildings within their borders; that these reports be examined by a grand committee of Congress composed of one member from each State; that the valuations be fixed by a vote of nine members; and that these serve as a basis for the adjustment of all accounts for the next five years. This motion was agreed to nine to one, New York alone voting against it, but according to Madison "with great reluctance by almost all, by many from a spirit of accommodation only, and the necessity of doing something on the subject. Some of those who were in the negative, particularly Mr. Madison, thought the plan not within the spirit of the Confederation, that it would be ineffectual and that the States would be dissatisfied with it."[29] The New York Delegates had objected on the ground that such a plan did not guarantee that New York's restricted resources during the war, due to the British occupation, would be duly regarded. Hamilton, who was spending most of his time on questions of the State and private accounts, moved that equitable allowances or abatements should be made in favor of those states which had been occupied for long periods by the enemy. The motion was referred to a committee which reported on February 26th

[27] *Journal Continental Congress,* XXV, 885. See also a plan by Madison. *Ibid.,* p. 877.

[28] *Ibid.,* pp. 887-888.

[29] *Journal Continental Congress,* XXV, 899. Hamilton wrote to Clinton, February 24, that there was really no satisfactory or equitable way of apportioning expenses. Any system would be merely a guess. *Hamilton's Works,* Const. Ed., pp. 313-322.

that because Virginia had already disagreed to such a measure it was not probable that a new proposal would have any better success, and that the difficulties of making such abatements were greater than the advantages to be expected from them. The Eastern Delegates, however, were in favor of keeping the question open. Madison was in favor of the principle but felt that it should wait and be incorporated in a general revenue plan. Accordingly the motion was postponed.[30]

The question of making a common mass of all the unusual State expenditures for carrying on the war not specifically authorized or assumed by Congress was brought up in these debates. In general, of course, those States whose expenses had been largely sanctioned by Congress were against the common mass plan. Madison drew up an interesting memorandum on the attitude of the various States toward abatements, a common mass, and an impost.[31] The following is a diagramatic summary of his views:

Abatements		Common Mass		Impost	
For	Against	For	Against	For	Against
R. I.	N. H.	Mass.	N. H.	N. H.	R. I.
N. Y.	Mass.	N. Y.	R. I.	Conn.	Md.
Va.	Conn.	Va.	Conn.	N. Y.	Mass. and
N. C.	N. J.	N. C.	N. J.	N. J.	Va.
Ga.	Del.	S. C.	Pa.	Pa.	undecided.
S. C.*	Md.	Ga.	Del.	Del.	
	Pa.†		Md.	N. C.	
				S. C.	
				Ga.	

*Voted against March 27th ⎱ *Jour. Cont. Cong.* **XXV, 946.**
†Voted for   March 27th ⎰

As might be predicted from this analysis, the plan for a common mass failed as did the clause for abatements in the general revenue act by the final vote of five to six.[32]

[30]*Journal Continental Congress,* XXV, 913-914. See also Chap. VII, pp. 195 f., for connection of this with the general revenue plan.

[31]*Journal Continental Congress,* XXV, 913-914 n.

[32]*Ibid.,* p. 937, Mar. 21, 1783. See *infra,* p. 147 f.

Notwithstanding their fear of a general apportionment based merely upon the peace-time value of property in the State, the New York Legislature passed the necessary law to carry out the estimates called for in the above act of Congress of February 20. The Surveyor-General was to submit the returns to the Legislature prior to February 1, 1784.[33] At the end of 1783, however, the Commissioners to settle accounts in the States reported that nothing had been accomplished, and recommended that the private accounts be settled before taking up the State governmental ones.[34] April 27, 1784, the New York Legislature asked that the act of February 20, 1782, be amended to take into account the fact that New York had furnished specific supplies at lower prices than most of the other States.[35]

Confronted with these difficulties Congress passed a comprehensive act which temporarily laid the matter of apportionment aside. Money and supplies furnished by the States would be reduced to a just specie value, and six per cent allowed from the original time of payment. The same rule would be carried out for money or supplies furnished to the States by Congress. Officers charged with receiving and disbursing public money should not be charged with the deprecation occuring while the money was in their hands, provided they transacted their business with all reasonable speed. Where the specie value of supplies furnished by individuals to the United States prior to August 26, 1780, could not be justly determined by the tables, an estimate was to be made by the Commissioners appointed by the Act of February 20, 1782. It was recommended to the States to compensate citizens who had suffered at the hands of the enemy or Continental troops, and that where any State should be burdened from this cause beyond the others a special allowance should be made by Congress. No allowance of this type, however, was to be made

[33]*Laws of N. Y.*, Chap. XLII, p. 288, March 21, 1783.
[34]*Journal Continental Congress*, XXV, 807-809.
[35]*Laws of N. Y.*, Chap. XLIV, pp. 58-63.

by the present Commissioners. New certificates bearing six per cent interest from the original date of issue were to be given in exchange for quartermaster's certificates, and other similar obligations.[36] These latter became a circulating medium passing at about two shillings six pence on the pound.[37] The further history of this subject is connected with the attempt to amend the basis of apportionment in Article VIII, and will be considered later.

REQUISITIONS

Taxation, or rather the lack of it, continued to be the key to the financial difficulties of the period. From the end of 1781 on, the military expenditures were scarcely more than those required for a small standing army, and the States should have started repaying the debts of the war or at least balancing the national budget by means of adequate taxation. Instead of this the situation grew steadily worse.

March 16, 1781, Congress passed a comprehensive act on the matter of finance asking: That the States remove all laws making Continental bills a legal tender except at their current ratio to specie; and that they furnish their proportions of $1,500,000 quarterly, starting June 1.[38]

Much as Morris desired to get hard money he felt that he could not refuse to receive the old or new Continental bills, at their proper ratio, in payment of requisitions. At first he reissued a part of this paper, thereby deriving some slight benefit from the payments, and making contraction very

[36]*Journal Continental Congress,* 1823 ed., IV, 442-443. See Appendix B.
[37]Bolles, *op. cit.,* p. 327.
[38]In discharge of this requisition as well as those of August 26, November 4, and January 15 the new Continental bills were to be considered as equivalent to specie. The States were to be credited with interest on payments made before due. They were to make exact returns to the Board of War by June 1 of the articles supplied by them in response to the first quota of specifics, levied February 25, 1780; and the United States would then call on the States for the full amount of their deficiencies by September 1. *Journal Continental Congress,* XIX, 266 f. March 16, 1781. Quotas set, *Ibid.,* p. 299.

gradual, but by the winter of 1781-82 he stopped reissuing altogether.[39] An even worse form of revenue than the old bills were the certificates issued by the Quartermasters and Commissaries in payment for supplies, and by law receivable for taxes. They were, of course, valueless as present revenue, and yet they made up a large part of the total receipts. They formed a particularly difficult medium with which to deal justly, as the officers, distressed at having to confiscate the goods of their own countrymen, usually issued these certificates for considerably more than the real value of the supplies taken.[40] Finally on November 12, 1781, Congress resolved that they should be no longer receivable for taxes.[41]

Three weeks after the surrender at Yorktown, Congress voted its greatest requisition. Not realizing that the war had come to a practical end, they asked for $8,000,000 in specie or its equivalent, to finance the next year's operations.[42] This large request was unfortunate in many ways; it made the people doubt the foresightedness of Congress, provided ground for the charge that Congress was trying to enrich itself, and through the impossibility of its collection added to the bad psychology of non-payment.

Although few payments had been made on this great requisition, Congress added another in the fall of 1782. They asked for $1,200,000 immediately in order to pay interest on the public debt, and suggested various taxes through which the States might raise the money.[43] Eight States including New York strove unsuccessfully to get their quotas reduced,

[39]Bolles, *Financial History*, pp. 278-279.

[40]*Dip. Cor.*, XII, 457-459.

[41]*Journal Continental Congress*, XXI, 1112.

[42]*Ibid.*, XXI, pp. 1087, and 1090. Oct. 30, 1781.

[43]*Ibid.*, XXIII, 545. September 4, 1782. The following taxes were suggested: a land tax of one dollar per hundred acres; a poll tax of a half a dollar on all free and able-bodied males between 16 and 21, a dollar on those between 21 and 60, and a half dollar on male slaves between 16 and 60; and an excess tax of one-eighth dollar per gallon on liquors.

but in all but one case every State except the petitioner voted nay.[44]

While the estimated expenses for 1783, composed chiefly of arrears, totaled $6,000,000 it was useless, in view of the fact that the States had paid less than $1,000,000 in the last two years, to call upon them for so large a sum. Accordingly a requisition of $2,000,000 was voted, and arrangements proposed to borrow the residue.[45] A motion was also passed by a vote of eight to one (Rhode Island nay) that it be impressed on the several States as absolutely necessary to lay separate taxes for raising their quotas of money due the United States; to the collectors to pay the same to officers appointed by the Superintendent of Finance; and to authorize such receivers to recover the monies for the use of the United States in the same manner as State taxes are recovered by the Treasurers of the respective States.[46] This last resolution, as we have pointed out before, really got at the heart of the matter. As long as the existing method of single assessment was retained the government would receive but a portion of the amounts asked for. The resolution was never acted on by the States. This same jealousy of Congressional collectors formed one of the chief impediments to the impost scheme.[47]

September 9, 1782, the Financier had to direct the loan officers to stop current interest payments on the domestic debt. This suspension was necessitated by the condition of our credit abroad and the failure of the States to take action on the impost proposals, which we will discuss presently.[48] Now that the war was practically over, France was no longer willing to continue advancing us money to pay domestic interest.

Congress did not adopt the quotas for 1784 until April 5 of that year, vainly hoping that the impost might be adopted and

[44]*Ibid.*, XXIII, pp. 564-571.
[45]*Ibid.*, XXIII, p. 659. October 16, 1782.
[46]*Ibid.*, XXIII, pp. 666-667.
[47]*Ibid.*, XXIII, 652.
[48]*Ibid.*, p. 576; XXII, 447.

permit a lessening of internal taxation. When this became unlikely, it was decided to call upon the States for payments sufficient to total, together with what had already been paid in, three-quarters of the $8,000,000 quota of December 1781, or in other words $4,577,591.[49] A week later three-quarters was changed to a half, only Pennsylvania, the great security-holding State, dissenting.[50] The total amount due from all the States was $2,670,987.98,[51] and New York was required to pay $147,734.09.[52] Only specie would be received according to the original act, but the next day a paragraph was added stating that a quarter of the sums called for could be paid for in the certificates called indents of interest issued by the loan officers in lieu of specie payments.

STATE FINANCES

During the year 1781 New York finances reached their lowest ebb. The money to pay the requisitions of February and May 1780 had to be borrowed. None of the officers of the civil government had received any salary for that year, and the money owing to the militia would use up any funds that might be raised through the sale of forfeited estates. Despite the fact that every cent in the Treasury had been paid to the troops, they had in many cases to be fed by private subscription. Only $62,500 of the State's quota of new bills had been put in circulation, and these largely to citizens of other states.[53] The Legislature, in a memorial to the Delegates in Congress, complained that as a result of selling practically the whole surplus product of the State to Congress for the past three years there was so little real money in the State that the officials collected in currency very little more than sufficient to defray the expense of collecting. "By our exertions, by a

[49]*Journal Continental Congress,* 1823 ed., IV, 360.

[50]*Ibid.,* IV, 365. The report was finally agreed to April 27.

[51]*Ibid.,* IV, 386-89. Not $4,000,000 as erroneously stated in Bolles, p. 322.

[52]On April 7, 1783, Congress had fixed New York's peace time percentage of requisitions at 8.5. *Journal Continental Congress,* XXV, 231.

[53]*Pap. Cont. Cong.,* no. 67, II, ff. 344-361.

series of compulsory laws, and by the use of the most vigorous means to execute them, our inhabitants feel themselves so aggrieved, that prudence forbids any further attempts on their patience. New requisitions on them before their demands against the Purchasing Officers are satisfied would be vain."[54]

At the end of November 1781 the Legislature resolved that they were "reduced to the necessity of informing Congress that they entertain very slender hopes of their ability . . . to comply with any of the requisitions of Congress." In explaining this situation they point out that in addition to the points raised in other letters they have 1800 additional men in the field, raised by bounties of $60 apiece, and therefore "Resolved: that . . . they do request Congress to suspend . . . any further requisitions."[55] Governor Clinton accompanied the copies sent to the President of Congress and Robert Morris with strong explanatory letters setting forth the difficulties and dangers of the situation.[56] Morris replied to these in a comprehensive letter of December 19 from which I will quote extensively, as it gives a good summary of the New York position at the end of 1781:

The Legislature are undoubtedly best able to discover and to describe the evils, which afflict their constituents, and I should almost in any case, bend before so high an authority. But the situation, in which I am placed, compels me to make some observations, which if they are not admitted to have weight, will not, I hope, be considered as foreign to the purpose.

It is contended by the State Agent, that the supplies, which he has delivered, and those which he holds ready to furnish, amount fully to the demand for specific supplies. And it is lamented, that the army have subsisted from the neighborhood of West

[54]*Ibid.,* 344-361.

[55]*Jour. N. Y. Sen. and Ass.,* 5th sess., II.

[56]*Clinton Papers,* VII, 520-523. He says: "I shall, therefore, only observe in addition that there is more than a hazard that we shall not be able without a change in our circumstances long to maintain our Civil Government." p. 520.

Point in former times, thereby leaving a great mass of certificates, which being useless to the inhabitants, the supplies obtained have to all intents and purposes, operated a tax. To this I will add, that the resolutions of your Legislature state an extra expense, which has produced a tax to the amount of one hundred and eighty thousand dollars. If these exertions joined to the ravages of the enemy, and the usurpations complained of, have occasioned distresses, they at least demonstrate the abilities of the State in former periods. You will perceive that I am now about to supply the troops by contract wherefore a ready market for their produce must immediately be opened to the inhabitants of your State. This will enable them to obtain hard money, and that will enable them to pay taxes. The great object, therefore, of the Legislature will be to adopt a vigorous and just system of taxation, and to take off all those restraints upon the people, which injure, afflict, and impoverish them, without producing any advantage to the public. . . .

As to the extra expense, which has accrued to the State by calling new levies into the field, it is the business of the United States in Congress to determine upon it. It is, however, my duty to remark, that exclusive of the great expense of additional officers, the sum there stated as a bounty is fully equal to that for pay and rations of so many men for six months. I am sure that I need not observe to your Excellency the impracticability of carrying on a war where it costs as much to enlist a man as it does to feed and pay him for six months. A few such extra corps raised in each State and the bounties charged to the United States, in payment of the quota would immediately compel Congress to disband the whole army for the want of the means of subsistence, or to permit the troops to plunder the inhabitants.

In the midst of those complaints of your situation I receive a particular pleasure from the assurance that the Legislature will contribute to the general service of the Union their proportion of the well established funds. I hope the recommendation for that purpose will soon come under the consideration of the United States and be duly expedited.[57]

[57] *Dip. Cor.*, 12, pp. 63-66. The last paragraph refers to the impost.

The unwillingness or inability of the people to pay taxes was still the main reason for lack of revenue. The tax arrears had become enormous, and during the years after Yorktown the Legislature made strenuous but futile efforts to collect them.[58] Each of the tax laws contained provisions for the punishment of delinquent Assessors, Supervisors, Collectors, and County Treasurers; and the Governor threatened prosecutions by the Attorney-General.[59] The language of the government was more vigorous than its action, however; these penalties were not actually enforced.

As can be seen from the table in Appendix B, the Legislature felt unable during this period even to try and keep pace with Congressional requisitions. The general state of affairs was well described by Alexander Hamilton, who served as the Continental Tax Receiver for New York during 1782.[60] On accepting his office he wrote: "The whole system (if it may be so called) of taxation in this state is radically vicious, burthensome to the people, and unproductive to the government. As the matter now stands there seems to be little for a Continental Receiver to do. The whole business appears to be thrown into the hands of the county treasurers, nor do I find there is any appropriation for Continental purposes. . . . "[61] Feeling that the only chance for him to be of use was to lobby for new tax laws at the July meeting of the Legislature, he asked Governor Clinton to allow him to confer with a joint commission of both houses, and present to them the views of the Superintendent. The request was granted and after the conference Hamilton wrote to Morris:

[58] *Laws of N. Y.*, Chap. XI, p. 214, Nov. 20, 1781.

[59] *Ibid.*, Chap. IX, p. 264, July 24, 1782; Chap. XLIX, pp. 290-99, March 25, 1783; *Clinton Papers*, VII, 510. It is interesting to notice that it was necessary in the law of July 1782 to provide for the drawing up of assessment lists where none had been made out in pursuance of the original acts!

[60] *Journal Continental Congress*, XXII, 336, June 18, 1782.

[61] *Hamilton's Works*, Lodge ed., IX, 269 ff.

I found every man convinced that something was wrong, but few were willing to recognize the mischief when defined, and consent to the proper remedy. The quantum of taxes already imposed is so great as to make it useless to impose any others to a considerable amount. A bill has, however, passed both Houses, payable in specie, bank notes, or your notes for £18,000.[62] It is at present appropriated to your order, but I doubt whether some subsequent arrangement will not take place for a different appropriation, [i. e.] for a quantity of forage. . . . I have hitherto been able to prevent this, but as it is of . . . importance . . . to leave this place immediately . . . it is possible, after I have left that contrary ideas will prevail. . . .

Should the bill for £18,000 go in its present form, I cannot hope it will produce in the treasury half the sum, such are the vices of our present mode of collection. A bill has also passed the Assembly for collecting arrearages of taxes . . . The arrearages are very large. . . .

The Legislature have also appointed at my instance a commission to devise, in its recess, a more effectual system of taxation.[63]

In August Hamilton wrote Morris a long letter on the condition of New York. He found the picture drawn by the legislation in their previous letters, a little highly colored but substantially accurate. "It is the opinion of the most sensible men with whom I converse . . . that [the states'] faculties for revenue are diminished at least two-thirds. . . . The efficient property, strength, and force of the state will consist of little more than four counties. In the distribution

[62]This act was partly the result of a special Congressional committee that visited the northern states in June to stimulate their payments. Clinton wrote: "I endeavored to explain to them as fully as I was able, our reduced and distressed circumstances and the impracticability of our complying with the requisitions of Congress on the subject of Finance . . . However, before we parted, I agreed to issue my Proclamation for convening the Legislature on the first Wednesday in July." Clinton to Scott, June 6, 1782. *Clinton Papers*, VIII, 11.

[63]July 22, 1782. This same session also adopted a resolution in favor of strengthening the Articles of Confederation by a convention of the States. *Clinton Papers*, VIII, 17.

of taxes before the war the City of New York alone used to be rated at one third of the whole . . . (too high due to country influence, . . . its proper proportion was . . . about one fourth)." Despite the influx of refugees from the occupied regions "labor is much dearer than before the war."

The State had made great exertions of the most exhaustive kind; sometimes from want of judgment, and sometimes from necessity. The general claim that the State trade balance was extremely adverse was true. He estimated it as follows in round numbers.

	Paid into the State annually	Paid out of the State annually
For expenditures of army contractors	$90,000	
For expenditures of Q. M. G. Department	90,000	
To New York City for luxuries, etc.		$75,000
To New England for salt and other supplies		150,000
To Pennsylvania and New Jersey for the same		75,000
	$180,000	$300,000
Net unfavorable balance		$120,000

The real reason that tax assessment was left in an indefinite form was so as to discriminate between Whigs and Tories. The collection of arrears was very difficult.

The supervisors have no interest at all in collections, and it will not on this account appear extraordinary, that with continual delinquencies in collection, there has never been a single prosecution. (!)

The temper of the State, which I shall now describe may be considered under two heads—that of the rulers, and that of the people. The rulers are generally zealous in the common cause,

130

though their zeal is often misdirected. They are jealous of their own power, . . . yet the immediate danger from the theatre of war . . . makes them very willing to part with power in favor of the Federal Government. . . . They also have great confidence in you personally, but pretty general exception has been taken to a certain letter of yours written, I believe, in the winter or spring.

The people . . . I fear if left to themselves, would, too many of them, be willing to purchase peace at any price . . . not from inclination to Great Britain or disaffection for independence, but from mere supineness, and avarice. . . .

Even with a judicious plan of taxation I don't think the state can afford . . . to pay more than £70,000 or £80,000 a year . . . Out of this must be deducted the expense of internal administration, and the money necessary for the levies of men. £15,000 and £10,000 respectively.

He added that he was endeavoring to find out how much was being paid into the Continental treasury, but found it hardly possible to get a tolerable idea of the subject. A few days later he wrote: "I find a singular confusion in the accounts kept by the public officers from whom I must necessarily derive my information."[64]

The committee of the Legislature on taxation met and parted without doing anything definite, despite Hamilton's exertions. None of them felt that the State could possibly raise over £70,000 annually.[65] Late in 1782 Benjamin Tillotson succeeded Hamilton, who had resigned to take his bar examination, and our interesting account comes to an end.[66]

In summarizing the history of taxes and requisitions for this period an important factor is lacking, that is a record of tax payments actually received by the State Treasurer. The State tax laws from June 1781 to November 1784, exclusive of the one for the southern counties which was not for national pur-

[64] *Hamilton's Works,* IX, 282. August 25, 1782.
[65] *Ibid.,* p. 294. Oct. 5, 1782.
[66] *Ibid.,* p. 303.

poses, total $330,250. From the discussion in this chapter it can be seen that while Congress at first made requisitions totaling $690,401[67] they subsequently scaled down the second one for $373,598 until only half of it was due by November 1784.[68] This fraction together with the full amount of the other requisitions totals approximately $503,602, which must be assumed to represent New York's liability, although this figure is nowhere definitely stated. The relation of the tax laws to requisitions is therefore about the same as in the earlier period. Because of the bad conditions collections reached a low ebb. The payments to Congress were only about half as large in proportion to the total sums voted as they had been prior to June 1781.[69] Up to the end of 1784 New York paid to Congress only $56,974.14 or about 11% of the amount called for.[70]

[67]*Journal Continental Congress*, IV, 360. The requisition of March 1781 is not included in the table.

[68]*Ibid.*, p. 589. See table, Appendix B.

[69]The actual figures for the money paid in to the State Treasurer cannot be found, but the language of each new tax law leaves little doubt that the arrears were mounting even faster than before.

[70]*Pap. Cont. Cong.*, no. 141, I, f. 153 and I, f. 47. This was worse than the general average. Up until the end of 1783 the States had paid an average of 17% of the requisitions of 1781, whereas New York had paid less than 11% (i.e., $59,064.01). Bolles, *Financial History*, p. 322.

CHAPTER VII

THE STRUGGLE FOR FEDERAL POWER BEGINS
1781-1784

THE IMPOST PLAN OF 1781

THE history of the attempts of Congress to get the States to agree to an impost best illustrates New York's change of attitude toward the power of Congress after the war. While the war was still in full swing in 1780 New York was one of the prime movers in efforts to give Congress greater powers; by 1784, the end of the period covered in this chapter, the Legislature became indifferent; and by 1786 the majority or Clintonian Party were decidedly hostile to any such proposals. The reasons for this change are not hard to discover. During the war New York was, with the exception of Georgia, the State most menaced by the British, and therefore its aim was to build up the powers of the central government in order to secure more adequate protection and support. There was also, as we have seen, the impending settlement of the Vermont question, which made the good will of the other States a matter of prime importance.[1] As an example of this attitude of coöperation we have the western land cession, discussed in Chapter IV. By 1783 the Vermont question seemed to be lost anyway, but the evacuation of New York by the British was the real turning point in New York's change of front. With the recovery of all its territory, and the removal of the British menace, the agrarian party of Governor Clinton no longer needed the aid of Congress, and the land taxes were considerably lowered by the State import duties. Subsequently as the up-state men became more and more conscious of the benefit derived from taxing the goods that poured in through

[1] See *supra,* Chap. IV, pp. 89 ff.

one of the great ports of the Atlantic coast, they became less and less willing to surrender this particular power to Congress. It was a beautiful system whereby, according to the economic views of the day, the city merchants paid the taxes. Also the politicians were becoming loath to give up power to anybody outside the State. It was this situation more than any other that underlay the difficulty in finally ratifying the Constitution in New York.[2]

In 1780, Governor Clinton addressed the Legislature on the subject of the "defect of Power" in the Confederation, and the same summer John S. Hobart and Egbert Benson were dispatched to a convention of the New England States at Hartford for the purpose of considering means of strengthening the Articles. They were the leaders in the meeting which recommended Congress be empowered to propose certain taxes on specific articles, or duties on imports.[3]

Even before this action on the part of the Northern States, the question of an impost had been initiated in Congress. A resolution passed the committee of the whole on March 18, 1780, that the States be requested to levy an impost of one percent on all exports and imports to provide a fund for sinking the emissions of currency made for carrying on the war. New York supported this resolution.[4] By November 1780, they were still debating specifically how the request should be stated, had raised the rate of the tax to two and a half percent, and inserted what was to become one of the storm centers of the whole problem, that Congress should have the power to appoint and remove the collectors.[5] The report was finally

[2]See: Hamilton, *History of the Republic,* II, 387, for a discussion of New York prosperity after 1783. The impost made up over half the State revenue. (See Appendix E.)

[3]Roberts, *History of New York,* II, 443. Hamilton, *op. cit.,* II, 198. Hough, F. B., *Proceedings of the Convention of the New England States at Hartford.*

[4]*Journal Continental Congress,* XVI, 261.

[5]*Ibid.,* XVIII, 1033-5.

amended to read: "That it be recommended to the several states as indispensably necessary that they vest a power in Congress to levy a duty of five percent upon the value of all goods, as well prize goods as others, at the time and place of importation, and all articles of foreign growth and manufacture after the first day of May 1781." This was agreed to February 3, 1781.[6] It is interesting to notice that on the amendment to insert the words "vest a power in Congress to levy" in the above, the motion barely passed, and that Floyd of New York voted nay.[7] A careful observer might well predict difficulty when the proposition reached the States.

Neither this 1781 request of Congress for additional power nor the similar one of 1783 was put in the form of an amendment to the Articles of Confederation. They must be regarded as unusual or extra-constitutional compacts between the States of a type that could only operate effectively through the coöperation of all of them.[8]

[6]*Ibid.*, XIX, 113.

[7]*Ibid.*, XIX, 105-106, and 111-112.

[8]Most historians refer to the impost proposals of 1781 and 1783 as amendments to Articles, apparently because the words "vest a power in Congress" are used. This is not warranted by either the language of the proposal of 1783, or in the light of similar proposals made by Congress. A clause of the act of 1783 alone should be almost conclusive on this subject. It reads: "That none of the preceding *resolutions* shall take effect until all of them shall be acceded to by every state, after which unanimous accession however, they shall be considered as forming a *mutual compact* among all the states, and shall be irrevocable by any one or more of them without the concurrence of the whole or a majority of the United States in Congress Assembled." *Journal Continental Congress*, XXIV, 259. Almost every phrase in the foregoing denies the possibility of it being a part of the Articles of Confederation. If it were to be an article it was unnecessary to insert that it would not be effective until agreed to by all the states. Furthermore this "mutual compact" was only to be effective for twenty-five years at the longest.

In a resolution regarding the Vermont question the three interested States were asked to "vest a power in Congress" to settle the question. This is obviously no addition to the Articles as it is in accord with the provisions of Article IX, *Journal Continental Congress*, XV, 1095. A perusal of the Journals of the New York Legislature when the impost was being

New York was one of the first States to agree to the request of Congress. March 19th the State Legislature passed an act authorizing Congress to levy the 5% impost, as provided in the recommendation, after May 1, but with the proviso that the assent was not to be effective until all the states had similarly agreed.[9] This action by the Legislature composed of much the same men as rejected the later impost proposals, including Abraham Yates, Jr., Melancthon Smith, and Henry Wisner, illustrates markedly the affect of the war conditions in New York. Abraham Yates said five years later: "The Legislature, as it were in a storm, without consideration, adopted the recommendation . . . , at a time when the enemy were in possession of two-thirds of the state. . . . [When they were] in a shattered vessel with water up to their

debated confirms this opinion still further. The proposal to change the basis of apportionment of requisitions was always referred to as the "amendment to the eighth article," whereas the impost proposal is never referred to except as a normal bill. *N. Y. Sen. and Ass. Jours.*, 9th sess., *passim.* In the New York Acts partially agreeing to both the proposals of 1781 and 1783 the clause is inserted that the act shall not become effective until agreed to by all the States, a wholly unnecessary reservation in the case of an amendment or new article. *Laws of N. Y.*, Chap. LXI, pp. 117-119, May 4, 1786 and Chap. XXXI, pp. 177-178, March 19, 1781. In April, 1785, a committee of Congress submitted a printed report calling for an amendment to article nine giving Congress the power to regulate commerce, providing the duties collected accrue to the use of the States. This report was considered by Congress at various times for over two years, and finally discarded with the calling of the Federal Convention. *Pap. Cont. Cong.*, no. 24, I, f. 135. This is entirely different language than was ever used in conection with the two impost proposals, and illustrates clearly the difference between the ordinary bill and a change in the Articles.

Most conclusive of all is the fact that when North Carolina agreed to the resolutions of Congress of April 30, 1784, asking for the power to regulate trade, couched in practically the same language as the impost proposal of the year before, she provided that the provisions should become an Article of the Confederation, and made the agreement unacceptable to Congress for this very reason. *Journal Continental Congress*, 1823 ed., IV, 621.

[9]*Laws of N. Y.*, Chap. XXXI, pp. 177-178. The bill passed the Senate without a roll call for votes. *Jour. N. Y. Sen.*, 1781, p. 79.

chins, . . . thus situated I say the Legislature might be excused hastily coming into and without consideration adopting the resolution of Congress.[10]

Clinton immediately enclosed the act in a letter to Congress, where it was read April 5.[11] In November of the same year Clinton wrote the President of Congress: "I do not hesitate to give assurances that this State will on her part cheerfully consent to vest the sovereignty of the United States with every Power requisite to an effectual Defense . . . and for the Preservation of internal Peace and Harmony."[12]

Massachusetts had meanwhile taken the lead in objecting to the impost, ostensibly for the reason that as a commercial State she would pay more than her share.[13]

In July 1782 the New York Legislature adopted resolutions written by Hamilton and introduced in the Senate by Schuyler declaring that the powers of the central government should be extended, that it should be authorized to provide revenue for itself, and that to that end "it would be advisable to propose to Congress to recommend to each state to adopt, measures for assembling a general convention of the states specifically authorized to revise and amend the Constitution." Schuyler took the resolution to Congress and tried to get the Delegates to take some action, but he was discouraged by their attitude.[14] This resolution is interesting from the standpoint of our discussion of New York's changing attitude toward Congress.

[10]*Political Papers addressed to the Advocates of a Congressional Revenue,* p. 9, N. Y. P. L.

During the summer of 1781 Hamilton wrote a series of Articles called the *Continentalist* which were published in Loudon's *N. Y. Packet.* Their aim was to arouse public sentiment in favor of a convention to improve the Articles of Confederation. Hamilton, *History of the Republic,* II, 231 f.

[11]*Journal Continental Congress,* XIX, 353.

[12]*Pap. Cont. Cong.,* no. 67, II, ff. 443-50. Clinton to President of Congress. November, 24, 1781.

[13]*Journal Continental Congress,* XIX, 421-27. April 19, 1781. The real reasons involved will appear later.

[14]*N. Y. Sen. and Ass. Jours.,* no. 60, pp. 89-90 and 119-120. Robert's *History of New York,* I, 444.

It represents practically the last victory of the group whom we may call the Coöperationists, the future Federalists, led by Hamilton, Schuyler, Duane, and Jay, and composed largely of the down-state interests.

By the fall of 1782 all the States except Rhode Island and Georgia had agreed to the impost proposal, although several had made reservations. A Grand Committee which had been considering the matter then proposed that Congress call on the States of Rhode Island and Georgia for an immediate definitive answer as to whether they would comply with the impost recommendation of Congress.[15]

The speaker of the Rhode Island lower house had presented that body's formal objections to Congress. They were based, as were those of Massachusetts, upon the fear that Rhode Island as a commercial State would pay more than her share. According to Hamilton, this was only a pretext to cover her disinclination to surrender the right to tax goods bound for Connecticut.[16] Hamilton, Madison, and Fitzsimmons, as a committee of Congress, wrote a letter in answer, and a deputation was appointed to proceed to Rhode Island to try and convince the Legislature of their error, but on December 24, 1782, the whole enterprise was dealt a crushing blow by the news that Virginia had taken the final refusal by Rhode Island as a pretext to repeal its law agreeing to the impost.[17] In this case Hamilton believed the real reason was that Virginia had little share in the debts to which the impost would be applied.[18] Their chief arguing point being taken away, the deputation was suspended, but a new committee was appointed to try and redraft the impost so as to avoid objections. Madison, in commenting on this, says, "The most intelligent members were deeply affected and prognosticated a failure of the

[15] *Journal Continental Congress*, XXIII, 643-644.
[16] *Ibid.*, XXV, 902.
[17] *Ibid.*, XXIII, 798-810.
[18] *Journal Continental Congress*, XXV, 902. Virginia had paid into the loan office only $313,741. *Ibid.*, p. 915.

Impost scheme, and the most pernicuous effects to the character, the duration and the interests of the Confederacy."[19]

ARMY PAY

At the beginning of 1783 the question of establishing funds for the payment of the public debt became involved with the question of how the army was to be paid off and demobilized. A memorial from the army was received on January 6, demanding that Congress take action, and notifying them that a special deputation would wait upon them.[20] Morris meanwhile said that there was no possibility of making any payment in the present state of the finances.[21] When the deputation arrived they were interviewed by a Grand Committee of Congress. General McDougall of New York outlined the army demands as: First, an immediate advance of back pay; second, adequate provision for the residue; and third, half pay for officers after the war, which had been promised by Congress in 1780.[22] The first two demands were recognized as obligatory by everyone, the only question was whether they should be paid by Congress or the States.[23] The third demand was not regarded as binding by many people, both in and out of Congress, and it became the key point of the long and bitter debates that followed.

Before going further it will be well to stop a moment to discuss the personnel of this all-important session of Con-

[19]*Ibid.*, XXIII, 831 and 872.

[20]*Journal Continental Congress,* XXV, 846. Washington would have preferred to have a plenipotentiary commission of Congress visit the army at headquarters, but Congress refused. Hamilton, *History of the Republic,* II, 513.

[21]*Journal Continental Congress,* XXV, 847. Morris was not in favor of making a payment under direct compulsion even if it were possible. He told Washington, however, that he had some secret financial measures which would soon meet the situation.

[22]*Ibid.*, p. 851. The fact that the civil service was paid regularly was a great source of grievance to the army. They were indignant at the States' refusal to establish a general revenue. *Ibid.*, p. 852.

[23]Men in the army suspected that Morris, Hamilton, and others were playing a game to disband them without pay. Hamilton, *op. cit.*, II, 500 f.

gress. Madison, at the height of his powers, was the recognized leader in debate. He had an ability for close political reasoning that was unequaled among his contemporaries in the government. Hamilton and Wilson were his chief lieutenants. Hamilton had the confidence of Robert Morris, and often appeared in the rôle of spokesman for the financier. He was still immature, however, and lacking in political experience. He displayed the same unwillingness to compromise that was to mark his labors in the Federal Convention, and consequently some of his arguments only tended to drive the States' rights men into corners that forced them to fight back. James Wilson has scarcely ever been given credit for the value of his services to the cause of federalism. He had the learning necessary to puncture the false analogies from history continually built up by R. H. Lee, Mercer, and others. As a dialectician he was the peer of either Hamilton or Madison, although he lacked their political grasp. Richard Henry Lee, John Rutledge, and John Mercer led the States' rights group. While Lee is the best known of these three, the speeches of Mercer present the keenest exposition of their case. Hamilton's colleague Floyd was later a leading Anti-Federalist, but he had not yet developed this philosophy sufficiently to withstand the arguments of the young financier. He took no recorded part in the financial debates, and consistently voted with Hamilton.

The stand of the States' rights men was a consistent and logical one, despite the fact that the superior brilliance of the nationalists made it appear unreasonable. They wanted a division of the entire public debt among the States on some just basis of apportionment. They correctly feared the establishment of a funded national debt as leading eventually to a national type of government. If Congress were divested of its financial obligations, the Confederation might well serve indefinitely as an offensive and defensive alliance guaranteeing to each State its right of self-determination.

The first clash of the two factions occurred on January 26 over the question of commuting half pay for life for officers to full pay for a limited number of years paid in a lump sum as a funded six per cent note. On this occasion the New England States and New Jersey prevented any specific number of years from being agreed upon by the necessary seven votes.[24] It soon developed that the Connecticut and Rhode Island Delegates were instructed against voting for half pay on any basis.[25] The fundamental reason for opposition to half pay was fear by the States' rights men of the establishment of funded debts dischargeable only by national revenues, but it was strongly reënforced in this case by the desire of the States which had supplied only a few troops to avoid contributing to the general fund.

As Congress allowed the weeks to slip by in argument the army grew continually more restless. Hamilton, who as an ex-army man and a New Yorker, was in communication with many men familiar with affairs at Newburgh, warned Delegates privately that the army was determined not to lay down their arms without pay, and that Washington was becoming every day more unpopular because of his adherence to Congress.[26] March 17 Congress received a letter from Washington warning them that there was reason to believe that the civil creditors were inflaming the army to the point of rebellion, and enclosing two anonymous exhortations to the troops to act for themselves. This communication was referred to a committee purposely made up of the leading States' rights men.[27]

This plan produced the desired effect. The New Englanders were scared into swallowing their arguments. Dyer of Connecticut was compelled to report a resolution for paying the

---

[24] *Journal Continental Congress*, XXV, 865. Arnold, Wolcott, and Dyer from Conn. questioned the validity of Congress' original promise, as it was made prior to the adoption of the Articles, and by a vote of only six States.

[25] *Ibid.*, XXV, 889.

[26] *Ibid.*, XXV, 907.

[27] *Ibid.*, XXV, 926.

troops and granting the officers full pay for five years, both in six per cent notes on the credit of Congress.[28] Ironically enough this motion was agreed to on the same day that a letter from Washington arrived telling of the successful termination of his Newburgh meeting. It is doubtful, however, whether anybody felt that the trouble would have been quelled for long if Congress had not acted quickly.

THE GENERAL REVENUE PLAN OF 1783

The formation of a plan for a reliable Congressional revenue involved not only the question of the desirability of a system of national finance, but also extremely controversial questions as to method of operation. The States' rights men after they had been beaten on the army question by outside influence were the more determined to make their views felt in regard to the rest of the debt. In Congress itself the friends of a payment of the national debt by a national revenue administered by Congress controlled the necessary seven votes to carry measures, but there was such a great divergence in their opinions regarding practical means that their opponents found it easy to play one group against the other. They also had the consolation that even if they failed in Congress they had the State Legislatures to rely on.

Morris had recommended a plan the year before that served as an initial basis for discussion. It proposed in addition to an impost duty of 5 per cent ad valorem, a land tax of one dollar per hundred acres, a poll tax of one dollar on each freeman, or male slave between sixteen and sixty, and an excise of one-eighth of a dollar per gallon on distilled liquors.[29]

There were three chief factors in determining every State's attitude toward such a comprehensive plan.

First, if their ports were used for the importation of goods bound for neighboring States they disliked to give to Congress

[28]*Ibid.,* XXIV, 207.
[29]Wharton, *Revolutionary and Diplomatic Correspondence,* V, 627-628.

the power of taxing imports. Massachusetts, Rhode Island, New York, Pennsylvania, and Virginia, were the States that benefited most from this ability to tax neighbors' trade.

Second, the question of the type of taxes that might be proposed as funds supplementary to an impost involved such fundamental considerations as the amount of land, its average fertility, and the population of the States.[30]

Third, the State's attitude depended on how much of the public indebtedness was in the hands of its citizens.[31]

In some cases two of these factors counterbalanced each other, or one was so much more important that it obscured the others. New York, for example, may have had more than her share of the public indebtedness and, let us assume, an average ratio of land to population, but it had such a large revenue

[30]The relation of supplementary funds to the vote of the Southern States is excellently treated in St. G. L. Sioussat's *North Carolina Session, Mississippi Valley Historical Society Proc.,* II, 1908.

New York and Pennsylvania were divided when the proposal to make the value of surveyed land the basis for apportionment was inserted in the original articles by a vote of all the Southern States, plus New Jersey. *Journal Continental Congress,* IV, 801. Duane was nay, Duer aye.

[31]It is impossible to estimate this accurately for any given year, such as 1783. The original loan office records give the following table of loans by individuals in the various states.

New Hampshire	$336,579
Massachusetts	2,361,866
Rhode Island	699,725
Connecticut	1,270,115
New York	949,729
New Jersey	658,883
Pennsylvania	3.948,904
Delaware	65,820
Maryland	410,218
Virginia	313,741
North Carolina	113,341
South Carolina	90,442

In general, as the certificates had changed hands, the drift had been northward especially into Pennsylvania, whose citizens were believed by Madison to hold certificates for over one-third of the total of the domestic debt. *Journal Continental Congress,* XXV, 915.

from taxing imports that it is not remarkable that the agrarian majority in the Legislature were not much interested in a general revenue bill which would deprive them of this source of income.

Ellsworth of Connecticut recommended only the establishment of permanent State funds for the use of Congress. Madison, however, pointed out the vital difficulty that this last plan could not be put into effect until the State proportions were accurately determined, and this would entail long delay. If an effective revenue were not speedily established, it appeared likely that the States would appropriate money required by Congress to the payment of the claims of their own citizens.[32] Madison felt that an impost might be supplemented by a poll tax, making allowances for blacks, and a land tax, "by considering the value of land in each state to be in an inverse proportion of its quantity to the number of people; and apportioning on the aggregate quantity in each state accordingly." Hamilton proposed in addition a house and window tax.[33] The point to be emphasized was that no form of taxation devised to supplement the impost should involve the moot question of adjusting State quotas.

All the commercial States regarded a land tax based on acreage alone as better than an impost, whereas the far Southern States were violently opposed to such a tax. The North Carolina Delegates regarded it as "insufferably unequal" because of the large barren tracts in their State compared with the uniform fertility of such States as Pennsylvania.[34] On the other hand Howell of Rhode Island said that his state would positively not agree to the impost until the other states

---

[32] *Journal Continental Congress*, XXV, 870-74. The situation in Pennsylvania was particularly dangerous in this respect. Hamilton, *History of the Republic*, II, 338.

[33] *Journal Continental Congress*, XXXV, 877. The Constitution of Maryland, however, forbade a poll tax.

[34] Sioussat, *op. cit.*, p. 45. This point was also urged by Rutledge of S. C., *Journal Continental Congress*, XXV, 871.

had agreed to the supplementary funds.[35] All in all the progress was not very encouraging. Many members seemed to feel "that the ideas of the states on the subject were so averse to a general revenue in the hands of Congress, that if such a revenue were proper it was unattainable."[36] In a discussion between Hamilton,, Madison, Peters, Carroll, Gorham, and Fitzsimmons only Hamilton felt that any supplementary tax could be devised that would bear equally on all the States.[37]

The question of the duration of any revenue grant occasioned long debates at various times. Hamilton was vigorously opposed to a twenty-five year limitation, but Madison felt that they were asking so much that they had better give way on this point.[38] As in 1781, a principal objection was to the collection under the authority of Congress, but Madison, Hamilton, and Wilson all regarded this provision as essential, and forced their point.[39]

Granting that a revenue was to be raised, there was the question of how the proceeds should be applied to reducing the debts. Rutledge, representing the general feeling of the Southern States which had few public creditors, argued for several days that the money should be used solely for the army, to which Hamilton, Madison, and Fitzsimmons of Pennsylvania replied that without the support of the other public creditors the measure could never be got through the State Legislatures.

[35]Staples, *Rhode Island in the Continental Congress*, p. 515 ff.

[36]Bland in *Journal Continental Congress*, XXV, 870. On the question of the constitutionality of an impost Madison said: "It has been objected that a general revenue contravenes the Articles of Confederation. They . . . authorize Congress to borrow money. Now in order to borrow money permanent and certain revenue is necessary, and if this provision cannot be made in any other way, as has been shown, then a general revenue is within the spirit of Confederation." *Ibid.*, p. 874.

[37]*Ibid.*, p. 906.

[38]The vote on suspending the twenty-five-year clause was Mass. and Va. nay, Conn. and N. Y. divided, rest aye (giving only six votes in favor).

[39]New York and Pennsylvania wanted appointment of collectors by Congress in addition to responsibility to that body. *Ibid.*, p. 904. This, however, had been partly responsible for the defeat of the proposal of 1781.

R. H. Lee made a suggestion prophetic of the debates to come after the adoption of the Constitution. He advocated distinguishing between the original holders of the loan-office certificates and those who had bought them for speculation.[40]

These conflicting sentiments made it appear as the debate wore on that a general revenue including both an impost and supplementary funds would have more chance of adoption than the impost alone, because it would give a better opportunity to counterbalance features objectionable to any particular State.[41] This was formally decided on March 21, by defeating a motion to complete the plan for the impost separately.[42] Try as they would, however, the advocates of supplementary funds could not devise a system acceptable to all sections. Wilson was willing to reduce the land tax to twenty-five cents a hundred acres, but the Southern States would not agree as a matter of principle.[43] Perhaps to bring pressure to bear upon Congress, Massachusetts in the latter part of March invited the Eastern States to a convention to regulate matters of common concern.[44] This implied threat of independent action was used by Gorham as an argument for speeding up the agreement to a general revenue. Hamilton, as usual, was in favor of calling a General Convention.[45]

As it became more and more obvious that the question of supplementary funds would have to be left to the discretion of the individual States, all the old questions of apportioning State quotas came up again. As we have seen in the early part

[40]*Ibid.*, p. 905.

[41]In Chapter IX it will be demonstrated that the members of Congress were not altogether right in this assumption. It was the agrarian element in the commercial States that were objecting to the Federal impost, and they would likewise object to land taxes, or almost any other kind of funds that could be devised.

[42]*Journal Continental Congress*, XXIV, 205, XXV, 937.

[43]*Ibid.*, XXV, 928. Such men as Wilson and Hamilton were in sympathy with the commercial classes, and therefore much more anxious for supplementary funds than were the people of their States.

[44]*Ibid.*, p. 951.

[45]*Ibid.*, p. 952.

of the previous chapter, abatements in favor of States that had suffered from the occupation of the enemy was defeated March 27. On April 7, a temporary list of quota percentages was adopted so that payments on the new supplementary funds could commence at once without waiting for a final settlement of the proportions.[46] It was as follows:

New Hampshire ...	3.5%	Pennsylvania	13.6%
Massachusetts	14.8	Delaware	1.5
Rhode Island	2.1	Maryland	9.4
Connecticut	8.7	Virginia	16.9
New York	8.5	North Carolina	7.2
New Jersey	5.5	South Carolina	7.2
	Georgia	1.1%	

At last, after almost four months of debate the attempt to reach an acceptable plan for general supplementary funds was given up and it was decided that the States should severally establish such funds as they thought best to produce the quota fixed in the proposal. To make up partially for this, specific duties were added to the impost in such a way that they would presumably bear more heavily on the South than on New England. The final bill was adopted as a resolution of Congress by the vote of nine States. Rhode Island voted "nay" and New York was divided; the rest of the represented States voted "aye."[47] The resolutions, which were immediately dispatched to the States, were as follows:

1. Specific duties were placed on certain articles such liquors, coffee, tea, pepper, sugar and molasses; five per cent ad valorem was to be collected on all goods at the place of importation.

[46]*Ibid.*, XXIV, 231.

[47]*Ibid.*, XXIV, 261. Hamilton voted nay because: (1) It did not designate specific funds for paying all the interest on the debt; (2) Twenty-five years would not be a long enough duration; (3) Nomination, and appointment of collectors resided in the States, whereas at least nomination should have been vested in the United States. Hamilton to Clinton, *Hamilton's Works*, Const. Ed., IX, 339-342.

2. Duties were to be applied only to the payment of principal and interest of the United States debts contracted for supporting the war.

3. The duties were to continue for only twenty-five years.

4. Collectors were to be appointed by the States within one month, or in case of non-action, by Congress, and were to be amenable to and removable by Congress alone.

5. The States were to establish such additional sources of revenue as they should think convenient to yield their quota of $1,500,000 annually, collected by persons appointed as for the impost, except that collections were to be carried to the separate credit of the State (the provisional quotas as given above p. 21 were here inserted).

6. The resolutions were not to be effective until accepted by all the States, but could be done away with at any time thereafter by a majority vote.

7. States not having completed land cessions were urged to do so.

8. Article VIII of the Confederation was to be amended to provide for apportionment of expenses by population counting five slaves as equal to three freemen.[48]

The Superintendent estimated the probable revenue from the impost at $915,956 annually, which, together with the $1,500,000 to be paid by the States, would just equal the interest charges on the foreign and domestic debt.[49]

THE STRUGGLE BEGINS IN NEW YORK

While this debate had been going on in Congress the New York Legislature had repealed their law agreeing to the Impost proposal of 1781, on the ground that there was no chance

[48]*Journal Continental Congress,* XXIV, 257-261. The "three-fifths" compromise was first agreed to March 28, 1783. On the vote only Rhode Island was against it and Massachusetts divided. The slave states were afraid that three to four might be adopted. (*Journal Continental Congress,* XXV, 949.)

[49]*Journal Continental Congress,* XXIV, 285-288.

of its acceptance by the States. The act of repeal, however, offered Congress the proceeds of a five per cent impost collected, by the State, as soon as the other States should do likewise.[50] Such was the initial defeat of the "vest a power to levy" clause.

The half-pay proposals met violent opposition from large numbers in New York even before the general revenue act attracted much attention. A town meeting in Dutchess County resolved that officers were not entitled to any special compensation. The resolutions were published in the papers, and gave rise in turn to several answers, one by "Publius" who was probably Hamilton.[51]

While this half-pay controversy was at its height the general revenue plan was published in the papers.[52] It was immediately attacked and defended by several writers. An anonymous writer argued for the revenue in a forceful way. "There is no such thing . . . as granting money to Congress. Does a man grant money when he pays his debts? Certainly not. A man's creditors may grant him an indulgence, but he certainly grants them nothing by paying them."[53]

The Legislature did not meet in the fall of 1783, and by the time they assembled at the beginning of the next year much of the excitement had quieted down. The enemies of a general revenue had a sizable majority, and rebuffed the Congressional proposal by the enactment of a State Impost Act on March 22,

[50]*Laws of N. Y.*, Chap. XVI, p. 279, Mar. 15, 1783. Abraham Yates, "Rough Hewer," held that the appointment of tax collectors by Congress would be an unconstitutional use of power. He cited the loss of Dutch liberties through centralization. *N. Y. Packet*, April 8, 1784.

[51]The reasons given in the Dutchess County resolves were: (1) the officers did not expect extra compensation when they enlisted, and the State never agreed to it; (2) they had had depreciation in pay adjusted whereas most citizens had not; (3) it was an unjust distinction between officer and private; (4) the State had promised a generous land bounty; (5) the State militia would receive nothing; (6) it would create idlers. *N. Y. Packet*, July 24, 1783, answered July 24, and July 31, *et seq*.

[52]*Ibid.*, Aug. 7, 1783.

[53]*N. Y. Packet*, July 17, 1783.

1784. This act imposed specific duties on certain enumerated articles, and 2½% ad valorem on all others, to continue in force until the rising of the Legislature at their next meeting. Goods for other States, however, could be bonded at double duty, and receive a drawback on re-exportation.[54]

In May of this year the New York Delegates again tried to get the principle of abatements incorporated in the general revenue plan, but their motion to consider the matter was lost seven to two, Rhode Island siding with New York and New Hampshire divided.[55]

It is best now to take up some of the other threads of finance before proceeding to the stormy and dramatic conclusion of the general revenue attempt.

[54]*Laws of N. Y.*, Chap. X, pp. 11-17.
[55]*Journal Continental Congress*, 1823 ed., IV, 411, May 24, 1884.

CHAPTER VIII

ATTEMPTS TO MAKE THE ARTICLES FUNCTION IN TIME OF PEACE 1783-1788

INTRODUCTION

T HE events of 1783 brought about a great change in the position of New York in the Confederation. With its lands restored and trade resumed through the city port, the State government enjoyed an immense increase in available resources. Whereas the States in general suffered a depression after the war, up-state New York seemed prosperous in comparison with its former hardships.[1] The merchants in the previously occupied districts probably lost rather than gained through the departure of the British, but they were not in a position to control State policies. As a result of these changed conditions the collection of taxes became easier and New York paid a larger percentage of her Congressional requisitions during this period than any other State.[2] It is not surprising that the up-state men became contented with the situation as it was, and unwilling to increase the powers of Congress. Perhaps one thing that prompted such generous responses to Congressional requisitions was a desire to prove that the existing Confederation could function adequately.

After the retirement of Morris no satisfactory man could be found to fill his place, and on May 27, 1784, Congress decided to return to the system of a board.[3] It was eight months more before a board could be selected. In the interim the Comptroller acted as "Superintendent" with limited powers. The new three-member board, beginning its labors on April 21, 1785, immediately started a system of quarterly reports which

[1] Hamilton, *History of the Republic*, II, 387.
[2] See Summary, pp. 216-17.
[3] *Journal Continental Congress*, 1823 ed., IV, 421.

from this time on to the close of the Confederation give us the exact amounts paid by the various States in answer to requisitions.[4]

THE ADJUSTMENT OF ACCOUNTS

Before taking up the two vital threads of financial history during this period, taxation and the impost, the history of the attempts to adjust State and private accounts will be considered. While the life of the Confederation did not depend on the settlement of accounts the way it did upon the means of raising revenue, these unsettled accounts in themselves formed one of the obstacles in the way of raising such revenue. Each State felt that it had done more than its share, and until this share could be determined the psychological effect made all the States less energetic.

During the year 1785 the question of settling State accounts was postponed until it could be determined whether or not the States would accept the general revenue recommendations of April 18, 1783, and the proposed changes in Article VIII.[6]

[4]The second quarter was started on April 21, but terminated June 30, 1785. *Pap. Cont. Cong.,* no. 141, II, ff. 197 and 361. The Comptroller kept the records from November, 1784 to April 21, 1785. New York paid nothing between June 1, 1784 and April 21, 1785, no. 141, II, ff. 53 and 205.

In fact, there is almost nothing connected with national finance during these last four years that cannot be found in the reports of the Board of Treasury in *Pap. Cont. Cong.,* no. 141, I and II.

[6]When the requisitions for 1785 were being debated in Congress it was moved by Rutledge of South Carolina that the States who had assumed debts owing by Congress to private individuals be allowed to stand in the place of the individuals. That is, to have these accounts settled as private ones rather than wait for the State settlement. On this motion every Northern Delegate voted nay, and every Southern one aye, except for one vote from Maryland. A similar motion was again defeated September 24, 1785. *Journal Continental Congress,* 1823, ed. IV, p. 555, July 26, 1785, and p. 583. During this same year some agitation was carried on for making the State Auditors the Commissioners to adjust accounts. *Pap. Cont. Cong.,* no. 26, III, f. 525; Wadsworth to Gerry, Feb. 24, 1785.

In February, 1783, a committee reported that all the States except New Hampshire, Rhode Island, South Carolina and Georgia had agreed to the change in Article VIII.[7] This inaugurated a fresh series of debates on the best means of adjusting accounts once the basis of apportionment was determined on. An ordinance replacing the Commissioners for settling accounts between the United States and the States, appointed in pursuance of the act of February 20, 1782, by a three-member board, any two of which should provide a quorum, was passed October 13, 1786.[8] Seven months later this ordinance was repealed and a new one substituted. Five Commissioners were appointed, each of whom was to go to a certain district and gather together the State accounts against the United States.[9] They were to submit all information regarding army accounts to the Commissioners already appointed by Congress for adjusting them, and all accounts regarding supplies and money furnished on requisitions prior to October 1781 to the Comptroller.[10] Another special board

[7]*Pap. Cont. Cong.*, no. 24, I, f. 153. New York had agreed April 9, 1785. *Laws of N. Y.*, Chap. LXIII, p. 55. It passed a census law Feb. 8, 1786. *Laws,* Chap. VIII, p. 9.

[8]*Journal Continental Congress,* 1823, IV, 711-12. During the debate New York and the New England States attempted to add an amendment that each State should receive compensation for troops raised above its quota, and that deficient States should be charged correspondingly, but all the other States voted against this. *Journal Continental Congress,* 1823, IV, 710. New York had actually provided more than her share of troops. B. Fernow, *New York State Archives,* I, Muster Rolls.

[9]New York and New Jersey constituted one district.

[10]Six per cent interest was to be allowed in all cases. Accounts must be presented to the Commissioners within six months after they notified the chief executive of the State that they were ready to receive them, or else they would not be honored. The Commissioners were to deliver their statements one year after they were appointed.

The five Commissioners for settling the accounts of the government departments were still functioning. These ordinances only did away with those created to settle the State accounts.

of three Commissioners was appointed to adjust on the basis of equity accounts not authorized by Congress.[11]

Despite this elaborate machinery the accounts were never settled. In fact, many of them were in such confusion that settlement was practically impossible. In May, 1788, a committee reported that after a careful examination they found "that many millions were advanced to sundry persons whereof proper accounts have not been rendered . . . though they have been frequently called upon. . . . Some of the accounts rendered are so general and inexact that revisions must be made." It was resolved that Congress commence suits against all persons who stood charged with public money or property; within three months if they had been previously called on or five months if they had not.[12] The following month the States were given three months longer in which to present their claims, and the Commissioners three months more in which to adjust them. By October 17, almost the end of the sittings of Congress, the necessary books and papers for any kind of a final settlement had been received only from New York, New Jersey, Pennsylvania, Maryland, and Georgia.[13] The whole matter was postponed at this point by the dissolution of the old government, and remained for Hamilton to deal with in 1790.

REQUISITIONS

The requisitions of Congress from 1784 on were primarily for the payment of interest and principal on the domestic and foreign debt. The cost of such civil and military authority as the Congress exercised was a small item compared with the annual interest charges. The problem of raising money to pay interest on the domestic debt naturally brought up the question of accepting indents for such in payment of requisitions. The

[11] They were to sit for a year and a half from the time of their appointment. *Journal Continental Congress*, IV, 743 ff., May 7, 1787. Passed unanimously.

[12] *Journal Continental Congress*, IV, 817, May 22, 1788.

[13] *Pap. Cont. Cong.*, no. 26, III, 701-8.

Southern States, holding proportionally little of the national debt, favored specie alone, but as the Northern States were in the majority a large percentage of each requisition was made payable in indents.[14] The provisions of the four requisitions made by Congress from January 1, 1785, on may be found in Appendix C. Late in 1786 Congress tried the expedient of a domestic loan, the first since 1779, but the attempt was futile. While Congress might borrow from Amsterdam bankers who could build on the future, the ordinary American could by this time have little faith in the immediate prospects of Congress.[15]

STATE FINANCES

The resumption of peace-time commerce, and the organization of means for disposing of the forfeited Loyalist estates relieved the State government of the necessity of laying heavy internal taxes. An examination of the State receipts during these years, Appendix E, shows that customs duties, and forfeitures and sequestrations made up the bulk of State revenue.[16] Only $285,000 in internal taxes was levied between the end of 1784 and the beginning of 1789.[17]

Early in 1787 Hamilton tried unsuccessfully to substitute definite tax rates for the county quota system. "What criterion," he said, "can the Legislature have for estimating the abilities of the various counties. The whole must either

[14]*Journal Continental Congress*, IV, 547-550, 552, 578, 579. It was provided, however, that if the indents were not paid in within a certain period the delinquent States would be liable for the balance in specie.

[15]*Journal Continental Congress*, IV, 714-15. The offering was withdrawn the following May. *Ibid.*, IV, 741.

[16]In February, 1784, a duty of four pence per ton was laid on all vessels entering New York ports except New York vessels on coasting voyages, and American vessels of under sixty tons. The next month a list of specific duties, and a general two and a half per cent ad valorem duty were laid on all goods. These acts were extended from time to time and the duties increased until in 1787 they ranged up to seven and a half per cent ad valorem on goods and eight pence per ton on vessels. *Laws of N. Y.*, Chap. I, p. 3, Feb. 12, 1784; Chap. V, pp. 11-17, March 22, 1784; and *infra*, Chap. IX, p. 167 f.

[17]See table of tax laws, Appendix C.

be a business of honest guessing or interested calculations," each member seeking to shift the burdens on some other county than his own. The same thing was true of the division by the County Supervisors of the quotas for the various districts, and finally of the assessment of individuals by the Assessors. This practice of discretion in taxation had been generally condemned by the leading authorities on the subject.[18] He was defeated in his attempt at reform by the same up-state majority in the Legislature that had refused to agree to the impost.[19]

The arrears of taxes had mounted so high in New York by 1784 that the efforts of the Legislature during this year and 1785 were devoted to trying to collect them, rather than assess new taxes. November 26, 1784, a long act was passed to compel the payment of arrearages. Fines to be levied on delinquent collectors and County Treasurers were increased fivefold, and they were liable to further prosecution in court. A most disorganized state of affairs is shown by the provisions of this act. In several counties there were no Treasurers, or Collectors. In others no assessments had been made. All the taxes since June 30, 1781, were in arrears. In some cases the collectors had died or moved away without ever giving an accounting. A statement from all Treasurers and Collectors was ordered for March 1, 1785, and payment in full by the first of the following October.[20] But the day of reckoning was postponed by subsequent acts until January 1, 1787.[21]

At the end of 1785 the taxes were $431,513.00 in arrears in the six counties that had not been occupied by the British.[22]

[18]*Works of Hamilton*, Const. ed., VIII, 33 f.

[19]*N. Y. Ass. Jour.*, 10th sess., p. 107.

[20]*Laws of N. Y.*, Chap. XVI, p. 24, Nov. 26, 1784.

[21]*Ibid.*, Chap. XXX, p. 16, March 10, 1785; and Chap. XXI, pp. 21-22, March 31, 1786.

[22]Report of Gerard Bancker to the Legislature. *Sen. and Ass. Jours.*, 11th sess., p. 14 f. The exact sums were as follows:

Albany County	£91,368	Orange County	£19,884
Dutchess County	34,498	Westchester County	1,234
Ulster County	24,005	Charlotte County	1,616

From 1786 on collection of current taxes seems to have been somewhat better, the act of March 29, 1786, the first post-war tax law, being 79.71% collected by the end of the following year.[23] But at the end of the period of the Confederation there were still large arrears due the State Treasury.[24] It is interesting to note that the time for collecting the 1788 tax for the maintenance of the poor and other contingent expenses arising in the City and County of New York had also to be extended. It was not only the taxes for Continental purposes that the people disliked to pay.

While on the subject of unsuccessful taxation, mention should be made of the question of quit rents. These had not been collected during the war. An act of April 1, 1786, stated that none should be charged for the period from September 29, 1775 to September 29, 1783. Those due from this latter date onward were made payable in any recognized securities if paid in prior to January 2, 1787, but after that date in gold or silver only, and when payments were three years in arrears the Treasurer might foreclose. In this same act it was provided that any landholder might commute his quit rents forever by paying fourteen times their annual value prior to May 1, 1787, or if commuted in gold or silver at any time prior

[23]

	Quota	Paid		Quota	Paid
New York	£13,000	£12,430	Ulster	£3,400	£2,078
Kings	2,400	2,328	Orange	2,800	1,594
Queens	4,500	4,015	Dutchess	5,000	1,958
Suffolk	4,500	4,365	Albany	4,700	3,156
Richmond	1,000	1,109	Columbia	2,300	2,031
Westchester	3,400	2,838	Washington	800	466
			Montgomery	1,600	1,483

Totals ....£50,000...£39,856, resp.

Report of Gerard Bancker, *N. Y. Ass. Jour.*, 11th sess., p. 26.

[24]March 15, 1788, the County Treasurers were given until June 1 to pay arrears. It was further provided that in cases where there was no property to condemn for arrears on previous taxes the sum due should be apportioned on the other taxpayers of the place. *Laws of N. Y.*, Chap. LXXVII, pp. 179-181. February 28, 1789, the time for collecting the tax of March 19, 1788 was extended from February to May 1. *Laws of N. Y.*, Chap. XXVII, p. 63.

to January 2, 1788. Quit rents on forfeited estates were re-mitted forever.[25] In April 1787 the time for commutation or payment of quit rents in paper was extended a year and the Treasurer ordered to submit to the County Clerks a statement of the quit rents due from their counties.[26] February 28, 1789, the period for commutation in paper was again extended to May 1, 1790.[27] It has been estimated that the collection of quit rents was usually about 60% in arrears.[28]

SUMMARY OF REQUISITIONS AND TAXES

The following is a summary of requisitions and taxes between October 30, 1784, and April 1, 1788, similar to those made for the two earlier periods. The Requisitions of Congress on New York for this period totaled $420,927.$52.4/90$ in specie and $544,913.$37.4/90$ in indents. The State payments to the national Treasury totaled $249,170.$22/90$ in specie and $399,358.$37.4/90$ in indents. Adding the specie and indents together New York paid to April 1, 1788, $648,528.$59.4/90$ or about 65% of all requisitions made upon it.[29] This sum is exclusive of money paid for pensions, etc., which was claimed to complete all but $24,583.$39/90$ of the specie sums required.[30]

---

[25]*Laws of N. Y.*, Chap. XXIII, pp. 24-27, April 1, 1786. The usual quit rent in New York was two shillings six pence per hundred acres. Sowers, *Financial History of New York*, p. 38.

[26]*Laws of N. Y.*, Chap. LXXVI, p. 137, April 11, 1787.

[27]*Ibid.*, XXXVIII, p. 63.

[28]Sowers, *op. cit.*, p. 38.

[29]*Pap. Cont. Cong.*, no. 141, I, f. 75. If we accept the figure in Hamilton's report of 1790 for specie payments, then New York had paid $774,380 by that time, or nearly 75% of all requisitions during this period. These reports of 1790, however, may include payments made after our period, and therefore the reports of the Board of Treasury are more exact for our purposes.

[30]*Laws of N. Y.*, Chap. XIX, p. 22. There seems to have been a discrepancy between the State's accounts and those of the Board of Treasury. March 31, 1788, a committee of Congress reported that, according to the latter record, New York still owed $171,757.30/90. Deducting the $93,750 paid by the State to disabled veterans between the end of 1783 and the beginning of 1788 still leaves a deficit of approximately $78,007. (Report of the Auditor, *Jour. N. Y. Ass.*, 1788, p. 16 f.). Subtracting from this sum

Neglecting this last item which cannot be verified from the records of the Board of Treasury or computed for the other States, this constituted approximately twice as good a record as that made by the State in either of the two preceding periods, and a better record than that made by any other State for this latter period. Pennsylvania stood next to New York in percentage of payments with 56%, and South Carolina a close third with 55.5%. In percentage of specie payments alone Pennsylvania stood slightly ahead of New York, having paid $615,735 out of $910,592$\frac{70}{90}$ required.[31] In indents no State even approached New York's percentage. None of these figures include the additional requisition for indents made August 20, 1788, but there are no records of any payments on this having been made to the Board of Treasury by any of the States.

The foregoing discussion illustrates strongly that New York's opposition to a Congressional impost was not based upon a disinclination to meet her obligations toward the central government. In fact, the large figure for payments in indents would indicate that New Yorkers held an abnormal percentage of the public debt, and would therefore be decidedly interested in a better general revenue. The real opposition arose partly from a disinclination to give up power, and partly from the disinclination of the up-state men to do what they felt would favor the city merchants and might increase the land

the $24,583 ordered paid in 1789 leaves a net deficit of $53,424, which accords tolerably well with Hamilton's statement that New York owed $45,902.40.4 in specie requisitions by 1790. (*American State Papers, Finance,* I, 56-57).

Congress had recommended to the States in 1778 that they make provision for persons disabled in the service of the United States and deduct the amounts paid from their proportion of the total expenses. The New York Legislature passed this act in compliance. *Laws of N. Y.,* 2d sess., Chap. XXX, p. 62, 1779.

[31] *Pap. Cont. Cong.,* no. 141, I, f. 75. South Carolina cannot be classified for specie payments, as she received large credit under this head for money spent for supplies within the State during 1781.

taxes.[32] How this worked out will be seen in the following chapter.

CURRENCY AND LOANS

The usual depression that follows the abnormal activity of a war period was accentuated in the United States by the disorganization of ancient trade relations, uncertainty regarding the future of the government, and contraction of the currency.[33] The hard times reached their maximum throughout the country in the winter of 1785-6, and the agrarian debtor group clamored for inflation. In view of the strength and political solidarity of this group in New York it is not surprising that in March 1786 the Legislature authorized the issue of $500,000 in paper currency on the old colonial plan.[34] In the Council of Revision the argument was long and bitter with Clinton and Yates representing the popular side and R. R. Livingston, Hobart, and Lewis Morris the creditors' side. At length, the Council having argued away the ten days allowed them to offer objections without being able to agree on any one report, the bill became law without their consent.[35] The Board

[32]The fact that Congress might levy a 5% impost did not mean that State imposts would necessarily be abandoned. See *Laws of N. Y.*, Chap. LXXXI, p. 156, April 11, 1787. Of course, it would act as a check on raising the State duties as high as they otherwise might be. In the act of 1786 the Legislature did agree to suspend all State duties on imports while the law was in force, but this was altered by the act of April, 1787.

[33]In New York on March 12, 1785, the Legislature passed an act commanding the Treasurer to destroy all State bills of credit in his possession, but on March 28 the effect of this was to some extent counterbalanced by declaring all State certificates or securities negotiable. *Laws of N. Y.*, XXXII, 18, and *Laws of N. Y.*, XIX, 21, respectively.

[34]The sum was to be divided among the counties and then lent as mortgages on land, houses, or plate at 5% annually repayable in installments over fourteen years. No loan was to exceed $750. When interest and principal repaid should equal $150,000 the Treasurer was to declare the remaining notes redeemable in specie. These notes were to constitute the only legal tender other than specie. *Laws of N. Y.*, XL, 61-78, March 18, 1786. The only concerted opposition came from the New York City delegates.

[35]*Minutes of the Council of Revision,* April 8 to 18, 1786.

of Treasury at once reported that they could not accept this new currency in place of payments in specie or Continental bills of March 18, 1780.[36]

A committee of Congress reported in February 1786 that money was imperatively needed to pay $577,307.25 in interest on the foreign debt by June 1, 1787, exclusive of $1,252,-938.72 which would come due for repayments of principal during this latter years. The receipts for the fourteen months preceding January 1, 1786, were only $432,897.81, less than enough to run the civil government. They concluded a vigorous peroration with: "the time of crisis has arrived."[37]

In response to this appeal, New York opened a loan of £585,950 for Continental purposes at six per cent. The subscriptions were to be paid at the State loan offices, and the State Treasurer was to turn the money over to the Continental Board. These certificates could be offered in payment for forfeited estates.[38] According to the record of the State debt, £565,000 of this sum was turned over to the national Treasury, or expended for national purposes.[39]

[36]*Pap. Cont. Cong.,* no. 139, I, ff. 125-127.
[37]*Journal Continental Congress,* IV, 620.
[38]*Laws of N. Y.,* Chap. LXXIII, June 30, 1786.
[39]*American State Papers, Finance,* I, 30.

CHAPTER IX

THE FINAL FAILURE OF THE CONFEDERATION
1784-1788

THE life or death of the Confederation really depended upon the result of the final attempt to get the States to agree to the five per cent impost. Had this power been granted, plus that of regulating commerce, which as we shall see had no insuperable obstacles in its way, the Confederation might have been able to stabilize its finances and survive. Without these powers the future seemed hopeless. Congress had never been able to pay interest alone, on either the foreign or domestic debt out of any year's revenue. The security-holders backed by the foreign interests represented the best organized, most active and powerful group in the country, and if agrarian State Legislatures would not agree to the measures necessary to repay them, then an overturn of the existing regime was inevitable. Before taking up this question, however, we should first examine a closely related topic, the regulation of trade.

THE REGULATION OF TRADE

While the impost proposal of April 18, 1783, was being discussed by the States, Congress took up the regulation of trade from another angle. In accordance with the resolves of Congress of October 29, 1783, "most favored nation" treaties had been concluded with France, Sweden, and the Netherlands, but the British situation presented difficulties. In 1783, William Pitt had attempted unsuccessfully to sponsor in Parliament the *laissez faire* theories of Adam Smith regarding Empire trade. The old navigation policy was so skillfully set forth in Lord Sheffield's "Observations on the Commerce of the United States," written in the same year, that Pitt gave up further efforts and let the mercantilists have their way.

As a result the navigation system was continued in its old form with the United States on the outside.[1] This meant, among other things which would affect New York, the prohibition of the West Indian trade in American vessels.[2] The Canadian trade was also restricted to British vessels, and the importation of all American goods into Canada forbidden except by executive proclamation in special emergencies.[3]

Unfavorable regulations, however, were not sufficient to alter the old habitual courses of trade. Americans were used to British products and preferred them to any other. American and British merchants were deeply involved in credit relationships which could not be easily terminated, and British merchants in general offered better credit terms than those of any other nation.[4] While entirely new trades such as the Far Eastern and Russian offered possibilities of profit apart from the trade with Great Britain, they were entered into very hesitantly by the conservative merchants, and probably formed a rather insignificant portion of the total commerce.[5] The Sheffield group seemed borne out in their statements regarding the

[1] 23 Geo. III., C. 39; and summary of all regulations in 28 Geo. III., C. 6. A good discussion of this whole topic may be found in S. F. Bemis, *Jay's Treaty*, p. 21 f.

[2] New York exported grain and general food stuffs to the West Indies.

[3] 25 Geo. III., C. 1. This did not really affect New York greatly as both areas produced much the same goods, and there was no incentive to extensive trade. For example, the principal Canadian exports were: furs; wheat; flour; peas; and lumber. (*A Memorandum on Canadian Trade, Chalmers Papers,* Canada, 1692-1792, N. Y. P. L.)

The Canadian authorities were afraid of the influence of American traders on the Indians, and tried strictly to prevent smuggling on the Great Lakes. (Haldimand to St. Leger 1784, pp. 12-13; and Dorchester to Sydney, May 17, 1788, in *Bancroft Transcripts of Papers in the Public Record Office,* N. Y. P. L.)

[4] Talleyrand-Perigord, *Memoir concerning the Commercial Relations of the United States with England.* London, 1806.

[5] As late as May 3, 1787, LeRoy and Bayard write that they will only take cargoes for these destinations on commission, although the market is undoubtedly a very good one. *Bayard, Campbell, Pearsall, Correspondence and Accounts,* N. Y. P. L.

necessity of the United States trading with Britain under any conditions, and the government turned a deaf ear to all American proposals for a commercial treaty.[6]

Congress, therefore, decided that only forceful coercion would be effective, and asked in April 1784 that it be given power, for fifteen years, to prohibit goods from being exported or imported in vessels belonging to or navigated by subjects of any power with whom the States had no treaties of commerce. They further resolved that Congress be given power, for fifteen years, to prohibit the subjects of any foreign state from importing goods which were not the products of the country whose subjects they were; provided that for such acts the consent of nine States in Congress should be necessary.[7]

The merchants of New York City did not favor any violent measures which would temporarily suspend trade. The continuous British occupation of New York City had permitted many mercantile houses to maintain uninterrupted relations with Great Britain during the war, and those whose business had been interrupted were eager to resume relations.[8] In the records of the merchants to which we have access there is no indication of any large accumulated indebtedness of New York concerns to their English correspondents.[9] In some cases the good will with which they parted is proved by the resumption

[6]The tonnage of foreign vessels clearing from the Port of New York between Nov. 21, 1785 and Nov. 23, 1786 was as follows:

British	9347	Danish	857
French	2218	Spanish	781
Dutch	1874		

(*Bancroft Transcripts, America and England*, 1783-1789, no. 47, N. Y. P. L.)

[7]*Journal Continental Congress*, IV, 393, April 30, 1784.

[8]Bayard, Campbell, Pearsall, *Correspondence*, 1751-1806; John Van Schaik, *Letter Book, Gansevoort-Lansing Papers; Taylor-Cooper Papers;* N. Y. P. L.

[9]This fact is born out by the table of mercantile debts due to Great Britain in 1783, *Chatham Mss.* Bdl. 3431, quoted in Bemis, *op. cit.*, p. 103.

of relations between the same two firms immediately after the war.[10] These firms had no scruples about trading in British ships to avoid the regulations, which constituted an added grievance to the radical group.[11]

The general tone of letters in the New York City press on the subject of trade reprisals was decidedly moderate during the spring of 1784, but this conciliatory attitude was not shared by the radical majority in the Legislature.[12] That body speedily replied to the request of Congress by granting them the power to forbid British West Indian trade in British vessels, provided all the other States concurred.[13] This partial compliance did not satisfy Congress, and the Legislature was urged at its next session to agree to all of the resolutions of April 30 last. They did so, but with two additional qualifications: That the powers should not become effective until agreed to by all the States, and that nothing in the act should enable

[10]John Van Schaik of Albany, for example, traded with Blackburn and Shirley both before and after the Revolution. LeRoy and Bayard also resumed their old connections.

There were naturally some minor examples of bad debts. Dixon and Lee of Leeds commissioned Alexander Hamilton to collect their debts July 18, 1786. *Bayard, Campbell, Pearsall, Correspondence and Accounts,* N. Y. P. L.

[11]LeRoy and Bayard to Col. Wm. Bayard, May 3, 1787. *Bayard, Campbell, Pearsall, Correspondence,* N. Y. P. L.

[12]British and American commerce was debated in a series of letters published in the *Independent Journal and General Advertiser,* May 10, 14, and 21, 1784. "Cincinatus" represented the pro-British feeling, and "Common Sense" the radical American attitude.

[13]*Laws of N. Y.,* Chap. LII, pp. 77-78, May 4, 1784. Both House and Senate agreed to this bill *without ever having a division* at any stage. The Legislature, as we have seen previously, was unusually anti-British at this session (for example: the delegation from New York County was made up of Willet, Lamb, Sears, Rutgers, Stagg, Macolm, Harpur, Van Zandt, and Hughes), and possibly their desire for vengeance overcame their repugnance to giving powers to Congress. *N. Y. Sen. and Ass. Jours.,* 1784, *passim.* Final passage of bill in House, p. 154.

Congress to raise or collect duties within the state without the sanction of the Legislature.[14]

While Congress was still waiting to hear from all of the States, New York in the spring of 1785 doubled the duties on British vessels.[15]

In the spring of 1786 a Congressional committee reported that all the States except Delaware, South Carolina, and Georgia had practically complied with the recommendations regarding the regulation of commerce, although only Massachusetts, New York, New Jersey, and Virginia had done so in full. A resolution was thereupon passed to call upon the three delinquent States for action, and upon the others to correct the irregularities in their agreements.[16] Neither of these actions was ever completed before the inauguration of the new government.

THE IMPOST IN THE LEGISLATURE

New York was already well on the way to becoming the greatest commercial State, and the collection of duties on imports was the most important source of state revenue.[17]

[14]*Laws of N. Y.*, Chap. LVI, p. 48, April 4, 1785. The qualification that the acts shall not become effective until agreed to by all the States shows that this act was not regarded as a new article.

This act was also passed without a division at any stage. The mercantile group were too poorly represented to even offer a show of resistance. *New York Sen. Jour.,* 1785, pp. 64, 68; Ass. Jour., pp. 126, 130.

[15]*Laws of N. Y.*, Chap. XIX, p. 5.

[16]*Journal Continental Congress,* IV, 621-622. It is worth noting that North Carolina's "irregularity" consisted in requiring that the resolutions should form an Article of Confederation.

[17]The receipts from the impost for the four years from 1784 to 1787, inclusive, were approximately $480,000, or over 51% of the total receipts of the Treasury, exclusive of the paper money issued in 1786. *N. Y. Sen. and Ass. Journal,* 11th sess., 1788, "Report of the Auditor." The New York State Laws laying duties on vessels and imports from 1784 to 1789 are as follows:

Feb. 12 1784. An act laying a tonnage duty of 4 d. per ton on all vessels, except N. Y. coasting vessels or American vessels of under sixty tons. *Laws of N. Y.*, Chap. X, pp. 11-17.

March 22, 1784. An act imposing specific duties on a long list of

Therefore it is only to be expected that the State would be one of the storm centers of the struggle for the impost.

The political alignment on the impost was almost identical with that on the adoption of the Federal Constitution. On the one hand there were the Anti-Federalists, men whose income was derived almost wholly from the cultivation of land, who had no direct interest in trade or commerce, and who had bought no government securities. On the other were all those who would gain either by better conditions of trade, or the payment of public obligations, more than they would sacrifice from increased land taxes. As has been pointed out before, many of the great "Manor Lords" had interests of this latter type which placed them on the Federalist side. A more clean-cut division in the Legislature can in fact be made on the basis of locality than social group. The representatives of the Southern District were almost invariably favorable to the Congressional impost because of the feelings of their con-

imports, and a 2½% ad valorem duty on all non-enumerated articles. To be in force until the rising of the Legislature at their next meeting. Goods for re-export to the other States could be bonded at double duty until reshipment. *Laws of N. Y.*, Chap. X, pp. 11-17.

November 18, 1784. Act of March 22 repealed and a new one with some modifications substituted. Indefinite in duration. *Laws of N. Y.*, Chap. VII, pp. 10-15.

March 15, 1785. An act doubling the duties, i. e., 4d to 8d, for one year on all goods imported in English vessels. *Laws of N. Y.*, Chap. XIX, p. 5. Continued until May 1, 1790, by Act of Feb. 4, 1786, Chap. V, p. 7.

April 11, 1787. An act greatly increasing the number of specific articles subject to duties, and classifying the goods paying ad valorem duties into three classes, those paying 7½%, those paying 5%, and those paying 2½%. There was also a short free list. All goods produced in the United States were admitted free. Goods imported in foreign vessels had to pay an additional 25% on all specific duties, and 2½% more ad valorem. Goods could be bonded for re-export. All old acts were repealed, but if Congress should accept the impost as granted by the previous act of May 4, 1786, then this act would be void, and the old act revived. *Laws of N. Y.*, LXXXI, 144-156. It is important to note that in accordance with this act New York intended to continue levying state duties even if Congress levied an additional 5%.

stituents, if for no other reason, whereas those from the other Districts were with few exceptions opposed.

It is notable that in all the recorded discussions on the impost proposal no attempt was made to emphasize the supplementary funds as a balancing feature. The reason is not hard to discover. In New York any readily establishable supplementary funds would be just the reverse of a balance. The theory of these funds was that they should compensate the mercantile group for having trade taxed by placing additional taxes on the farmer. Whereas in New York, as explained above, and, it must be added, in probably all the other commercial States, it was the mercantile class that wanted the impost, and the farmer who was opposed. This paradoxical situation had arisen because Congress had taken the objections of the members from Rhode Island and Massachusetts too literally, even though Hamilton had pointed out at the time that these were not their real reasons.[18] As a result a system of supplementary funds was built up which tended only to obstruct the impost rather than aid it.

Despite the enactment of the State impost law of 1784, the friends of the general revenue prepared to exert strenuous efforts for the adoption of the Congressional impost in 1785. A heavy barrage of propaganda was laid down. The "Inhabitants of the City of New York" sent a lengthy petition to the Legislature, and published the same in the newspapers.[19] The New York City Chamber of Commerce sent a memorial to the Assembly pointing out that trade had not prospered under the system of State regulation, and that this in turn had depressed industry and agriculture.[20] The Legislature was flooded with private petitions of the same type.[21]

[18]See *supra,* Chap. VII, p. 190.

[19]*N. Y. Packet,* March 7, 1785.

[20]*Ibid.,* March 14, 1785. They incidentally pointed out that nothing could be done about the Barbary pirates until Congress secured some money.

[21]*Ibid.,* March 17, 1785, as reported by a spectator at one of the meetings of the Assembly who signed himself M. Dives.

The agrarians were not backward in replying to this fire. They filled the press with page after page on the danger of a Congressional revenue beyond the control of the State. Abraham Yates, the most prolific of these pamphleteers, wrote under three names in both the city and up-state papers. He attacked the power to collect the money as the most vulnerable spot in the proposal: "The power to erect judicial courts, ascertain the mode of trial, and the trying of offenders" would constitute an intolerable tyranny by Congress. He also pointed out that funding the national debt was what had started England on the road to ruin.[22] The day the Senate started debate on the impost he wrote: "The legislature which shall give the last fiat to the recommendation of Congress will sign the death warrant of American liberty."[23] It was useless to point out that Congress was only composed of men selected annually by the States. With a sure revenue once in their hands they were pictured as buying elections from corrupted Legislatures and intimidating the people in their special courts.[24]

In the Legislature the chances of the impost men were not promising. An amendment to the State impost law doubling the duties on goods brought to port in British vessels had been introduced early in the session. This was vetoed by a three-member meeting of the Council of Revision, with Clinton, R. R. Livingston, and Hobart in attendance, on the grounds that any attempt to regulate trade by one State without the concurrence of the others would produce injury to such State and might contravene the terms of the treaty of commerce being negotiated with Great Britain.[25] The House and Senate promptly overruled the Council by large majorities, even some

[22]*Political Papers,* pub. by Kollock, Albany, 1786, pp. 5-6.

[23]*N. Y. Packet,* March 17, 1785.

[24]*Political Papers,* pub. by Kollock, pp. 7 ff.

[25]Street, *Minutes of the Council of Revision,* pp. 267-268.

of the Southern Delegates disagreeing with the reasons advanced.[26]

It was felt that because of the presence of Schuyler from the Western District the impost had a better chance in the Senate than in the Assembly. March 17 the Senate started consideration of the Congressional proposal. After a month of debate in the Committee of the Whole, the bill granting the necessary powers to Congress was defeated ten to eight, only Schuyler and one other up-state Senator voting with the six from the Southern District.[27] After this defeat in the Senate the Assembly committee did not even report a bill.[28]

The Federalists now turned their attention to the next election, and on May 1 elected a strong delegation from the Southern District, but up-state the situation was hopeless.[29] Victory would have to depend on finding arguments to convert at least six up-state Assemblymen and four up-state Senators. To help in this campaign the New York Chamber of Commerce called a large meeting in June to "consider the critical situation of American trade," at which they appointed a committee of correspondence to circularize the various counties and keep in touch with the progress of the impost in other States.[30]

By the beginning of 1786 the men in Congress were convinced that there was no way of raising an immediate and adequate revenue without the impost, and this tax was now concentrated on as essential to the life of the government.[31] New York had agreed to the proposed change in the basis of apportionment in Article VIII the preceding April, five days

[26]*Jour. N. Y. Sen.*, p. 48, *Ass.*, p. 85.

[27]*Jour. N. Y. Sen.*, 1785, p. 86.

[28]*Jour. N. Y. Ass.*, 8th sess., *passim.*

[29]*N. Y. Packet,* May 2, 1785. Duer, Troup, and Sears were among those selected from New York County.

[30]*Ibid.,* June 20, 1785.

[31]*Journal Continental Congress,* IV, 614-15. Report of a five-member commission, February 2, 1786.

before the Senate defeated the impost.[32] In the middle of
February 1786 a committee reported to Congress the exact
state of the agreements to date. Delaware and North Carolina had passed acts in full conformity with the general
revenue plan. New Hampshire, Massachusetts, Connecticut,
New Jersey, Pennsylvania, Virginia, and South Carolina had
complied with the impost provisions of the plan. Rhode Island
had complied, but not in an acceptable form. Maryland had
lately complied fully with the proposal of 1781, but had not
yet acted on the one of 1783. New York and Georgia had
done nothing about the impost. The cash receipts of the
Treasury for the last fourteen months had been less than
enough to pay the civil establishment. They concluded with
the peroration referred to in chapter VIII . . . "the time
of crisis has arrived." Congress agreed to the report without
a division. Then resolutions were adopted calling on each of
the States individually for the specific actions required and
asking that all considerations except the act of April 18, 1783,
be suspended.[33]

During the spring of 1786 the various States except New
York agreed to the requests of Congress in forms which
might be considered satisfactory.[34] Therefore, the final crisis
of the Confederation must really be traced in the New York
Legislature. A bill to agree to the impost provisions of the
general revenue act was introduced in the Assembly in March,
but the real battle commenced when, on April 13, it was suc-
cessfully moved that the clause in the original bill reading,
"to be collected under such regulations as the United States in
Congress Assembled shall direct" be erased and the provisions
for collection of the State impost law of November 18, 1784,

[32]*Laws of N. Y.*, Chap. LXIII, p. 55, April 9, 1785.

[33]*Journal Continental Congress*, IV, 618-20.

[34]Printed Report of a Committee of Congress, August 1786. *Pap. Cont.
Cong.*, no. 20, I, Part II, f. 318. *Journal Continental Congress*, IV, 669-670.

be substituted.[35] This struck at the vital spot of the whole system. Unless the collectors were responsible to Congress there was no reason to suppose that the impost would be paid into the Continental Treasury any better than other requisitions. The vote on the above amendment was thirty-three to twenty-two, and clearly indicated the conflicting economic interests in the Legislature. The twenty-two nays included two Livingstons, William Duer, Gerard Bancker, and other holders of public funds, and New York City merchants. The thirty-three ayes represented the up-state farmers and their political leaders such as Vrooman and De Witt.

Two days later Duer, who had been sent to the Legislature expressly to use his magnetic and persuasive personality for securing agreement to the impost,[36] moved as another amendment that whenever Congress should devise a good and uniform means of collection New York should adopt it, providing it would not subject any citizen to being tried outside the State. This compromise amendment won no agrarian support and was lost by the same type of vote as before. The financial interests then gave up and the bill was passed without a division.[37]

When the bill reached the Senate Schuyler, the General in charge of the security holders, and strong government interests, moved that the collection clause be struck out and the words "paid under such regulations as . . . Congress shall direct . . ." be inserted. The amendment was defeated ten to six, by the same alignment as in the House. Most of the names of the six senators who voted aye will be recognized by any student of the general history of this period.

[35]N. Y. Ass. Jour., 9th sess. p. 134. The clause of the act of November 18, 1784, reads in part "Res. that the present Collector and all other Officers of the Customs shall hold and exercise their respective offices until they shall be reappointed or until other persons shall be appointed" by the Governor. Laws of N. Y., Chap. VII, pp. 10-15.

[36]S. J. Davis, op. cit., p. 124.

[37]N. Y. Ass. Jour., pp. 137-38.

They were: William Floyd, Lewis Morris, Nicholas Roosevelt, Philip Schuyler, Ezra L'Hommedieu, and William Stoutenburgh.[38] Schuyler then tried to get the Senate to agree to a clause giving Congress the right to remove any Collector at its pleasure, and if the vacancy were not filled by the Governor within a month to appoint a new one. This proposal was lost eleven to five, Stoutenburgh having gone over to the opposition. The only alteration made in the end was the insertion of a clause that the monies paid to Congress should be the equal of gold or silver; by a vote of nine to seven.[39] The act as finally passed contained the following provisions:

1. The State granted to the United States the required duties on imports to be levied and collected, and applied as prescribed in this act.

2. The collection was to be *in the manner designated in the State impost Act* of November 18, 1784,[40] the Collector to render an account from time to time as required by Congress.

3. The Collectors were to pay the whole amount collected to Congress less a deduction for salaries not exceeding eight per cent.

4. Congress was to have the power to proceed against delinquent Collectors in the New York Courts, and collect all fines or penalties arising from such actions.

5. All monies arising from the act were to be applied to the war debt, and an annual account was to be sent to the Governor who would lay it before the Legislature. The account must contain the money arising from each type of duty, the total from each State and the disposition thereof. If this should not be done the Legislature reserved the right to repeal the act.

6. The act was to go into effect for twenty-five years from the time when Congress should notify the State that all the

[38]*Ibid.*, Senate, p. 92.
[39]*Ibid.*, p. 93.
[40]That is, by collectors appointed by and responsible to the State.

other States had agreed acceptably, unless the war debt was discharged before this time. All other acts laying duties on imports were to be suspended while this act was in force.[41]

THE FINAL DEFEAT

On July 27 the committee of Congress to whom the Act of New York had been referred made its report. After reviewing the provisions of the act they proposed that Congress be "Resolved: That the Act of the State of New York . . . so essentially varies from the system of impost recommended by Congress that the act is not a compliance with the same." This resolution was postponed, at the request of the New York Delegates.[42] At the same time a committee was appointed to draft an ordinance for collecting the duties as soon as New York should agree, and Pennsylvania and Delaware should repeal their clauses suspending operation until the supplementary funds were agreed to.[43] After some debate a resolution was passed calling upon the Governor of New York immediately to convene the State Legislature in order to reconsider its agreement to the impost. All the Delegates except those from New York voted in favor of the resolution.[44]

Governor Clinton answered this resolution without delay. He refused to convene the Legislature because the Constitution gave him power to do so only on extraordinary occasions, and as the Legislature had already considered this matter repeatedly and passed on it at their last meeting this could not be regarded as such an occasion. The letter was exceedingly polite and apologetic in tone.[45] From the legal standpoint Clinton was unquestionably within his rights in exercising his discretion, and it is highly probable that a meeting of the Legislature would have been of no use.

[41]*Laws of N. Y.*, Chap. LXI, pp. 117-119, May 4, 1786.
[42]*Journal Continental Congress*, IV, 669-670.
[43]*Ibid.*, IV, 671.
[44]*Ibid.*, IV, 681-682, August 11, 1786.
[45]*Pap. Cont. Cong.*, no. 67, II, ff. 539-542.

The committee to whom Clinton's reply was referred proposed three resolutions, which were adopted August 22. The first declared the New York Act to be inadequate; the second, that since New York was the only State that had not agreed, the occasion was extraordinary, and that Congress demanded that the Legislature be convened; the third, that it be recommended to the executive to convene the Legislature.[46]

Clinton replied in a letter admonishing and reproachful, but still dignified and polite in tone. He said: "I cannot discover a single matter stated in the Report on which the present Resolutions are founded, but such as were fully within the knowledge of the Legislature before, and at the time when they adjourned their last meeting. . . . I conceive it would be criminal to yield up my judgment from motives of complaissance. I have the Honor . . . etc."[47]

The deliberate wrecking of the Confederation by one who believed so strongly in State sovereignty seems shortsighted in the light of later events, but we must remember that the Anti-Federalists at the time did not believe that any movement for a stronger government could succeed. Representing the feelings of the great mass of the American people, they felt secure in defying the champions of the small mercantile class, and even the historian must still be somewhat amazed at the final success of the movement for the Constitution.

Clinton's letter really ended the hope of saving the Confederation without a general convention, but the strong government men had, at least, a chance to protest at the opening of the next session of the Legislature. Hamilton and two others in the Assembly prepared the reply to the Governor's address, and omitted all mention of his explanation regarding

[46] *Journal Continental Congress,* IV, 686-687.

[47] *Pap. Cont. Cong.,* no. 67, II, 547-50. It is interesting to note that at no time between June and September 1786 was any mention made in the *Independent Journal* or the *New York Packet* of these vital political questions. (This statement should be qualified in so far as the available files are not absolutely complete.)

the calling of a special session.[48] The followers of the Governor immediately proposed an amendment approving the Governor's actions.[49] This gave Hamilton the opportunity to make a powerful speech condemning the Governor's reasoning. He regretted that Congress had made the call for the special session, in the first place, as it placed the Governor in a bad situation. If he refused to comply Congress lost dignity, but if he assented the Legislature would assemble in a bad humor because of being called from home at that season. In the next place he regretted the Governor's flat refusal when he might easily have had a conference with Congress, and discussed the matter. Then he launched his main attack. While the precise meaning of ordinary and extraordinary was a matter of opinion, the only workable rule would seem to be that ordinary meant the normal routine details of State administration. The earnest call of Congress on "a matter of great national magnitude" must be an extraordinary event. In fact for national safety it must be possible for Congress to have the State Legislatures convened without stating specific reasons. The fact that the last Legislature had considered the matter was not a valid argument. The new Legislature was a different body having a large proportion of new members. Nor had the members of the last Legislature known that their act would not be acceptable to Congress. He did not deny that the Governor had a right to use discretion in the matter, but he did claim that in basing his refusal to act on constitutional impediments he was clearly wrong, and hence his course should not be approved by the House.[50] Despite the eloquence of Hamilton the amendment was adopted by a vote of thirty-six to nine, an indication of what would have happened had a special session met.[51] The Senate agreed to a reply approving the Governor's actions without debate.[52]

[48]*Jour. N. Y. Ass.*, 10th sess., pp. 7 & 9.
[49]*Ibid.*, 10th sess., pp. 15.
[50]*Works of Alexander Hamilton*, Const. Ed., VIII, 5-17.
[51]*Jour. of N. Y. Ass.*, 10th sess., p. 16.
[52]*Jour. of N. Y. Sen.*, 10th sess., p. 8.

The strong government men were not ready to give up, however, without one last effort. Again a law complying with the impost recommendation was introduced in the Assembly, and the argument was resumed in the newspapers at greater length than ever before. "Cimon" argues that the impost involved "in its consequences, perhaps the fate of this new empire." He attacked such men as "Rough Hewer" (Abraham Yates, Jr.) as placing their selfish interests before the good of the community, and the whole discussion took on an increasingly personal tone.[53]

"Candidus" pointed out that since the State had passed the act of 1786 the whole argument now turned upon the matter of collection, and therefore had no bearing upon the question of shifting the burden of taxes.[54] "A Farmer" argued that Congress might at least have tried the impost under a system of State collection, before asking for this power.[55] "Patroticus" wrote a long indictment of the whole policy of the up-state politicians. To avoid paying taxes they had taxed trade, sold the forfeited estates at a fraction of their real value, and issued paper money to help pay off their obligations in a depreciated medium. Now they were afraid of being forced to assume finally some of their just burden by granting Congress the impost.[56]

February 15th Hamilton made a great plea for the impost before the Committee of the Whole. He started with a long analysis of the power and situation of Congress, and the absurdity of thinking it would be a menace to the State. Aside from all else the States might always rely on "the natural imbecility of federal government." Jealousy of the federal power was really the greatest danger to the Confederation. Wars or quarrels with each other were the greatest dangers to the liberties of the States. It was only by trusting their own

[53] *N. Y. Daily Advertiser*, Jan. 31, 1787.
[54] *Ibid.*, Feb. 6, 1787.
[55] *Ibid.*, March 3, 1787.
[56] *Ibid.*, Feb. 13, 1787.

representatives in Congress that they could achieve the benefits of union.[57]

After listening to the unanswerable logic of Hamilton supported by the eloquence of several others, the majority quietly defeated the proposal by striking out the vital clauses, thirty-eight to nineteen.[58] It was said that "the impost was strangled by a band of mutes."[59]

Two days later Hamilton moved for instructions to the Delegates in Congress to have that body summon a convention to revise the Articles of Confederation by a majority vote, and render them adequate to the government of the nation.[60] This resolution passed the House but met stern opposition in the Senate. The up-state or Clintonian leaders, John Haring and Abraham Yates, Jr., in this branch were among the ablest of their party. The Federalists led by Schuyler and L'Hommedieu finally prevailed, however, and the resolution passed by a margin of one vote.[61] The fact that there were many of the refugees from Shay's rebellion in the State who might cause trouble may have had considerable influence in getting this resolution through both houses. It served to revive some of the old wartime dependence on the help of Congress.[62] The same public alarm was taken advantage of in pushing through Congress on February 21 resolutions for the calling of a convention similar to those drawn up at Annapolis the preceding fall.

A few days later Hamilton in the Assembly and Schuyler in the Senate moved that five Delegates be jointly elected by

[57]Hamilton, *History of the Republic,* III, 222-227. Published in full in the *N. Y. Daily Advertiser,* Feb. 26, 1787.

[58]*Jour. N. Y. Ass.,* 10th sess., p. 52.

[59]Hamilton, *op. cit.,* p. 228.

[60]*Ibid.,* 10th sess., p. 55. Miner, C. E., *The Ratification of the Federal Constitution in New York,* has a detailed account of these actions.

[61]*Jour. N. Y. Sen.,* 10th sess., pp. 35. February 20, 1787.

[62]This theory is advanced by J. C. Hamilton, *op. cit.,* p. 240.

the two houses to represent the State.[63] In both houses the Clintonians amended the number from five to three before agreeing to the motions.[64] The majority displayed a degree of magnanimity in the election of delegates, allowing what might be termed proportional representation to the minority. As a result a delegation was nominated, in both houses, composed of John Lansing and Abraham Yates, Jr.—two Clinton men—and Hamilton.* On May 6 they were elected without a division by a joint meeting of both houses.[65] Hamilton tried until the end of the session to have five men sent, and proposed the names of R. R. Livingston, Egbert Benson, James Duane, and John Jay as a list from which to choose two additional delegates. It is a great tribute to the energy and persuasive power of Hamilton that he actually won the Assembly over to his plan, but the Clintonians in the Senate defeated it.[66]

Lansing and Yates ceased attending the meetings of the Federal Convention in July when the success of the strong government men seemed assured. This left New York without a vote in the final proceedings although Hamilton helped as an individual.

[63] *Jour. N. Y. Ass.,* 10th sess., p. 68, February 26, 1787. *Jour. N. Y. Sen.,* 10th sess., p. 44, February 28, 1787.

[64] *Jour. N. Y. Ass.,* 10th sess., p. 71. *Jour. N. Y. Sen.,* 10th sess, p. 45.

[65] *Jour. N. Y. Ass.,* 10th sess., p. 82 f.

[66] *Jour. N. Y. Ass.,* 10th sess., pp. 165, 166, April 16, 1787. *Jour. N. Y. Sen.,* 10th sess., p. 95, April 18, 1787.

CONCLUSION

THIS study of the period from 1775 to 1788 has suggested the formulation of some new generalizations and the questioning of some established ones.

The patent weakness of the governmental machinery set up by the Continental Congress has obscured the fact that the states were pitifully weak internally. The good will of their constituents was so sedulously cultivated by the elected minor officials that the enforcement of the laws often came to a complete standstill. The Confederation functioned better in the financial relations between Congress and the New York Legislature than the State Government did in the financial relations between the Legislature and the people.

There can be no doubt in the mind of anyone who has examined the political situation in New York that in this State, at least, the movement for the Federal Constitution was primarily a financial one. It was the desire of the security holders to provide for the repayment of the public debt, rather than an interest in strengthening the American commercial or diplomatic position that motivated the followers of Hamilton and Schuyler. The five per cent impost plan of 1783 was the crucial effort of the security holders to bolster up the credit of the Continental Government, and its final defeat in the New York Legislature sounded the death knell of the Confederation.[1]

New York, when we consider the difficulties under which it labored, made greater financial efforts than any other State. The New York opposition to a stronger central government was not based as much on a fear of the volume of taxation as on the type of taxes proposed, and the collection of them by federal agents.

[1]Neither this plan nor the proposals of 1784 to give Congress the power to regulate commerce took the form of an amendment to the Articles of Confederation. See note, p. 135 for the proof of this statement.

The powerful anti-Tory sentiment in the State was a natural result of the strength and activity of the Tories during the war. The confiscation of the large Tory estates also appealed to a people who desired to avoid taxation. It does not appear that debts owed to British merchants were an important factor in the New York situation.

New York played a more influential rôle in the Western land cessions than has been realized. The New York claim was as firmly advanced as those of the other States, and its cession set an important precedent that paved the way for the ratification of the Articles of Confederation.

There was no great gain in democracy within the State as a result of the Revolution. The franchise was not essentially altered in the new Constitution. The great landlords and merchants still kept control of affairs in the State. Many of the Loyalist holdings which were broken up and sold found their way into the hands of other large landholders. The State land system was administered in favor of the large grantees just as the British had been. All in all, the Revolution may be said to have had a comparatively small social effect in New York.

APPENDIX A

REQUISITIONS AND TAXES
1775-1780

Congressional Requisitions				*New York State Taxes*	
Date	Total Amount	Medium	N. Y. Quota	Amount of Tax	Date
ιn. 4, 1777	As much as Convenient[1]	Continental Currency	As much as Convenient		
΄ov. 1777	$5,000,000[2]	"	$200,000	See Note[1]	Mar. 28, 1778
ιn. 2, 1779	15,000,000[3]	"	800,000		
ιn. 2, 1779	6,000,000 annually[4]	"	319,998*	See Note[2]	Mar. 2, 1779
΄ay 21, 1779	45,000,000[5]	"	2,400,000		
ct. 6, 1779	15,000,000[6]	"	800,000	2,500,000[3]	Oct. 23, 1779
΄ar. 18, 1780	10,000,000[7]	"	533,333*	5,000,000[4]	Mar. 6, 1780
ιug. 26, 1780	3,000,000[8]	Specie	159,999*	2,500,000[5]	June 15, 1780
				150,000[6]	Oct. 10, 1780

our. Cont. Cong. VII, p. 37.

"   "   " IX, p. 955.

"   "   " XIII, p. 21-23.

For eighteen years from and after the ear 1779."

Before Jan. 1, 1780. *Ibid.* XIV, p. 614 : 616.

Payable February to October 1780. *bid.* XV, p. 1147f.

Payable at once. Period of $15,000,000 monthly payments extended to April 781. *Ibid.* XVI, p. 261-269.

bid. XVII, p. 782-785.

Estimated.

[1] 3d. per £ on Land, 1½d. on personal property and 50£ per 1000 on money gained by trade since Sept. 12, 1776. *Laws,* Chap. XVII, p. 19f.

[2] 1s. per £ on land, 6d. per £ on personal property. *Laws,* Chap. XVI, p. 51.

[3] *Laws,* Chap. XXVII.

[4] *Laws,* Chap. XLVII, p. 112f.

[5] *Laws,* Chap. XLIV, p. 131f. Old Continental currency.

[6] *Laws,* Chap. XVI, p. 163. Suspended in its operation by Chap. XLIII, p. 184, 1781; and repealed by Chap. V, p. 208, 1782.

APPENDIX B

REQUISITIONS AND TAXES
1781-1784

Date	*Requisitions* Sum called for			N. Y. State Taxes Date	
of Act	Total	Specie	Indents	of Act	Amount
Jan. 15, '81	$879,342[1]	$77,589			
Mar. 16, '81	1,500,000[2]	43,200.75		June 30, '81	$27,500[1]
Oct. 30, '81	8,000,000[3]	373,598		Nov. 20, '81	62,500[2]
Sept. 4, '82	1,200,000[4]	54,000		Apr. 11, '82	90,000[3]
Oct. 16, '82	2,000,000[5]	90,000		July 22, '82	45,000[4]
Apr. 27, '84	(2,670,997.98)[6]	(110,800.57)	(36,933.52)	Mar. 25, '83	105,250[5]
				May 6, '84	(250,000)[6]

[1] An emergency requisition to pay the troops. *Jour. Cont. Cong.*, XIX, 58-61.

[2] Quarterly starting June 1, 1781. In discharge of this requisition the new Continental bills were to be considered as equivalent to specie. Interest would be paid on payments made before due.

[3] Superceding the previous requisition. To be paid in during 1782. *Ibid.*, XXI, 1087, 1088, and 1090.

[4] Payable at once. Land and poll taxes recommended to the states. Eight states including N. Y. tried unsuccessfully to get their quotas reduced. *Ibid.*, XXIII, 545, 564-571.

[5] Payable during 1783. *Ibid.*, XXIII, 659.

[6] To be counted as equalling, together with payments already made, one half of the $8,000,000 quota of Oct. 30, 1781. *Ibid.*, 1823 ed. IV, p. 386-389, and 390-391. This sum is erroneously stated as in $4,000,000 in Bolles, *Financial History*, p. 322.

[1] *Laws of N. Y.*, Cha LVII, p. 198.

[2] Payable in wheat at si shillings a bushel. *Ibid* Chap. X, p. 210.

[3] Payable in two install ments, June 1st and Octo ber 1st in specie or whea at six shillings per bushe *Ibid.*, Chap. XXXVII, ﹐ 242.

[4] Payable in bank notes c specie. A $25,000 loan wa also authorized to be pai to the Continental Treas urer, or expended for an exigencies that might arise. *Ibid.*, Chap. VI, ﹐ 260.

[5] $87,500 to be paid t the Superintendent of Fi nance. The tax was pay able only in specie or th notes of the Bank of th U. S. *Ibid.*, Chap. XLIX pp. 290-299.

[6] A special tax on th southern counties whic had not paid state taxe during the war. To b expended for state pur poses. Vetoed by th Council of Revision an speedily repassed. *Ibid* Chap. LVIII, p. 83.

1785-1788

Requisitions

Date of Act	Sum Called for Total	N. Y. Quota* Specie	Indents
Sept. 27, '85	$3,000,000[1]	$85,495	$170,991.00
Aug. 2, '86	3,777,062[2]	185,567	137,434.00
Oct. 21, '86	(500,000)[3]	(45,368)	
Oct. 11, '87	1,700,407[4]		145,555.00
Aug. 20, '88	1,686,541.1%0[5]		144,185.59

N. Y. State Taxes*

Date of Act	Amount of Tax	Orders to State Treasurer to Pay Money to U. S. Treasurer Date	Amount
Mar. 29, '86	$112,500[1]	Apr. 4, '85	$147,734.%0[4] (¾ in specie)
Apr. 11, '87	112,500[2]	Apr. 28, '86	85,495 spec.[5] / 170,991 ind.
Mar. 19, '88	60,000[3]	Apr. 13, '87	185,567 spec.[6] / 137,434 ind.
		Feb. 2, '89	24,583.38%0[7]

[1] This was to be considered as ¾ of the remainder of the old $8,000,000 quota of 1781. *Journal Continental Congress,* IV, 587-89.

[2] In response to the demands of South Carolina the first million dollars of this quota was regarded as the final payment on the quota of 1781. *Ibid.,* IV, 674-676.

[3] A special emergency requisition to be paid before June 1787 for the support of the army. In May 1787 it was resolved to credit all payments made on this quota to the balances due on those of 1784, 85 and 86. *Ibid.,* IV, 714-15, & 741.

[4] $1,309,391.04%0 in specie was also needed but for this sum the states were asked to pay up their deficiencies on previous quotas. *Ibid.,* IV, 794-95.

[5] It was still planned to collect specie in the form of arrears on former requisitions. *Ibid.,* IV, 851-54.

* For table of N. Y. State payments made to the U. S. Treasury see Appendix D.

[1] Payable in gold, silver, or new bills of credit. *Laws of N. Y.,* Chap. XVI, pp. 101-105.

[2] In this act Hamilton tried to substitute a general assessment for the county quota system but was defeated by the Clinton faction in the house 31 to 21 (practically the same vote that defeated the impost). *N. Y. Ass. Jour.,* 10th sess., p. 107. *Laws of N. Y.,* Chap. LXXVII, p. 140.

[3] *Ibid.,* Chap. LXXXVI, p. 189.

[4] This was in payment of the requisition of April 27, 1784. Reference should be made to the table of state payments, Appendix D, to see how well these orders were executed *Laws of N. Y.,* Chap. LIII, p. 46.

[5] In payment of requisition of Sept. 27, 1785. *Ibid.,* Chap. LXVIII, pp. 93-95.

[6] In payment of the requisition of August 2, 1786. A deduction of $29,363.24%0 was made for amounts expended on invalid pensions, etc. *Ibid.,* Chap. LXXXIII, p. 162.

[7] In full settlement of all specie requisitions. *Ibid.,* Chap. XIX, p. 22.

APPENDIX D

PAYMENTS MADE BY NEW YORK TO THE CONTINENTAL LOAN OFFICERS BETWEEN OCTOBER 1, 1784 AND APRIL 1, 1788[1]

Period	Specie	Indents
10/1/84—12/31/84	$2,774.20	None
1/1/85— 3/31/85	None	"
4/1/84— 6/30–85	20,000.00	"
7/1/85— 9/30/85	51,000.00	"
10/1/85—13/31/85	39,800.51	"
1/1/86— 3/31/86	None	"
4/1/86— 6–30/86	10,212.59	"
7/1/86— 9/30/86	11,688.73	"
10/1/86—12/31/86	8,542.15	"
1/1/87— 3/31/87	13,760.35	"
4/1/87— 6/30–87	6,000.00	36,933.48
7/1/87— 9/30–87	37,307.44	165,995.00
10/1/87—12/31/87	15,869.80	196.429.60
1/1/88— 3/31/88	None	None
Totals	$269,155.20	$399,358.19

[1]*Pap. Cont. Cong.,* no. 141, I and II, *passim,* collected from the scattered quarterly reports. The difference between the specie total of $269,155.20 in the table and the $249,170²%₀ reported as paid in to the Board of Treasury is probably due to the fact that John Cochran, the last N. Y. Continental Loan Officer still had $14,166.85 in his hands, and Benjamin Tillotson, his predecessor, still had $1,075.31. Abraham Yates who had preceded Tillotson probably had a little also. All of which forms an interesting example of the laxness of government finance.

See Appendix E for Condensed Treasury balance sheets 1784-1787.

Appendix E

A CONDENSED ACCOUNT OF STATE EXPENDITURES AND RECEIPTS 1784-1787 INCLUSIVE

From the Report of George Banker to the Legislature January 16, 1788
New York Assembly Journal 11 ses. pp. 14 ff.

January 1, 1787—September 20, 1785

Expenditures		Receipts	
To invalid pensioners	£3,483[1]	Balance brought forward	£1,515[1]
To deranged officers	1,053	Received on arrears of taxes.	5,993
For supplies furnished during the war	1,107	Commissioners of Sequestration	141
Civil list	15,187	Commissioners of Forfeiture Southern district	9,891
To Robert Morris	2,766	Collector of Customs	20,356
To N. Y. Line for pay	1,048	Vendue masters, duty on their sales	1,392
To Clothing commissioners	1,214	A debt collected	15
Miscellaneous	5,367		
Balance in treasury	8,081		
Totals	£39,306		£39,306

September 21, 1784—December 31, 1785

Expenditures		Receipts	
To Continental Treasury for requisitions of 27 & 28, April 1784	£44,320[1]	Balance brought forward....	£8,801[1]
To ditto on account of former requisition	924	Special tax on the Southern counties May 6, 1784	62,670
Civil List	18,210	Arrears of taxes	3,946
Money borrowed and goods purchased on Long Island during the war	44,514	Customs collector of New York City	90,431
Invalid pensions	6,640	Customs collector of Sag Harbor	258
To Commissioners of Forfeiture	6,628	Commissioner of Forfeiture Southern District	4,500
To Commissioners of Conspiracy	3,560	Commissioner of Forfeiture Southern District	8,051
New York Line for pay	15,956	Vendue Masters, duty on their sales	5,876
To Commissioners of Indian Affairs	6,063	Commissioners of Sequestration	423
Stationery and printing	3,865	Old Loan-Officers	247
Goods & property destroyed during the war	20,017		
To New York Custom House officers	3,261		
Miscellaneous	4,370		
[1]Balance in the treasury	6,106		
Totals	£184,486		£184,486

[1]Shillings and pence omitted.

TREASURY RECEIPTS AND EXPENDITURES (ABRIDGED)

January 1, 1786 to December 31, 1786 inclusive

Expenditures		*Receipts*	
Deranged officers	£1,376[1]	Balance in Treasury	£6,106[1]
War supplies	3,027	Cash from tax of 5/6/84...	3,485
Civil list (excluding customs collectors and special commissions)	15,665	Vendue masters	2,581
		Customs Collector of N. Y. C.	32,749
Continental money purchased	7,565	Customs Collector of Sag Harbor	103
Paper money delivered to Loan Officers	150,000	From forfeited property ...	37
Invalid pensions	5,519	Arrears of taxes	1,720
Miscellaneous	19,673	Paper money issued	200,000
Balance in Treasury	46,173	Old Loan Officers	2,237
		Seizure of flour	15
Totals	249,038[1]		249,038[1]

January 1, 1787 to December 31, 1787 inclusive

Expenditures		*Receipts*	
To persons whose property was sold and forfeited ...	£4,970[1]	Balance in Treasury	£46,173[1]
For services and supplies during the war	3,751	Vendue masters	2,622
		N. Y. Customs Collections..	48,023
To Commissioners of Forfeiture	8,622	Sag Harbor Customs Collections	81
To Continental Treasurer on requisition of Sept. 27, 1785	22,322	Arrears of taxes	275
Civil list	14,490	Tax of May 29, 1786	39,856
Invalid pensions and arrears	19,305	Interest on paper emitted and loaned in 1786	6,554
Redemption of paper emitted 1780	8,707	Commissioners of Forfeiture for the Southern District.	5,647
1/5 interest on public securities loaned to the state ...	38,098		
Miscellaneous	23,495		
Balance in treasury	11,519		
Totals	149,279[1]		149,279[1]

[1]Shillings and pence omitted.

Appendix F

THE RECEIPTS OF THE CONTINENTAL LOAN OFFICES FOR THE WHOLE PERIOD, IN "OLD" CONTINENTAL CURRENCY

N. H.	....	$972,700	Del.	$537,000
Mass.	....	8,092,907	Md.	3,993,300
R. I.	....	1,866,800	Va.	2,957,800
Conn.	....	4,293,200	N. C.	1,209,800
N. Y.	....	3,509,800	S. C.	3,846,405
N. J.	....	4,549,900	Ga.	951,000
Pa.	....	28,522,500		

From *Pap. Cont. Cong.*, no. 12, f. 58.

Appendix G

BALANCE SHEET OF CONGRESS TO JANUARY 1, 1789[1]

Interest on Foreign Debt accrued prior to 1784 .... $265,548

Total interest due on Foreign Debt to 1788 inc. .... 2,442,101[2]

Portions of Principal of the Debt due during 1788 925,927

Expenses for Foreign, Civil, Military, Indian, Invalid, and Geographers service, plus contingencies through the year 1788 2,668,889

Total $6,036,917

Sums actually paid $3,168,442

Parts unpaid:
	Foreign interest	...................$1,521,116
Foreign Principal	....	925,925
Debts of Gov. Depts.	....	421,432

Total remaining due $2,868,474

Specie Requisitions since Jan. 1, 1784................$5,173,673

Loans contracted since   "   "   " 1,600,000

Still due from the States $3,292,594

Due from Holland on Loan 71,093

"   "   Jones' Captures 20,772

Total due $3,384,459

Surplus of Total Expected Receipts above Expenditures 854,625

[1]*Journals of Congress,* IV, 851-852.

[2]Cents or ninetieths have been omitted.

APPENDIX H

NEW YORK STATE DEBT IN 1790[1]

Costs of loan of 1786	£111	13	3
" ". " " "	741	6	0
Houses bought in 1780	904	5	0
For depreciation of pay to August 1780	54,520	1	7
Army pay for 1780	17,972		
Pensions for Officers	8,104	8	2
Pay for levies of militia	42,871	4	3
Received on loan for U. S. April 18, 1786	523,848	5	1
For four fifths of interest due on this loan	105,669	9	8
Claims on forfeited estates	25,897	8	10
Bills of credit issued June 30, 1780	3,612	16	0
Miscellaneous	1,047		
Demands against forfeited estates	41,017	12	5
Total interest charges	206,297	15	0
Total debt £1,032,616		2	0
Due from U. S. Treasurer for loan	565,586		
Balance £467,030		2	0
or......$1,167,575			

[1]*American State Papers*, Finance, I, 28-30.

Appendix I

MISCELLANEOUS FIGURES FROM *AMERICAN STATE PAPERS, FINANCE,* VOL. I

Monies of every kind, reduced to specie value, which were received from or paid to the State by Congress, from the beginning of the Revolution to April 23, 1790.

Paid to New York. . $622,803.06   Received from New York. . $1,545,889.45.

Only Massachusetts and Virginia had a large net balance. p. 53.

New York stood next to Massachusetts in the balance due to the State after pro-rating the expenses of the war on the basis of representation in Congress in 1790. New York had $21,000 credit. p. 26.

New York owed $45,902.40.4 in specie and $289,740.57 on indents in April 1790, on all quotas since October 30, 1781. This constituted the best record of any State. pp. 56-57.

Appendix J

TIME OF LEGISLATIVE SESSIONS AND MEETINGS

Session	Meeting	From		To	
1	1	February	6	June	30, 1788
2	1	October	13	November	11, 1788
	2	February	17	March	13, 1799
3	1	September	4	October	25, 1799
	2	February	9	March	13, 1780
	3	June	14	July	1, 1780
4	1	September	21	October	10, 1780
	2	February	21	March	31, 1781
	3	June	24	July	4, 1781
5	1	November	6	November	22, 1781
	2	March	20	April	6, 1782
6	1	July	12	July	25, 1782
	2	February	14	March	27, 1783
7	1	February	12	May	12, 1784
8	1	November	11	November	29, 1784
	2	February	12	April	27, 1785
9	1	January	31	May	5, 1786
10	1	January	26	April	21, 1787
11	1	February	6	March	22, 1788
12	1	January	5	March	3, 1789

BIBLIOGRAPHY

GUIDES

Bancroft, George, *Chronological Index to the American Correspondence in the Bancroft Collection, 1742-1789.* 2 vols. in Manuscript in the New York Public Library.

Beer, William, *Checklist of American Periodicals, 1741-1800,* in *Proceedings of the American Antiquarian Society,* New Series, 1917-1922, Worcester, 1917-1922.

Bowker, R. R., *State Publications,* 4 vols., New York, 1899-1908.

Brigham, C. S., American Newspapers, 1690-1820 in *Proceedings of the American Antiquarian Society,* New Series, Vols., 23-34, Worcester, 1913-1925.

Congress, Library of, *Monthly List of State Publications, 1910-25,* 16 vols., Washington, 1910-26.

De Puy, H. F., *A Bibliography of the English Colonial Treaties with the American Indians,* New York, 1917.

Green, E. B. and Morris, R. B., *A Guide to the Principal Sources for Early American History in the City of New York,* New York, 1929.

Griffin, A. P. C., *Index to Articles in Historical Collections Relating to New York Colony and State,* Boston, 1887.

Hasse, A. R., Materials for a Bibliography of the Archives of the Thirteen Original States in *Annual Report of the American Historical Association for 1906,* Vol. II, pp. 239-572.

Hasse, A. R., References to Documents, Reports and Other Papers in the New York Public Library Relating to the Boundaries of the State of New York. *New York Public Library Bulletin,* Vol. IV, pp. 359-378, New York, 1900.

Henckels, S. V., *The Bibliographers Manual of American History* (State, Territory, Town, and County), 4 vols. and Index, Philadelphia, 1907-1910.

Hickox, J. H., *A Bibliography of the Writings of Franklin B. Hough*, Washington, 1886.

Jewett, A. J., Official Publications of the State of New York Relating to its History as a Colony and State, in *New York State Library Bulletin, Bibliography*, Vol. 59, 1917.

New York State Library Bulletin, History No. 3, Albany, 1899. Annotated List of the Principal Manuscripts in the New York State Library, edited by G. R. Howell and C. A. Flagg.

Catalogue of the New York (State) Library (1856) of Maps, Manuscripts, etc., Albany, 1857.

Catalogue of the General Library, 1855, Albany, 1856.

Palsitts, V. H., *Calendar of Manuscripts in the New York Public Library*, 1900, New York, 1900.

Palsitts, V. H., *Calendar of Additional Manuscripts in the New York Public Library, 1900-14*, New York, 1914.

Society of Colonial Dames of New York, *Catalogue of the Genealogical and Historical Library of the Colonial Dames of New York*, New York, 1912.

United States Rolls and Library Bureau Bulletin No. 1, 1893, Catalogue of the *Papers of the Continental Congress*.

University of the State of New York, Albany, 1916: *A List of Books Relating to the History of the State of New York.*

MANUSCRIPT SOURCES

American Correspondence, 3 vols., New York Public Library.

Index to the American Correspondence, Bancroft, 2 vols., New York Public Library.

American Papers, 1779-1781, New York Public Library.

Articles of Agreement, Box 9, D. S. Pennsylvania Historical Society.

Bibliography

Bayard Campbell, Pearsall, *Correspondence and Accounts*, New York Public Library.

Continental Congress, Papers, Library of Congress.

Clinton Papers, New York Historical Society.

Clinton Papers, New York State Library (largely destroyed by fire in 1911).

Dreer Collection, Soldiers of the Revolution, Pennsylvania Historical Society.

Duane Papers, New York Historical Society.

Duer and Scioto Papers, New York Historical Society.

Etting Papers, Pennsylvania Historical Society.

Etting Papers, Bank of the United States, Pennsylvania Historical Society.

Etting Papers, The Ohio Company, 2 vols., Pennsylvania Historical Society.

Gratz Papers—The Ohio Company, and General Collection, Pennsylvania Historical Society.

Hooe, Stone & Co. *Account Books*, New York Public Library.

Hart Collection—Morris Correspondence, Pennsylvania Historical Society.

Jay Papers, New York Historical Society.

Letters of Members of the Old Congress, 5 vols., Pennsylvania Historical Society.

Letters of Members of the Federal Convention, Pennsylvania Historical Society.

Livingston Papers—Bancroft Transcript, 2 vols., New York Public Library.

Livingston, Philip Van B., *Treasury Book of Entries, 1775-78*, New York Historical Society.

Lansing, Family Papers, New York State Library.

Lamb Papers, New York Historical Society.

Morgan Lewis Papers, New York State Library.

Miscellaneous Papers, New York Historical Society.

Livingston Papers, Miscellaneous, 2 vols., New York Public Library.

Letters of George Mason—Transcript 1857, New York Public Library.

Miscellaneous Letters, from general MSS catalogue, New York State Library.

McKean Papers, Vol. II, Pennsylvania Historical Society.

Samuel Osgood Papers, New York Historical Society.

Peters Papers, Pennsylvania Historical Society.

Schuyler Papers, New York Public Library, including letters to and from General Schuyler 1776-1788, and letters on *Land and Indian Affairs*. A Calendar made in 1851.

Philip Schuyler Papers, 1773-1788, New York State Library.

Samuel Wharton Papers, American Philosophical Society.

Taylor Cooper Papers, New York Public Library.

Treasury Records of Gerard Bancker (largely destroyed by fire), New York State Library.

Van Rensselaer Papers, 1774-1795, New York State Library.

Van Schaick Papers in the Gansevort-Lansing Collection, New York Public Library.

Wharton Papers, Pennsylvania Historical Society.
    Case 23. Letter Book of Thomas Wharton.
    Case 27. Copies of the Deeds of the Indiana Co.

Yates Papers, New York Public Library.

PUBLIC DOCUMENTS

American State Papers, Finance, 5 vols., Washington, 1832.

American Congress, Journals of the, 1774-1788, 4 vols., Washington, 1823.

BIBLIOGRAPHY

Continental Congress, Journals of the, ed. by W. C. Ford and Gaillard Hunt, 25 vols., Washington, 1904-22.

Elliott, Jonathan, *Debates in the Several State Conventions on the Adoption of the Federal Constitution,* 2d ed., Washington, 1836.

Force, Peter, *American Archives,* 9 vols., Washington, 1837-53.

French Foreign Office Correspondence, ed. by A. F. Doughty. *Report of the Public Archives of Canada, 1913,* Ottawa, 1914.

Haldimand Papers, Catalogue, ed. by D. Brymer, *Rep. Pub. Arch. of Canada,* 1885-1889.

Hough, Franklin B., *Proceedings of the Commissioners of Indian Affairs,* Albany, 1861; also comprises vols. 9 and 10 of *Munsell's Historical Series.*

Hough, Franklin B., *Proceedings of a Convention of Delegates from Several of the New England States at Boston, in 1780,* Albany, 1867.

Hough, Franklin B., *New York Civil List from 1777,* Albany, 1860.

Lincoln, Charles Z., *Messages of the Governors,* 10 vols., Albany, 1909.

Maryland, Archives of, 32 vols., Baltimore, 1883-1912.

New York, Colonial Laws, 1664-1775, 5 vols., Albany, 1894-96.

New York State, Archives, 1 vol., Pub. by Board of Regents, Albany, 1887.

New York State, Chamber of Commerce, *Colonial Records, 1768-1784,* ed. J. A. Stevens, New York, 1867.

New York State, Comptroller's Office, *New York in the Revolution as Colony and State,* compiled by J. A. Roberts, 2 vols., Albany, 1904.

New York State, *Journals of the Provincial Congress, Provincial Convention, Committee of Safety, and Council of Safety of the State of New York,* 2 vols., Albany, 1842.

New York State, *Journals of the Senate and Assembly.* Sessions 1 to 12, published separately for each session, 1778-1789 by Samuel Loudon Fishkill.

New York State, *Laws,* 1778-1789.

O'Callaghan, E. B., *Documentary History of the State of New York,* 4 vols., Albany, 1849-51.

O'Callaghan, E. B. and Fernow, B., *Documents Relating to the Colonial History of New York.* Materials collected from Holland, England and France, ed. by J. R. Brodhead, Albany, 1856-1883.

Privy Council of England, Acts of, Colonial Ser., 6 vols., ed. by J. Munro and W. L. Grant.

Sparks, Jared, *Diplomatic Correspondence of the American Revolution,* 12 vols., Boston, 1830.

Sparks, Jared, *Diplomatic Correspondence of the United States, 1783-89,* 7 vols., Washington, 1833-34.

Street, Alfred B., *The Council of Revision of the State of New York and its Vetoes,* Albany, 1859.

Thorpe, Frances N., *Federal and State Constitutions,* 7 vols., Washington, 1909.

University of the State of New York, *Report of the Regents for 1873,* ed. by D. J. Pratt, 2 vols., Albany, 1874 & 78, also as New York Senate Document, 96th session, Vol. 5, No. 108.

Documentary History of the Vermont Question, *Proceedings of the Vermont Historical Society,* Vols. I-II.

Vermont State Papers, 1749-1791, ed. by William Slade, Middlebury, 1823.

Virginia, Statutes at Large, ed. by W. Hening, 13 vols., Richmond, 1809-1823.

Wharton, Frances, *The Revolutionary and Diplomatic Correspondence of the United States,* 6 vols., Washington, 1889.

BIBLIOGRAPHY

GENERAL SOURCES

Adams, John, Works of, ed. by Charles Francis Adams, 10 vols., Boston, 1850-56.

Bland Papers, The, ed. by Theodoric Bland, Jr., 2 vols., Petersburg, 1840-1843.

Boundary between Connecticut and New York, New Haven Colonial Historical Society Collections No. 3.

Burnett, E. C., *Letters of Members of Continental Congress,* 4 vols., Carnegie Institute Publication, 1921-28.

Burr, Aaron, Memoirs of, with miscellaneous selections from his correspondence, Mathew T. Davis, 2 vols., New York, 1836-37.

Carroll, Charles, *Life and Letters of Charles Carroll of Carrollton,* by K. M. Rowland, New York, 1903.

Clinton, George, *Public Papers,* prepared by The State Historian, 12 vols., Albany, 1899-1911.

Cox, Tench, *A View of the United States of America,* Philadelphia, 1795.

Cutler, Manasseh, *Journal of Life and Correspondence,* ed. by W. P. Cutler and J. P. Cutler, 2 vols., Cincinnati, 1888.

Franklin, Benjamin, Writings, ed. by A. H. Smyth, 10 vols., New York, 1907.

Hamilton, Alexander, The Works of, ed. by John C. Hamilton, 2 vols., New York, 1850-51.

Hamilton, Alexander, The Works of, ed. by Henry Cabot Lodge (Constitutional Edition), 12 vols., New York, 1903.

Henry, Patrick, Life Correspondence and Speeches of, by William Wirt Henry, 3 vols., New York, 1891.

Jay, John, The Correspondence and Public Papers of, ed. by Henry P. Johnston, New York, 1890.

Jefferson, Thomas, The Writings of, ed. by P. L. Ford, 10 vols., New York, 1892-99.

Jefferson, Thomas, The Writings of (Library Edition), ed. by A. A. Linscomb and A. E. Bergh, 20 vols., Washington, 1903.

Johnson, Sir William, Papers, 6 vols., University of the State of New York, Division of Archives, 1929.

Jones, Thomas, *History of New York During the Revolution,* ed. by Floyd De Lancey, 2 vols., New York, 1879.

Kent, James, Memoirs and Letters of, by William Kent, New York, 1898.

King, Rufus, The Life and Correspondence of, ed. by Charles R. King, 6 vols., New York, 1894-1900.

Lee, Arthur, Letters to, New York Public Library Bulletin, vol. VII, pp. 162-163.

Madison, James, The Writings of, ed. by Gaillard Hunt, 9 vols., New York, 1900-1910.

Morris, Gouveneur, Diary and Letters of, ed. by A. C. Morris, 2 vols., New York, 1888.

Morris, Gouveneur, Life and Writings of, ed. by J. Sparks, 3 vols., Boston, 1832.

New York Claims to Vermont, Evidence in Favor of, *New York Historical Society Collections,* 1869, pp. 281-528.

Paine, Thomas, Writings of, ed. by D. E. Wheeler, 10 vols., New York, 1905.

Pendleton, Edmund, Unpublished Letters of, Massachusetts Historical Society Proceedings, ser. 2 XIX (Feb.), pp. 107-167.

Preston Papers, 1774-1783, Magazine of History, vols. VIII and XVII.

Scoville, J. A., *The Old Merchants of New York City,* New York, 1885.

Spanish Regime in Missouri, ed. by Louis Houck, 2 vols., Chicago, 1909.

Stokes, I. N. P., *Iconography of Manhattan Island,* 6 vols., New York, 1915-28.

BIBLIOGRAPHY

Thompson Papers, The, New York State Historical Society Collections, 1878.

Washington, George, Writings of, ed. by W. C. Ford, 14 vols., New York, 1889-1893.

Washington, George, *Account with the United States, 1775-1783,* Reproduced in facsimile by J. C. Fitzpatrick, New York, 1917.

Wharton, Samuel, *Plain Facts,* Philadelphia, 1781.

Webb, Samuel B., Correspondence and Journals of, ed. by W. C. Ford, 3 vols., New York, 1893-1894.

Webster, Peletiah, *Essays on the Nature and Operation of Money, Public Finance and Other Subjects,* Philadelphia, 1791.

(Yates, Abraham Jr.) under various pseudonyms such as Sydney, Rough Hewer, and Rough Hewer Jr.), *Political Papers Addressed to the Advocates of a Congressional Revenue in New York.* Pub. by Kollock, Albany, 1786.

NEWSPAPERS

Daily Advertiser (N. Y. C.), 1785-1806. Daily. Published to 1789 by F. Childs and Co.

New York Gazette and *Western Mercury* (N. Y. C.), 1768-1783. Weekly. Published by N. Gaine.

New York Gazetteer (Albany), 1782-1784. Weekly. Published by Sol. Ballentine and C. R. Webster.

New York Gazetteer (N. Y. C.), 1783-1787. Weekly, tri-weekly, semi-weekly, and daily at various times. Published by S. Kollock.

New York Independent Gazette (N. Y. C.), 1783-84. Weekly. Published by John Holt (A Continuation of his *New York Journal* published until 1782 at Poughkeepsie).

The New York Journal, 1777-1782 (Kingston, 1777), (Poughkeepsie, 1778-1782). Weekly. Published by John Holt (revived at New York as the *Independent New York Gazette,* Nov. 22, 1783).

New York Journal & the General Advertiser (N. Y. C.), 1784-93. Weekly. Published by W. D. and Ely Holt. (Daily Nov., 1787 to July, 1788).

New York Mercury and General Advertiser (N. Y. C.), 1779-1783. Weekly. Published by William Lewis.

New York Morning Post (N. Y. C.), 1783-1792. Semi-weekly, and from 1785 on daily. Published by Morton and Horner.

New York Packet and American Advertiser, 1777-1792. (Fishkill, 1777-1783; New York City, 1783-1792). Weekly. Published by Sam Loudon.

New York Royal Gazette (N. Y. C.), 1777-1783. Weekly. Published by J. Rivington.

Royal Gazette (N. Y. C.), 1777-1783. Weekly and semi-weekly. Published by James Robertson.

GENERAL HISTORIES

Bancroft, George, *History of the United States,* 6 vols., Boston, 1876.

Hildreth, Richard, *History of the United States of America,* 6 vols., Boston, 1877.

Winsor, Justin, *Narrative and Critical History of America,* 8 vols., Boston, 1884-89.

McMaster, J. B., *History of the People of the United States,* 8 vols., New York, 1884-1913.

Fiske, John, *The Critical Period,* Boston, 1898.

Channing, Edward, *History of the United States,* 6 vols., New York, 1905-25.

Van Tyne, C. H., *The American Revolution,* American Nation Series, vol. IX, New York, 1905.

McLaughlin, A. C., *The Confederation of the Constitution.* American Nation Series, vol. X, New York, 1906.

BIBLIOGRAPHY

STATE HISTORIES

Eastman, F. S., *A History of the State of New York*, New York, 1833.

Dunlap, William, *History of New York*, 3 vols., New York, 1839-40.

Barber, J. W. and Howe, H., *Historical Collections of the State of New York*, New York, 1844.

Hammond, J. D., *History of Political Parties in the State of New York*, 3 vols., Albany, 1852.

Carpenter, W. H. and Arthur, F. S., *The History of New York*, Philadelphia, 1853.

Comley, W. J., *Comley's History of the State of New York*, New York, 1877.

Sharff, J. F., *History of Maryland*, 3 vols., Baltimore, 1879.

Prentice, William R., *History of New York State*, Syracuse, 1900.

Bruce, Gen. D. H. (ed.), *The Empire State in Three Centuries*, 3 vols., New York, 1901.

Anderson, J. J. and Flick, A. C., *A Short History of the State of New York*, New York, 1902.

Morey, W. C., *The Government of New York, its History and Administration*, New York, 1902.

Redway, J. W., *The Making of the Empire State*, New York, 1904.

Roberts, E. H., *New York*, 2 vols., in American Commonwealth Series, Boston, 1904.

Alexander, DeAlva S., *A Political History of the State of New York*, 3 vols., New York, 1906.

Lincoln, C. Z., *The Constitutional History of New York*, 5 vols., Rochester, 1906.

Conant, C. A. (ed.), *The Progress of the Empire State*, New York, 1913.

Williams, Sherman, *New York's Past History* (A series of Essays), New York, 1915.

Horne, Charles F., *History of the State of New York*, Boston, 1916.

Smith, Ray B. (ed.), *History of the State of New York*, 6 vols., Syracuse, 1922.

Flick, A. C., *The Revolution in New York*, Albany, 1926.

Abbott, Wilbur, *New York during the Revolution*, New York, 1929.

MONOGRAPHS AND SPECIALIZED HISTORIES

Sheffield, Lord, *Observations on the Commerce of the United States*, London, 1784.

Talleyrand-Perigord, *Memoir Concerning the Commercial Relations of the United States with England*, London, 1806.

Hotchkin, J. H., *A History of the Purchase and Settlement of Western New York*, New York, 1848.

Turner, Orsamus, *Pioneer History of the Holland Purchase*, Buffalo, 1849.

Turner, Orsamus, *History of the Settlement of Phelps' and Gorham's Purchase*, New York, 1851.

Barrett, Walter, *The Old Merchants of New York City*, New York, 1863.

Doniol, Henri, *Participation de la France a l'Establissment des Estats Unis d'Amerique*, 5 vols., Paris, 1863.

Sabine, Lorenzo, *Biographical Sketches of Loyalists in the American Revolution*, Boston, 1864.

Stevens, John A., *Colonial Records of the New York Chamber of Commerce, 1768-1784*, New York, 1867.

Hamilton, J. C., *History of the Republic*, 7 vols., Philadelphia, 1868.

Staples, W. R., *Rhode Island in the Continental Congress*, Providence, 1870.

Adams, H. B., *Maryland's Influence in Founding a National Commonwealth*, Fund Publications of the Maryland Historical Society, Vol. II, 1886.

Sato, Soshuke, *History of the Land Question in the United States*, Johns Hopkins Studies in History and Political Science, Vol. IV, 1886.

Hinsdale, B. A., *The Old Northwest*, New York, 1888.

Roosevelt, Theodore, *Gouveneur Morris*, Boston, 1888.

Griffis, W. E., *Sir Wm. Johnson and the Six Nations*, New York, 1891.

Johnston, H. P., *New York After the Revolution, Magazine of American History*, Vol. XXIX, pp. 305-31, New York, 1893.

Friedenwald, Herbert, *Continental Congress, Pennsylvania Magazine of History*, July, 1895.

Silver, J. A., *Provisional Government in Maryland*, Johns Hopkins Studies in History and Political Science, Series 13, 1895.

James, J. A., *Some Problems of the Northwest in 1779*, New York, 1896.

Roosevelt, Theodore, *The Winning of the West*, 3 vols., New York, 1896.

Winsor, Justin, *The Westward Movement*, Boston, 1897.

Friedenwald, Herbert, *The Journals and Papers of the Continental Congress*, Philadelphia, 1898.

Thompson, Gilbert, *Colonial Boundaries of Virginia and Maryland*, District of Columbia, Society of Colonial Wars History Papers No. 1, 1899.

Flick, A. C., *Loyalism in New York During the American Revolution*, New York, 1901.

Halsey, F. W., *The Old New York Frontier, 1614-1800*, New York, 1901.

Baldwin, Simeon E., *American Business Corporations Before 1789*, American Historical Association Report for 1902.

Hamm, M. A., *Famous Families of New York*, New York, 1902.

Dale, B. M., *The Continental Congress at Work*, Chicago, 1904.

Hatch, L. C., *The Administration of the American Revolutionary Army*, New York, 1904.

Johnston, H. P., *New York City Under American Control*, in *Memorial History of New York*, Vol. 3, New York, 1904.

Bond, Beverly, *State Government in Maryland*, Johns Hopkins Studies in History and Political Science, Series 23, 1905.

Sioussat, St. George L., *The North Carolina Cession*, Mississippi Valley Historical Society Proceedings, Vol. II, 1908.

Van Tyne, C. H., Sovereignty in the American Revolution, *American Historical Review*, Vol. 12, 1907.

Randall, Ruth R., *Parties and Controversies in the Continental Congress, 1774-81*, Chicago, 1908.

Becker, Carl, *The History of Political Parties in the Province of New York, 1760-1776*, Bulletin of the University of Wisconsin Hist., series Vol. 2, No. 1, pp. 1-290, Madison, 1909.

Treat, P. J., *The National Land System*, New York, 1910.

Beard, C. A., *Economic Interpretation of the Constitution*, New York, 1913.

Hulbert, A. B., *Andrew Craigie and the Scioto Associates*, American Antiquarian Society Proceedings, 1913, N. Ser. Vol. 13.

Phillips, P. C., *The West in the Diplomacy of the American Revolution*, University of Illinois Studies in the Social Sciences, Vol. II, Nos. 2 and 3, Urbana, 1913.

Phillips, P. C., *American Opinions Regarding the West, 1778-1783*, Proceedings Mississippi Valley Historical Association, Vol. VII, Cedar Rapids, 1914.

BIBLIOGRAPHY

Hulbert, A. B., *Methods and Operations of the Scioto Group of Speculators,* Mississippi Valley Historical Review, Vol. II, 1915.

Walker, M. G., *Sir Johnson, Loyalist,* Mississippi Valley Historical Review, III, No. 3, 1916.

Corwin, E. C., *French Policy and the American Alliance,* Princeton, 1916.

Hulbert, A. B., *Records of the Ohio Company,* 3 vols., Marietta, 1917.

Alvord, C. W., *Mississippi Valley in British Politics,* Cleveland, 1917.

Schlesinger, A. M., *The Colonial Merchants and the American Revolution, 1763-1776,* New York, 1917.

Miner, C. E., *Ratification of the Federal Constitution in New York,* Columbia University Studies, No. 214, 1921.

Nevins, Allan, *The American States During and After the Revolution,* New York, 1924.

Bemis, S. F., *Jay's Treaty,* New York, 1924.

Fay Bernard, *L'Esprit Revolutionaire en France et aux Etats Unis,* Paris, 1925.

Harmon, G. D., *Amendments to the Articles of Confederation,* South Atlantic Quarterly, Vol. XXIV, Nos. 3 and 4, 1925.

Seymour, F. W., *Lords of the Valley,* New York, 1930.

BIOGRAPHIES

Marshall, John, *Life of George Washington,* Philadelphia, n. d.

Thomas, D. H., *Life of John Hanson,* Baltimore, n. d.

Jay, William, *Life of John Jay,* New York, 1833.

Jenkins, J. S., *Lives of the Governors of the State of New York,* Auburn, 1851.

Anonymous, *Life of Duer, Knickerbocker Magazine,* Vol. XL, pp. 95-103, New York, 1852.

Leake, J. Q., *Memoir of the Life and Times of General John Lamb,* New York, 1857.

Rives, W. C., *Life of James Madison,* Boston, 1857.

Stone, W. L., *Life and Times of Sir William Johnson,* 2 vols., Albany, 1865.

Morse, J. F., *Alexander Hamilton,* 2 vols., Boston, 1876.

Lodge, H. C., *Alexander Hamilton,* Boston, 1883.

Lossing, B. J., *Life and Times of Philip Schuyler,* 2 vols., New York, 1883.

Conway, M. D., *Life of Edmund Randolph,* New York, 1889.

Sumner, W. G., *Alexander Hamilton,* New York, 1890.

Pellew, George, *John Jay,* Boston, 1891.

Rowland, K. M., *Life of George Mason,* 2 vols., New York, 1892.

Sumner, W. G., *Robert Morris,* New York, 1892.

Ganrud J. E., *Five Years of Alexander Hamilton's Public Life, 1786-1791,* n. p. 1894 (Cornell Ph.D.)

Boudinot, H. H., *Life of Elias Boudinot,* 2 vols., Boston, 1896.

Oberholtzer, E. P., *Robert Morris, Patriot and Financier,* New York, 1903.

Tuckerman, Bayard, *Life of General Philip Schuyler,* New York, 1903.

Hamilton, A. M., *Intimate Life of Hamilton,* New York, 1910.

Davis, J. S., *William Duer, Entrepreneur,* in *Essays on the Earlier History of American Corporations,* no. II, Harvard Economic Studies, Vol. XVI, Cambridge, 1917.

Volwiler, A. L., *George Croghan and the Development of Central New York, 1763-1800,* New York State Historical Association Publications, Vol. XXI, Albany, 1923.

BIBLIOGRAPHY

Volwiler, A. F., *George Croghan and the Westward Movement*, Cleveland, 1926.

Minnigerode, M. and Wandell, S. H., *Aaron Burr*, 2 vols., New York, 1925.

Delaplaine, Edward S., *Life of Thomas Johnson*, New York, 1927.

Bryce, P. H., *Sir William Johnson*, New York State Historical Association Publications, Vol. XXV, Geneva, 1927.

Wilbur, James B., *Ira Allen, Founder of Vermont*, 2 vols., New York, 1929.

Pound, Arthur, and Day, R. E., *Johnson of the Mohawks*, New York, 1930.

FINANCIAL HISTORIES

Pitkin, Timothy, *History of the United States*, 2 vols., 1828.

Gouge, W. M., *Short History of Paper Money and Banking in the United States*, 1833.

Pitkin, Timothy, *Statistical View of the Commerce of the United States*, 1835.

Breck, Samuel, *Historical Sketch of Continental Paper Money*, 1843.

Bronson, Henry, *Historical Account of Connecticut Currency, Continental Money, and Finances of the Revolution*, New Haven Colonial Historical Society Papers, Vol. 1, 1865.

Hickox, J. H., *History of the Bills of Credit or Paper Money, 1709-1789*, Albany, 1866.

Phillips, Henry, *Historical Sketches of the Paper Currency of the American Colonies, Prior to the Adoption of the Federal Constitution*, 2 vols., 1865-1866.

Schucker, J. W., *Brief Account of the Finances and Paper Money of the Revolutionary War*, 1870.

Bayley, Rafael, *History of the National Loans of the United States*, New York, 1880.

Dommet, H. W., *History of the Bank of New York, 1784-1884,* New York, 1884.

Schwab, J. C., *History of the New York Property Tax,* American Economic Association Publications, Vol. V, no. 5, 1890.

Sumner, W. G., *The Financier and Finances of the American Revolution,* 2 vols., New York, 1891.

Bates, T. G., *Rhode Island and the Impost of 1781,* American Historical Association *Report,* 1894.

Bullock, E. J., *Finances of the United States, 1775-1789,* Madison, 1895.

Bolles, Albert S., *The Financial History of the United States, 1774-1789,* New York, 4th ed., 1896.

DeKnight, Wm. F., *History of the Currency and Loans of the United States,* Washington, 1900.

Dewey, Davis R., *State Banking Before the Civil War,* National Monetary Commission Publication, Washington, 1910.

Sowers, D. C., *The Financial History of New York, 1789-1912,* New York, 1914.

Hepburn, A. B., *A History of Currency in the United States,* Rev. ed., 1915.

Dewey, Davis R., *Financial History of the United States,* 9th ed., New York, 1924.

INDEX